# Faster! Faster!

## THE QUEST FOR SAILING SPEED

## DAVID PELLY

HEARST MARINE BOOKS
NEW YORK

# Contents

Foreword by Timothy Colman    v

Author's Preface    iv

1 War and peace    1
2 The clippers    21
3 Dinghies and catamarans    40
4 Offshore yachts    64
5 Offshore multihulls    83
6 Hydrofoils: what and why?    103
7 Hydrofoil record breakers    120
8 Flying surfboards    134
9 Speed trials    145
10 The Portland Speed Weeks    161
11 The *Crossbow* story    194
12 What makes sailing boats fast?    222

Appendices

Rules of World Sailing Speed Record    231
Results of RYA Speed Weeks, Portland Harbour    235
History of the World Sailing Speed Records    238
Standing records for various ocean passages    240
Time and speed for a 500 metre distance    242

Index    243

# Foreword

*by Timothy Colman, holder of the World Sailing Speed Record since 1972.*

I count it a privilege to be invited to write an introduction to David Pelly's book about sailing at high speed and I do so with pleasure. It is a story that I am sure will prove compelling reading for sailors the world over. The author, as journalist and yachtsman of wide experience, is ideally suited to present what is likely to become a definitive work.

As he explains in the earlier chapters, tracing the need for speed under sail through history, from the ancient Greeks to the nineteenth-century clippers, there is nothing new about man's desire to travel faster. What is remarkable is that it is only so recently that attempts have been made to measure with accuracy the speed of boats under sail. Aeroplanes, cars, power boats and indeed athletes have been concerned for decades with absolute speed.

Speed, 'the one genuinely modern pleasure' as Aldous Huxley once described it, is clearly of concern to every racing yachtsman. To 'those magnificent men in their sailing machines' however, as Hugh Somerville once so aptly described the assembly on the beach at Portland Harbour, speed is nearer to a fixation. For the past twelve years a fascinating variety of experimental craft have presented themselves, rich in hope and with varying degrees of success, to be timed over a measured distance. It is a happy development that regular speed events are now being staged in several different countries. They are fun, they bring people together and encourage the exchange of ideas.

One easily overlooked feature of the search for new records is that whatever the design configuration of a particular boat, as speed levels rise, new records will increasingly depend on a narrow range of suitable conditions, namely stronger winds (the only motive force) and smooth water. The likelihood of achieving such conditions during the course of a meeting is slender. Record breaking requires patience and some luck as well as endeavour.

In many traditional yachting events most opportunities for radical experiment are either already explored or limited by a rule. One of the hallmarks of recent high speed sailing trials has been to keep rules at a minimum so that designers have an almost unlimited opportunity for original thought and lightweight construction.

David Pelly has done a great service to yachting by chronicling with remarkable clarity many of the thoughts and developments which have helped to enhance the speed of a whole range of boats from the smallest sailboard with a displacement less than the weight of its sailor to the largest offshore multihull. His first-hand experience and understanding of hydrofoils has enabled him to write with authority on a very important aspect of speed sailing.

As one who has had the good fortune to witness at least some of the events and boats described in this book, I commend it for its entertaining style, its accuracy and refreshing objectivity. I am sure it will bring pleasure and inspiration to readers of all ages and I wish it every success.

# Author's Preface

I feel I should warn the reader that the title of this book is a misnomer; it should really be Slower! Slower! in recognition of the quite inordinate length of time it took to complete. As most 'amateur' authors discover, there always seems to be something more pressing than getting down to work on the next chapter and it is only thanks to persistent needling from the publisher and my wife that the text was finally completed. Actually it isn't complete and never can be because people's desire to sail faster is what the TV producers call 'an on-going story'.

Originally this book was conceived as a joint project by the author and James Grogono and with a somewhat narrower and more specific aim. Even after the wiser judgement of the publisher prevailed and it became a single-handed craft with wider horizons, James remained its staunchest ally and has given the project every assistance that I could have wished including the loan of several precious photographs from his own collection. My thanks to him also extend to the rest of the *Icarus* team who have known for some time that they had a mole in their midst.

Sending out drafts of a chapter to people who know more about a subject than oneself can be at once a rewarding and humbling process. Beecher Moore has been at the forefront of small-boat development for more than half a century as well as being the man who invented the trapeze so it is not surprising that he was able to take the chapter on dinghies apart and put it back together in considerably better shape. I went to Austin 'Clarence' Farrar because he was the designer of the famous *Lady Helmsman* wing rig, and came away with a completely fresh outlook on the history of the International 14ft dinghy and the hitherto underestimated part in it played by Tom Thornycroft.

Any book about speed under sail could hardly overlook the rôle of Timothy Colman, Roderick MacAlpine-Downie and the rest of the *Crossbow* team. It was therefore particularly satisfying to have received complete cooperation from this quarter including the generous foreword contributed by 'Tim' Colman. I am sure that I can speak for all speed sailing enthusiasts if I say that the return of *Crossbow* to the water is eagerly awaited.

Andrew Wolstenholme did the beautiful tracings of line drawings and Jack Hemmings, the editor of *Multihull International* compiled a complete set of reports of Speed Week which yielded invaluable facts. To my surprise, the library of the Cruising Association proved to be much the best source of books on yachting subjects, including racing!

I guess that having a budding author in the family is even worse than a wilful child so I have to thank my wife Philippa not merely for many hours of typing and much needed encouragement but for patience considerably beyond the call of duty.

*Great Plumstead*
*January 1984.*

# 1
# War and peace

Speed is one of man's most enduring obsessions. Ever since *homo sapiens* first hauled himself up onto his hind legs he has been trying to stagger along faster than the next chap. Over the ages, as more and more forms of transport have become available, they have provided more and more outlets for man's apparently insatiable competitive instinct.

This desire to travel faster than others can be rationalized in a number of ways. At the most primitive level it was doubtless very useful for our antediluvian ancestors to be able to run fast in order to obtain a limited food supply before the others got to it or, just as important, to escape the clutches of some snaggle-toothed predator intent on turning you into its next meal.

As soon as men began to be organized into tribes, politics was invented and conflict with other tribes became inevitable. Thereafter speed became associated with military effectiveness. It seems remarkable that in an era when armies moved only as fast as their infantry, who moved only as fast as their legs could carry them, that speed was nevertheless of the essence. Yet history tells us that it was above all the superior speed of reaction of the great commanders of the ancient world, such as Alexander the Great and Julius Caesar, that gave them the key advantage over more ponderous or less well-organized opponents. This business of needing to move fast in order to surprise or outrun an enemy has made itself felt in just about every possible medium of transport. Furthermore, since societies generally attach a lot of importance to winning wars, large resources are made available to develop faster military vehicles and the knowledge so gained tends to be useful in other spheres.

Although less spectacular in its demands, commerce has always provided a gentle but steady demand for improvements in speed. Since the dawning of trade, it has frequently been vital to get goods to market sooner than the rival merchants and, nearly as important, to pass

1

commercial messages from one part of the world to another.

Hunting, self-preservation, war and commerce are all powerful primal urges which demand speed, and there are elements of all of them in the final great speed-producer – sport. The sporting ethic and the competitive instinct that goes with it is so thoroughly ingrained in the human spirit that it would be pointless to try to justify it. It is sufficient to say that whenever we feel compelled to try to do something better than others for no obvious reason, then it must be sport!

# Early boats

Man's earliest boats were purely load carriers and must have been lamentably slow. It is safe to assume that the earliest form of propulsion was quanting, that is, pushing against the river bottom with a pole and that as soon as primitive boat-man accidentally ventured into deeper water he quickly found out about paddling. Rowing, which is a clever form of paddling, took a lot longer to develop.

After many centuries of refinement and competition, a team of super-fit and specially trained rowers in a boat of extreme lightness and fineness can maintain a speed of around 12 knots for a few minutes at a time. It follows that all other forms of rowing or paddling boats must be slower – and in most cases very much slower. We can put out of our minds immediately any picture of Greek or Roman war galleys skimming at thrilling speeds across the calm waters of the Mediterranean. From their size, shape and large cargo of armed men, it is clear that these galleys must have been of considerable displacement, and the arrangement whereby two or even three banks of rowers struggled to handle long heavy oars in unison must have been, to put it mildly, a somewhat clumsy business. I think it is fair to assume that oar-powered war galleys went into action at no more than a medium walking pace. The advantages of an oar-powered warship lay in manoeuvrability rather than speed.

When and where did the first sails appear? This appears to be an impossible question to answer, especially as the earliest known illustrations of sailing vessels – trading vessels on the River Nile – are quite advanced types. We therefore have to resort to inspired guesswork and postulate that somewhere in the eastern Mediterranean area – either in the Nile or Tigris–Euphrates basin, simple boatmen realized that if they held up a mat or rug against the wind, then their boat would be driven down-wind. It surely does not require any great creative genius to perceive this since it is a matter of common observation that leaves blow along with the wind, trees lean, tents billow and men and animals find it easier to walk with the wind than against it. Sailing in its simplest form thus consists of no more inspired an action than providing some kind of surface for the wind to push against.

It is easy to picture some kind of very simple square sail, made perhaps of rush matting, extended by a wooden pole along its uppermost edge and supported by a short pole mast. Neither is any great analytical thought required in order to discover that a boat with such a sail is not limited to a directly down-wind heading. It would be a matter of common experience that with the square sail drawing, the boat could be turned one way or the other without immediately coming to a stop, and furthermore, that if the sail begins to flap as the boat is turned, then it should be trimmed so that it stayed full. The simplest type of boat with the simplest type of sail can generally manage to sail on a square reach, that is, at right-angles to the wind direction.

Armed with this knowledge and a good deal of patience, it is possible to sail all over the World, as was demonstrated by the great European voyages of exploration from the 15th to 18th centuries, all of which, without exception, were made in ships that were totally incapable of sailing to windward. The simple square sail gives, in effect, a choice of downwind courses and one reached one's objective by waiting for favourable winds or rather by following a route which prevailing winds made possible. From this point of knowledge there stretches a long unbroken line of development which stretches right down to the great four and five-masted barques built around the turn of the present century that were the final expression of ocean-going cargo carrying under sail.

We now come to a very big step which is central to our story – the ability to sail to windward. For reasons that will become clear, it will be understood that it is never possible to sail very fast except in a vessel that is capable of going to windward and it undoubtedly requires an intellectual jump of some magnitude even to believe that it may be possible to sail towards the wind. What is unclear is whether the discovery of how to sail to windward was a matter of gradual improvement of existing types, or whether at a certain point in time someone came to the conclusion that it could be done and then set about finding the means.

It is as if one asked the question 'Who first thought of flight?' But no-one needed to since one only has to look up into the air to see birds happily flying around. Knowing, therefore, that it *must* be possible, the development of manned flying machines was more a matter of working

3

away persistently at the engineering rather than having truly original ideas. If, on the other hand, one asked 'Who first thought of space flight?' then there indeed is a question since there is nothing in nature that might suggest that such a thing might be possible.

In the same way, it seems that there is little in nature that would lead one to the conclusion that it must be possible to sail towards the wind. We now know that certain types of soaring bird such as the albatross do effectively sail to windward though to come to that conclusion requires a fairly sophisticated consideration of the dynamics of soaring flight including wind-gradient, surface effect etc. I cannot see that watching a gracefully soaring sea-bird would necessarily lead to the conclusion that sailing towards the wind ought to be possible. Observing the effect of wind on most everyday objects, from smoke to whole trees, would surely lead one to conclude that motion is always away from the wind.

An interesting exception to this rule is that the sails of windmills are a kind of windward-going rig, though it is perfectly possible to build a successful windmill and never realize this. Nevertheless there are in Crete and Greece windmills of very ancient origin, which have cloth sails, and it would be interesting to know which came first: windmills or boats capable of sailing to windward.

It is not just idle speculation that leads me to wonder how the windward-going boat originated. The puzzling fact is that as far as is known the first boats to achieve this were Arab or eastern Mediterranean vessels with 'lateen' rig. This beautifully efficient sail system with its high aspect-ratio, low drag and excellent aerodynamic drag angle is so totally different from the simple square sail that one wonders how it can have been arrived at without some understanding of aerodynamics.

If one reads David Howarth's book *Dhows* (Quartet) or Tim Severin's *The Sindbad Voyage* (Hutchinson) one discovers that a big lateen rig was an absolute monstrosity to handle, requiring a large trained crew in order to carry out a simple manoeuvre, such as a tack. In any kind of a seaway, the immensely long, unstayed luff-spar must have been a nightmare to handle and it does really seem that the only reason for adopting such an un-handy rig was its efficiency to windward. How did the Arab or Egyptian sailors of 2000 BC come to this conclusion and how did they devise the rig in the first place?

The important point is that they did and that they ended up with a boat capable of going to windward. The Nile Felucca and its first cousin the seagoing Dhow are amazingly elegant vessels compared to the northern European commercial sailing vessel with its jungle of spars and rigging. With the Dhow's short pole mast there is either no standing

*Small native craft with lateen rig. The paradox is that this rig, one of the first to be developed, was hardly improved upon for windward efficiency until the advent of modern yacht rigs within the last 100 years*

rigging at all or the bare minimum, thus eliminating a major source of drag. Running rigging is confined to halyard, downhaul and sheet, and since the rig has balanced sail areas ahead of and abaft the mast, there should never be much weight on the sheet. The sail is all leading edge – it has what the aerodynamicist calls high aspect-ratio. Thanks to the lack of standing rigging, the sail can be trimmed close to the fore-and-aft line of the boat so that it acts as a proper foil rather than merely a wind-break. Finally, that long flexible yard has the desirable characteristic of progressively flattening the sail as the wind increases. The Arabs were always very clever people, pioneers of mathematics and astronomy, and it seems quite plausible that they did to some degree understand the dynamics of sailing to windward. However, this is fairly idle speculation because unless someone uncovers a new Dead Sea scroll which turns out to be a treatise on naval architecture, we will never know the truth. What is clear is that sailing boats capable of going to windward did appear both in the Mediterranean and Persian Gulf areas and that over the centuries they gradually got faster. Now we can turn our attention to what they achieved, and how.

# The Mediterranean

For many centuries, warships of the Mediterranean were rowing boats: sail was reserved mainly for trade. These oared galleys gradually grew larger and more elaborate and very surprisingly continued to be the main type of warship right up to the middle of the 18th century. These reached their most extreme form in the French *Reales* which were up to 200ft (61m) in length overall and were rowed by 450 galley-slaves, sitting 7 to an oar, an arrangement which was apparently better than the classical one of two or three banks of oarsmen above each other. They did have sails as well as oars – normally two big lateen ones – but these were always furled before going into battle. One reason was that to have any performance a galley had to be slim, and low freeboard is a prerequisite of an oared vessel; therefore they could not stand up to much sail. The *Reales'* cannons could only shoot forward because the sides of the vessel were taken up with rowing paraphernalia and so they were in grave danger of being shot to pieces if they met up with something like a British frigate which had heavy broadsides of cannon. Their only chance of success was in light weather when they could avoid the broadside by rowing up from astern. Because of their great length, they were very slow to turn and in almost every respect a silly kind of warship.

The immensely long history of the oared galley in the Mediterranean meant that shipbuilders in that area well understood that a long, slim, lightweight hull would be fast and so when the smugglers and Barbary priates of the 17th century wanted speedy ships, they knew where to look. Piracy seems to have been the main incentive for the development of the Chebec or Xebec which became one of the most elegant and speedy of craft. Based on the galleys, they were originally combined rowing and sailing boats but gradually became pure sailers. They gradually became beamier and deeper in order to improve sail-carrying power but retained the fine bow and long tapering run of the galley. They also had long overhangs, consisting of a ram-like beakhead and bowsprit forward and a grating deck extending the poop aft above the waterline. These extended decks helped them to set a big spread of sail and in their final versions, Xebecs could set a quite amazing variety of sails. They normally had three masts and on these could be set large or small lateen sails for going to windward or square sails if the wind was abaft the beam and sometimes a combination of both. In his *Marine Dictionary* (1771) Falconer says: 'By the very complicated and inconvenient method of working these vessels it will be readily believed that one of their captains

The Xebec or Chebec was a fast Mediterranean vessel often used by pirates because of its superior sailing qualities. It could be rigged in a number of ways but the lateen rig shown here was the most usual

of Algiers acquainted the author, viz: *That the crew of every Xebec has at least the labour of three square-rigged ships, wherein the standing sails are calculated to answer every situation of the wind.'* This was really missing the point because if the Barbary pirate had had at his disposal a vessel that was faster than anything else on any point of sailing, then he was assured of rich pickings from among the lumbering merchantships of the area and could well afford a big crew and lots of expensive sails.

In the mid-17th century, the French Navy was in an awful state mostly due to the fact that the ruling classes at the time considered such things beneath their notice. When Jean-Baptiste Colbert was appointed Chief Minister by Louis XIV in 1663, he had to re-build the navy virtually from scratch. To do this, he imported two of the leading naval architects of the era, Anthony Deane from England and Biagio Pangallo from Naples. Deane was the author of the *Doctrine of Naval Architecture*, while Pangallo was responsible for a total shake-up of French design and shipbuilding practice. As is so often the case, starting from scratch was an advantage and by the beginning of the 18th century, French warship design was considered to be superior to that of England. That is why some of the most famous ships in the Royal Navy, such as *Téméraire*,

*Bellerophon* and *Tonnant*, were in fact captured French ships. Pangallo, who became known as 'Maître Blaise', designed some very nice frigates which, though full-lined, were much less tubby than most contemporary warships.

The strong French interest in America meant that many warships and merchant vessels made the transatlantic passage and were familiar to the colonists, so it is not at all surprising that when American shipbuilding got under way, it should base itself on a mixture of English and French models.

# The Atlantic

For any lover of boats, a visit to the Viking Ship museum in Oslo is a profound experience. It contains the two well-preserved vessels known as the Gokstad Ship and the Oseberg Ship, which were both excavated around the turn of the present century. Their graceful sheer and superb sweeping clinker planking immediately shows that you are looking at the products of a race that knew and understood the sea and shipbuilding. The Gokstad ship is the larger of the two at 76ft 6in (23·3m) LOA and 17ft 3in (5·25m) beam. She was a rowing and sailing ship with a good performance. This was proved beyond doubt in 1893 when a replica of the ship was built and crossed the Atlantic in the very respectable time of 28 days.

Yet the Gokstad ship, according to no less an authority than Björn Landström, was no more than a Karv or coaster and a very insignificant vessel compared to the mighty Drakkars or fighting long-boats. Although none of these vessels survive, they are well-described in the Viking sagas, which tell us how big they were in terms of *rums* or rowing thwarts. Olav Tryggvason's famous Drakkar *Ormen Lange* was 34-rummed which means that she would have been rowed by 68 men. The Gokstad ship provides a handy scale as her oar-holes are 3ft 2½in (98cm) apart and on this basis the *Ormen Lange* was about 150ft (46m) overall. For several centuries, the Vikings rampaged around northern Europe in these tremendous open boats carrying on the rape and pillage for which their name has become exemplary. Although it really is extraordinary that they chose to go on lengthy ocean passages in low-freeboard open boats, there is no doubt that the Drakkar was a highly developed vessel.

It is obvious that even eighty men could not row a 150ft (46m) ship very fast, but this was not the idea. Rowing was used for penetrating inland up the rivers in search of the richest settlements, as is

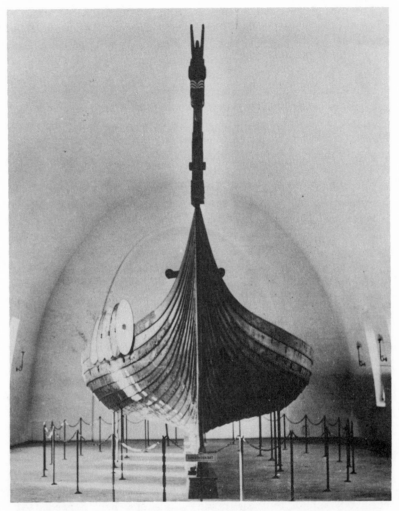

*The Gokstad Ship in the Viking museum at Oslo. The superb form and line of the Viking ships has never been bettered* (Norwegian Information Service)

demonstrated by the Sutton Hoo ship which was buried on a hill opposite Woodbridge on the upper reaches of the Deben. For passage making, they sailed and the ships were far better designed for this than the Mediterranean galleys, having relatively much more waterline beam and a firm turn to the bilge. Rather surprisingly, even the big Drakkars apparently only ever had one mast and sail, a straightforward square-sail laced to a yard. The small trading vessels were nearly flat-bottomed but the long-ships seem to have had more rise of floor and hence would have been able to sail well on a reach and perhaps even to windward. They had a special spar called a beitass which was used for pushing the tack of the sail forward; later a bow-line was used for the same purpose. Although the Vikings were obviously superb boat-builders, it seems they were less great as sailmakers, not through lack of skill but lack of suitable materials. They had no cotton or even flax canvas, so their sails were probably made of a soft woven cloth; illustrations seem to show a criss-cross pattern of reinforcement, perhaps leather. Although it is to be doubted whether they could really beat to weather effectively, the Viking long-ship must have slipped along beautifully on a nice quartering reach. The hull had all the right ingredients – lots of length without being too heavy, slim ends and very nice easy lines. With a better rig they could have really flown!

The sad thing is that after the end of the Viking era, north-European shipbuilding seemed to get worse rather than better. As far as merchant ships are concerned it is understandable that they abandoned the Viking model because to carry more weight, greater beam and depth were inevitable. The reason for the same thing happening to warships seems to be concerned with the weapons systems in use. The Vikings were strictly spear and arrow men, until they could get close enough to use their swords, so in a ship-to-ship fight the only defence was to cower behind a barrier of shields ranged along the bulwarks. However, if you could shoot from above, the men in the waist of the ship would be at your mercy so ships were given raised platforms at the ends, which can be seen even in late illustrations of Viking ships. This feature gradually became more pronounced as the platforms turned into castles, which eventually were two or three stories high. They also built little platforms on top of the masts so that one could shoot arrows or throw stones down on the enemy. To support these castles and fighting tops, the ships needed to be stronger and more stable and thus wider and heavier, and so the simple elegance of the Viking ship was gradually lost.

In fact the whole idea of the specialist warship seems to have been lost for much of the Middle Ages when kings who wanted to wage war simply commandeered whatever merchant shipping was available. This all changed with the invention of gunpowder. Guns were first fitted on ships in the mid-14th century and in the next century proper cannons came into use. These had an immediate and marked effect on ship design. Cannons are heavy so ships needed much more stability to carry them.

Since they were also liable to be on the receiving end, they needed thick, shot-proof planking. For these reasons it was essential to have specialized warships once again but because of the guns they were bound to be heavy, beamy structures.

This line of development went right on to the very end of sailing warships and culminated in the vast wooden battleships of the Napoleonic wars. These 'wooden walls', with as many as three gun-decks, were tremendously heavy and correspondingly slow. However, navies still needed speed for scouting, message carrying and the like and we will be looking in that direction in a moment. From the 17th century, the idea of the frigate was born. This was a single-decked, lightly armed warship with improved sailing performance, suitable for chasing pirates or intercepting merchant ships. They were found especially suitable for colonial wars such as the American War of Independence simply because there was no point in deploying a battleship unless it was liable to meet another of its kind.

It was during this period that shipbuilding generally became more scientific. The Anglo-Swedish designer Frederick Hendrik af Chapman published his *Architectura Navalis Mercatoria* in 1768, which showed for the first time how proper lines drawings should be developed. In 1775 his *Treatise on Shipbuilding* appeared and these books gradually had a profound effect on shipbuilding. Chapman was the first to carry out model tests and establish the connexion between speed and fineness. The designers of the handsome Xebecs learned from experience the value of length and fine ends but Chapman put it on paper in a way that others could follow. After centuries of awful, tubby ships, better shapes started to appear. For instance the Blackwall frigates that were among the last sailing ships built for the Royal Navy sailed extremely well considering their weight. Rigs too, were vastly improved although for big ships at least, the square rig continued to predominate. Small boats however, often had fore and aft sails and the Dutch must receive credit for the schooner rig.

The greatest improvements in ship design in the 18th century were made by American shipbuilders. They were expatriate Europeans so they naturally, at first, built European style ships. However, because of their situation they seem to have been much more open-minded and ready to experiment. First they used the best examples of European ships as their models and then began to make their own improvements. The drawings on page 12 show the first American-built ship whose lines survive, the despatch-boat *St Ann*. Not much is known about her except that she was said to be American. In 1736 she visited Portsmouth with

11

despatches from Lisbon, flying the Portuguese flag. She obviously made a big impression because arrangements were made by the Navy to have her dry-docked so that her lines could be taken off, a relatively new technique at the time. An Admiralty draught of her was made and this was subsequently borrowed or copied by Hendrik Chapman on a visit to England, which is why it can now be seen in the Statens Sjöhistoriska Museum in Stockholm.

Although she had the 'cod's head and mackerel tail' hull form typical of the period, the *St Ann* is interesting because she was so narrow and fine-ended, particularly aft. Her midship section shows quite a lot of deadrise which would have helped her to grip the water and sail well to

*1. St Ann a despatch-boat built in America in 1736. Her form, with a bluff bow and long tapering run, perfectly illustrates the expression 'cod's head and mackerel tail'. Notice how far forward her masts are stepped and how correspondingly far forward is the point of maximum beam. Also that even at this early date pronounced mast rake was thought necessary in a fast boat. With such narrow beam she must have been a tricky little thing to sail*

Principal dimensions
*Length of keel: 46ft 9in*
*Beam (moulded): 11ft 10in*
*Draught (aft): 5ft 2in*

*Length at rail (moulded): 58ft 2in*
*Depth (rabbet to deck): 6ft 10¼in*
*Displacement: 956 cu ft*

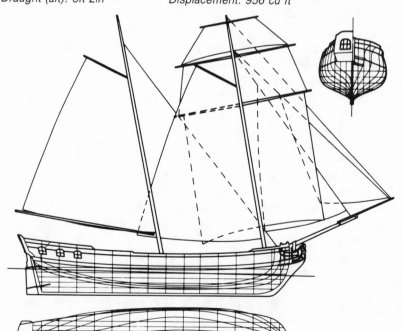

windward. She was rigged as a topsail schooner which became the most popular and successful of all rigs for small sailing ships, because it offered a good compromise between windward and off-wind performance. With so little beam, *St Ann* must have been a tricky vessel to sail but an impressive performer compared to the lumpen generality of ships.

Britain's shipping took a pasting in the French wars of 1757–63, mostly at the hands of privateers. These were really pirates who were given 'letters of marque' to operate against enemy shipping. For France it was a very clever arrangement; they did not have to pay the privateers anything because their reward was the booty they captured from merchant shipping. By terrorizing the sea-lanes, the privateers inflicted a lot of damage, particularly on Britain's trade with her American colonies. This conflict had a rapid effect on ship design because everyone suddenly needed more speed: the privateers to catch the merchant ships, the merchants to evade them and the Navy to catch the privateers.

The vessels used by the privateers were themselves very interesting. A number of Mediterranean style Xebecs and even some rowing and sailing galeasses ended up in the Caribbean where they took part in piratical conflicts for which the area became infamous. Nearer home, there were the big, open luggers that preyed on Channel shipping from ports such as St Malo which the Royal Navy could not penetrate. These were probably the fastest sailing craft of the era – since they did not stay at sea for more than a day or two, they were lightly-built open boats, generally rigged with two very big balanced lug-sails. From their lair behind the Minquières rocks, they would dart out to pounce on merchant ships. The Royal Navy's only answer to this was blockade of the ports, a most expensive and tedious procedure.

The British shipbuilders did not seem able to respond quickly to the need for faster ships, but the Americans did and rapid development of better ships began to take place in centres such as Marblehead and the Chesapeake Bay area while Bermuda supplied the Caribbean. Not only were fast merchant and despatch vessels needed but the Royal Navy itself was forced to buy American-built vessels to answer their urgent need for small fast patrol ships. A nice example is provided by the *Swift* which was probably built as a mail-packet and then purchased by the Navy in 1778, to serve as a lightly-armed patrol boat. Her lines are most attractive and show the great progress that American yards had made by this date. In particular, her elegant raked stem and fine forward waterlines are a great improvement over the bluff entry of the *St Ann*. Her midship section has considerable deadrise enabling her to carry her ballast low and a pronounced keel to help her grip the water. She draws

2. Swift *an American-built brig of 1778, probably designed as a mail or despatch-boat and bought by the Admiralty at a time when the Royal Navy was short of good small vessels. This very attractive and sensible-looking hull shows the progress that had been made in America in the 40 years since the building of the* St Ann. *Notice how much better balanced she is fore and aft and how the extra rake of the bow has helped to reduce the bluffness of the entry. The need to keep such a boat reasonably light was lost on the Admiralty who cut down her rig and added more ballast*

Principal dimensions
*Length between perpendiculars: 75ft 6in    Beam (moulded): 20ft 5in
Depth in hold: 7ft 9in*

more aft than forward, which was to become a characteristic 'Baltimore Clipper' feature. Her displacement of 87·8 tons was light for a vessel of the period and she carried 18 tons of pig-iron ballast. Her brigantine rig is generous in area but well-proportioned, avoiding the exaggerated mast-rake that was to become such a feature of the later Baltimore Clippers.

Her lines were taken off at Deptford in 1783 when she had already been in Naval service for some time. The fact that this was done shows that the Admiralty took an interest in this attractive little vessel but the dead hand of beaurocracy is evident in the Royal Dockyard's proposal that she be re-rigged with considerably less sail and more ballast, which would without doubt have transformed her into a slow, wet and ordinary ship. This mistake was made repeatedly during the American War of Independence. Naval officers serving in American waters would buy or capture a ship with an especially good reputation for speed and then send it home to England to be fitted for naval service. The dockyard would then load it up with guns and stores until the decks were practically awash and cut down the sail area. Afterwards, they would complain bitterly about the unsuitability for Naval service of these 'native' vessels.

The American War of Independence (1775–83) only increased the need for fast ships, for the revolting colonists now needed to run the blockade of Royal Navy cruisers in order to carry on any kind of sea-borne trade, and the French Revolution increased still further the possibilities for illegal trade. These two events of history brought the Baltimore shipbuilders to the acme of their reputation as the leading builders of small, fast ships and the 'Baltimore Clipper' became known throughout the world for speed and smartness.

Hull design continued to develop along the lines provided by the *Swift*. Fine waterlines and steep deadrise were the main features of the 'sharp built' ships – the idea of an external ballast keel did not occur until much later. Rigs showed a more dramatic change: the Baltimore designers decided that rake was an essential feature of a fast vessel and their predominantly topsail schooner rigs gradually acquired more and more pronounced rearward slope. No-one seems entirely certain of the thinking behind this rake of the masts. It seems as if the main point was that they were trying to pile on more and more sail area at the same time as fining away the waterlines forward. The weight of a tall foremast would then make the vessel pitch heavily into a head sea and the rake was supposed to alleviate this by moving the centre-of-gravity of the rig aft somewhat and by getting some lift from the sails. Just as important was the fact that American ships now had sails made from cotton duck rather than flax canvas. The excellent Louisiana cotton was far superior as a sail material, being both smoother and stiffer compared to the coarse, hairy flax. As a result, sailmakers began to get a decent curve into their sails and to build bigger, better fore-and-aft sails. It does not matter that they were not sure exactly how the curve of sails worked: they were not stupid men and were just as capable as we are today of judging from experience the effectiveness of different cuts and shapes.

The ultimate and disgraceful employment of the Baltimore Clippers was the 'black ivory' or slave trade. After Britain renounced slavery in 1833 the only way to carry on the business was by employing ships fast enough to evade the British frigates deployed on the West Coast of the African continent to prevent it. Ships built in the Baltimore area were generally sold to mysterious owners in Cuba and then put into the trade under false papers. Humans being a 'light cargo' made it possible to continue the trend to ever deeper, sharper hulls and the predominance of light airs on the middle Atlantic route meant that sail areas grew and grew. An extreme example is shown by the brig *Diligente* whose deadrise is so steep that it begins to be hollow. She was captured in 1837 and condemned as a slaver. However, this merely meant that she turned up later under a different name with different owners but in the same trade. She was taken again in 1838 by HMS *Pearl* and this time was probably broken up to stop her from going back into the business for a third time.

*3.* Diligente. *The lines of the slaver* Diligente *were taken off at the Admiralty shipyard in Bermuda after she had been captured for the second time. She represents an extreme example of the Baltimore Clipper type which had developed during the War of Independence. The hull sections show the extraordinary amount of deadrise, sharp waterlines and hard bilges of a vessel whose survival depended upon being able to keep to windward of contemporary British frigates, particularly in light airs. Her huge sail area and exaggerated mast rake are also characteristic of the Baltimore Clipper type. This line of development was a blind alley because such a sharp hull would be a very poor weight-carrier and anyway the slavers were doomed as soon as steam frigates came into service*

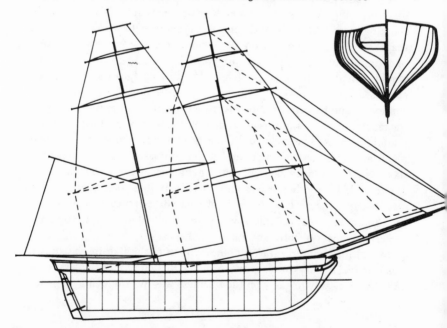

However, before this her lines were taken off at the Royal dockyard in Bermuda which indicates she must have had an outstanding reputation as a sailer.

It is interesting that when we get to the Clipper era, only about 15 years later, the hull form is quite different. *Rainbow*, which was considered to have a 'daring' amount of deadrise, in fact had a modest 11 degrees, nothing remotely approaching that of *Diligente*. The reason of course is that the clippers were freighters, albeit fast ones, and had to be able to sail on both light and loaded displacement. A really sharp hull like *Diligente* could not carry a useful load.

With the end of slavery and the appearance of the clippers, the Baltimore line of development more or less died out, except in one respect. The same general theme was carried on in the famous pilot boats of the US east coasts. The leading designer of these was George Steers who had also designed a very extreme small clipper ship, the *Sunny South*. She proved too small and sharp to be profitable and became a slaver out of Havana. Steers then started to concentrate on pilot boats and designed a number including the outstandingly fast and attractive *Moses H. Grinnell*. This had the typical Baltimore Clipper midship section with very steep deadrise and a high, sharp turn to the bilge but as well she had a really long, lean bow with the hollow waterlines then being used on the clippers. This very attractive schooner caught the attention of Commodore Stephens of the New York Yacht Club who ordered Steers to build him an improved version, as a yacht. This was the schooner-yacht *America*, whose exploits led to the America's Cup. Steers was killed in an accident at the age of 36, so he never had the opportunity to follow up the phenomenal success of *America*.

It must not be supposed that American shipbuilders were the only ones capable of coming up with design improvements. It was more a question of their being best placed to make use of them. Lack of opportunity, or straightforward conservatism were responsible for various excellent ideas being stillborn on the European side of the Atlantic. For instance, Sir William Petty designed and built a sea-going catamaran and demonstrated it in the Dublin Bay area in the mid-18th century. It easily outperformed other sailing craft but this was regarded as no more than a freak and the matter was not taken further.

Even sadder is the story of the schooner *Transit* which was completed in 1800 at Itchenor to the designs of Captain Gower, who appears to have been an exceptionally far-sighted gentleman. *Transit* was at least fifty years ahead of her time in almost every respect: she had a revolutionary mid-ship section with a deep keel and sharp reverse curve in the garboards. This made it possible to fit permanent ballast beneath the hold in the form of shaped iron castings, exactly in the manner used in racing yachts until the external ballast keel was invented. Her rig was even more revolutionary; she was originally fitted as a five-masted schooner with rectangular fore-and-aft sails set on sprits. The sprits gave trouble and were replaced by an ingenious kind of double-decker gaff rig. Two of the same rectangular sails were set one above the other on each mast, hanging from horizontal gaffs and topped off by a leg-of-mutton topsail. The gaffs were prevented from sagging off by vangs to the next mast astern. The masts were stayed independently in a thoroughly modern manner with fore-and-aft spread shrouds leading up over cross-trees and the upper panels were stiffened by jumper stays. As well as having mostly fore-and-aft sails, her whole rig was far lighter and cleaner than contemporary square rig, which contributed in large measure to her outstanding windward performance.

With some difficulty, Gower succeeded in arranging a series of trials against HMS *Osprey* a fast sloop of similar size. In their very first trial, with both ships on the wind, *Transit* took station dead astern of *Osprey*, then hauled out to weather, passed ahead, gybed round and regained her original position after 25 minutes. The remainder of the trials told a similar story, *Osprey*'s log recording '*Transit* beat us every way we tried.' For reasons one can only guess at, neither the Navy or the East India Company, which observed the trials, decided to take the matter further and Gower put the vessel into trade. Because the country was at war, she had to sail in convoy so the benefit of her superior speed was lost. However the Peace of Amiens was signed at the conclusion of her first voyage to Portugal and she was able to return home unescorted. She left the Tagus four days after the Post Office's mail packet *Duke of York* but caught and passed her in the Western Approaches, beating to windward in heavy weather. *Transit* passed the Lizard 14 days out of Lisbon while *Duke of York* took 23 days to reach the same point!

No-one in authority took the least notice of this achievement so *Transit* was put into the Mediterranean fruit trade. On her first voyage, she left Smyrna bound for the Thames 18 days after a well-known fast trader the *Pelican* and eight days astern of another named *Queen*. She docked in the Thames a thumping 13 days before the *Pelican* and when outward bound on her next voyage passed *Queen* still bound up-Channel. You would think that with this kind of record, every shipping agent in the country would be beating a path to Gower's door but for some extraordinary reason she remained 'one of a kind'. She continued to trade successfully until 1810 when she was wrecked on a reef. Gower subsequently wrote a paper about his brain-child which showed that he knew all about stability, fineness ratio, wind and water resistance, balanced ends and so on. It is tragic that Gower's work was not properly recognized because it is clear that he had managed to achieve outstanding performance while retaining a full, cargo-carrying mid-ship section, something the American clipper-designers claimed to have 'invented' fifty years later.

History is full of 'might-have-beens' unfortunately and as the saying goes, if you want to sail your race again, you must let the others do so as well. A fascinating race that never happened was that between the schooner *America* and the Yarmouth beach-yawl *Reindeer*. The Suffolk beach-yawls were a fascinating type of specialized fast pilot-boat. In the 1850s a vast number of sailing ships plied up and down the North Sea, many of them passing close by Lowestoft, which is England's most easterly point. The yawls would dash out to passing vessels to offer pilotage, supplies, mail or salvage as appropriate and naturally, the first boat on the scene got the best business. They gradually developed into quite extreme craft being long, narrow open luggers of around 60ft (15·2m) in length, this being the practical limit for a boat launched from the beach. Like the old Mediterranean galleys, they were pulling or sailing boats as occasion demanded and for this reason had to be quite narrow and low in freeboard. To overcome their lack of stability, they carried bags of shingle ballast which were shifted to windward on tacking and there is also some suggestion that they would lie out to windward on oars rigged across the gunwale. They had a hefty iron centre-plate to give them lateral plane and a couple of whacking great standing lugsails to drive them along.

The beach yawls were owned and sailed by a series of beach 'companies' who shared the costs and profits. This obviously competitive situation led to steady improvement of the boats and in the estimation of their crews at least, the yawls were the fastest working boats in existence. When *America* came over to England in 1851 and won her famous victory over the massed fleet of the Royal Yacht Squadron, the owners of the yawl *Reindeer* knew where their patriotic duty lay and slapped in a challenge for a match with a purse of £200. The owners of *America* responded by offering to race for a stake of £1,000 on either side. The longshoremen couldn't raise this kind of money so the challenge was dropped. This was probably just as well as it is very hard to imagine that the beach yawl would have stood much of a chance. *Reindeer*'s dimensions were 69ft (21m) LOA, 12ft (3·6m) beam and she was alleged to have sailed at 16 knots on a reach. *America* was considerably bigger at

19

90ft (27·4m) waterline and was at her best to windward. It is difficult to believe that the yawl, giving away 25ft (7·6m) of waterline, could have given her much trouble to windward, especially in a breeze when the open boat would probably need to ease off just to stay afloat. Off the wind it might have been a different story, with the yawl surfing away nicely down the waves and if the final leg had been down-wind they could have thrown the ballast over and really flown. Well, we'll never know the truth, unless someone would like to build a replica beach-yawl to race against the existing replica of *America*.

There were annual regattas at Yarmouth to which yawls from Aldeburgh, Sizewell, Southwold, Yarmouth and Lowestoft would come to race. The best racing record was that of the Yarmouth yawl *Georgiana*. Considerably smaller than *Reindeer* at 48ft 6in (14·7m) LOA, she was probably a good deal handier too. They raced with around 15 men aboard plus half a dozen bailer-boys! One reason for the large crew was that the big lugsails were so clumsy to handle. Apparently they overcame the difficulty of tacking a big lug by having two; one for each tack! An interesting side-line to the yawl story is that in 1894 one of the beach companies commissioned G. L. Watson to design them a new boat. Watson's masterpiece *Britannia* had been completed the previous year so the longshoremen reckoned he ought to be a good chap. The Watson yawl, which was named *Happy New Year*, was slightly larger than *Georgiana* at 50ft 2in (15·3m) LOA, 10ft 5in (3·2m) beam but failed to beat the latter in racing.

The decade 1850 to 1860 was really the climax of the age of sail. Steamships and railways were only just starting to make an impact. The clipper ships were racing round the globe with their premium cargoes while smaller fast ships such as the West Country schooners were dashing to and from the Mediterranean with fresh fruit. The slave trade was in its final throes with extreme Baltimore clippers such as the *Diligente* being chased, and caught, by the fast Blackwall frigates designed by Sir William Symonds. From 1860 onwards steam had the upper hand and although commercial sail survived until the 20th century, from about this date onwards commercial sailing vessels were built for economy rather than speed. Therefore, in the search for speed under sail, the lead passed to yachtsmen.

# 2
# The clippers

In the whole history of shipping, there is no more exciting or romantic story than that of the clippers; indeed their very name has passed into the language to indicate speed and smartness. When we look at their performances today they may seem modest but judged by the standards of their day they were tremendous and represented an enormous step forward in speed under sail.

It is important to realize from the outset that there were two quite separate 'fleets' of clippers: the British and the American. It was more or less an accident of history that they were built at approximately the same time and a very fortunate one because it created a rivalry of design and a useful cross-fertilization of ideas. It was the irresistible power of economics that created the clippers and then after a remarkably short time dropped them again.

The American clipper era was particularly short – hardly more than ten years. Although there was a steadily increasing demand for fast passages between the east and west coasts of the United States as colonization of the west proceeded, it was not until the California Gold Rush of 1849 that the pace became really hectic. At this time there was, of course, no Panama Canal and no railway across the continent. Land transport by horse-drawn wagon was slow, difficult and dangerous. Trans-shipment of cargo across the Isthmus of Panama was also very uncertain and expensive so for the short period until the depression of 1857, the most reliable way of getting men and cargo to California was by sailing ship around Cape Horn. Such was the demand for cargo space at this time that shippers could charge almost what they liked and it was not unusual for a ship to pay off her building cost in a single round trip. An extreme example is the Mackay clipper *Staghound* which was built in frantic haste in 1851, taking only 60 days to complete. She then loaded for San Francisco whence she crossed the Pacific to China where she loaded tea for New York. At the end of this first round trip she not only paid off her building cost but made a profit of $80,000.

With profits like this around, everyone concerned was prepared to take big risks. The shipbuilders were not only permitted but begged to build the most extreme vessels they could. Owners were able to pay for ships to be lavishly equipped and heavily crewed. Above all, in this intensely competitive situation, masters of ships were urged to sail their vessels with a ruthless disregard for either expense or safety that has never been seen either before or since.

The American clippers reached their zenith in 1853 when over 50 'extreme' clippers were built, but it was almost immediately obvious that shippers had over-reached themselves in their rush for profits. Freight rates to the west coast, which reached a peak of $60 per ton at the height of the Gold Rush, began to tumble as soon as available tonnage exceeded the supply of cargo, and fell right back to $10 within the following three years. In 1855 a railway was completed across the Isthmus of Panama and the long haul around Cape Horn became an anachronism overnight. The clippers, which were built for speed rather than capacity and were very costly to maintain because of their insatiable appetite for new sails and spars, were priced out of the market in a very short time.

The era of the American clipper ships was short, hectic and depended on freak economic conditions but while it lasted, ship design was completely transformed.

Although the 'Yankee Clippers' only achieved their full glory in the 50s they naturally had their origins much earlier. It seems as if the first ships to be called 'clippers' were the fast schooners from the Baltimore area that were described in Chapter One. Their main features were their deep, slack-bilged shapes with very fine run and large sail area compared to their displacement. However, their builders did not hit upon the idea of concave waterlines, which were such an essential feature of the later clippers. They did develop more efficient sail plans: first brigs and later schooners, one of whose features were raked masts which apparently gave rise to the adjective 'rakish' to describe a fast and ominous-looking vessel.

We have seen already that the development of faster sailing vessels follows from either military requirements or the availability of large commercial profits. The next important commerce to interest us was the Chinese opium trade which flourished between approximately 1830–50. Opium was supposed to be banned in China but was openly available in India. A fleet of specially built fast ships sprang up to carry on the business of smuggling opium into China. From a design point of view this was an extremely demanding requirement: the ships had to be fast in light airs but seaworthy enough to survive the dreaded typhoons and had also to carry an armament sufficient to drive off Chinese pirates and government vessels. The trade attracted a mixture of American and British vessels and was sufficiently profitable for ships to be specially built for it. One of the most interesting of the opium clippers was actually built as a yacht. The *Falcon* was built in Wooton Creek, Isle of Wight in 1824 for the Earl of Yarborough, Commodore of the Royal Yacht Squadron. He was one of those enlightened British noblemen who liked to see things improved, one of them being the Royal Navy. *Falcon* was a kind of miniature warship, being of 350 tons and mounting a broadside of 11 small guns. She was ship-rigged and heavily sparred and when in Yarborough's ownership frequently took part in trials against new naval vessels, which she generally outsailed. She still had the 'cod's head and mackerel tail' form that was typical of the period, but her lines were quite slim and refined and she had much more sail for her displacement than contemporary warships and merchant ships. *Falcon* was the pride of the Squadron but Yarborough became ill and sold her in 1836, whereupon

*Built as a yacht but later put into service as an opium smuggler, Falcon shows the English idea of a fast sailing vessel shortly before the clipper era. She is essentially similar to the frigates of the period but having somewhat finer lines and a higher sail area/displacement ratio, she was a bit faster. In the background can be seen a couple of heavily canvassed brigs and a schooner which were other examples of the effort to increase performance to meet the needs of the opium trade (National Maritime Museum)*

she disappeared 'out east', bought by the famous traders Jardine, Matheson who fitted her out for the opium trade. She then became one of the most celebrated vessels engaged in that trade and the only ship-rigged smuggler, so we can see that it was not only American influence that led to faster sailers.

American east coast builders produced a series of small brigs and schooners for the opium trade, generally around 90–100 tons and bearing some resemblance to the already mentioned Baltimore clippers. There was nothing really revolutionary about their design except that hull lines gradually got finer and sail areas bigger. American ships, however, did have the advantage of cotton duck sails which were superior to the flax canvas used by European ships of the period.

It is amusing that the humble beverage tea provided one of the more powerful economic forces of the 19th century and one of the most important of all time as far as ship design is concerned. The rapid rise in the standard of living at this time meant that many more people could afford to indulge their taste for a cup of tea, which remained an expensive luxury until the end of the 19th century, and it rapidly became one of the most important trades. Tea for Britain had for a long time been transported by the East India Company who had a monopoly of trade with both India and China. They used beamy, lumbering 'East Indiamen' which did not include speed among their virtues. However, in 1813 the Company lost its monopoly of trade with India and in 1833 with China, and when in 1849 the Navigation Act, which gave British ships the exclusive right to import goods into Britain or her colonies was repealed, the field was wide open for the first time. Tea is seasonal and the new crop of Chinese tea becomes available for loading into ships around the end of May each year. From that moment on, the ship that could get the tea to its market in Europe or America would get the best prices and so the 'tea race' was born. Like the race to the American west coast, it did not last very long. The Suez Canal opened in 1869 and destroyed the economic viability of the tea clippers at a stroke. The *Cutty Sark*, built in 1870, was thus an anachronism from the day she was launched and soon had to be put into the Australian wool trade which was about the last economic route for fast sailing ships.

To start with, fast American ships took the pickings of the China tea trade. They could make a rather profitable round trip starting from New York, thence to San Francisco with passengers and general cargo, then to Foochow to load tea either for New York or London and finally home again with general cargo, the whole thing taking approximately a year. After a short time, however, British shipowners and merchants were

24

stung into response and developed a breed of tea clipper that was finally superior to the American ships and culminated in masterpieces such as *Thermopylae* and *Cutty Sark*.

Probably the greatest ocean race of all time was the tea race of 1866. A whole fleet of purpose built tea clippers left Foochow on or after 29th May, bound for London. Among the best known were *Ariel*, *Fiery Cross*, *Serica*, *Taeping*, *Falcon*, *Flying Spur*, *Black Prince*, *Chinaman*, *Ada*, *Coulnakyle*, and *Taitsing*. The leaders raced neck and neck for 16,000 miles, often within sight of each other, and after 99 days of constant racing *Ariel* and *Taeping* reached London on the same tide and shared the prize for the first ship home. This stirring contest attracted a tremendous amount of attention at the time and their captains were public heroes. But of course it was not a game: *Ariel* loaded 1,230,000lbs (558,076kg) of tea that year at a rate of £7 a ton. Tea was a very high value cargo so that shipowners could afford to use ships that sacrificed carrying capacity for speed. So when the shipowners went back each year to their Scottish builders their demand was a simple one: faster, faster!

Having now outlined the circumstances which led to the demand for faster sailing ships, we can now go back to see how this demand was met by designers and builders. The Baltimore clippers had already developed the raked bow and improved sail plan but it was a draughtsman named John Griffiths of New York who proposed that ships should have concave or 'hollow' waterlines forward. To seamen and builders who for generations had believed that nature was the best model and that the shape of the cod and the salmon presented the ideal hull shape, this was heresy indeed and Griffiths was initially ridiculed. However, he kept up his campaign for what he claimed would be improvements by giving lectures and by displaying a model of the ship that he wanted to see built. Perseverance was finally rewarded when Howland and Aspinall commissioned Griffiths' employers Smith and Dimon to build them an experimental ship along the lines he proposed. She was the *Rainbow* of 750 tons, often called the first of the American clippers. The improvements Griffiths introduced were not confined to the bow. His midship section had much more deadrise than normal for a full-sectioned cargo ship and he lifted and fined the transom and quarters to balance the fineness of the forebody. Because she was so small, he could not make her nearly as narrow as the later, larger clippers, so she had the unremarkable ratio of just under 5 beams to the length. Critics said that she was 'inside out' and would never sail but they were soon proved wrong. With hindsight we can say that the hollowness of her waterlines was less important than the fact that the point of maximum beam was brought back to amidships so that something like a fair curve of areas was created for the first time. However, the slim, sharp bow did make a very useful contribution to windward performance because sailing vessels at that time had an amazing lack of lateral resistance. They would have made appalling leeway but for the fact that their rigs were so inefficient that they could not point up anyway. *Rainbow*'s hollow bow gave much more 'grip' on the water and resisted the tendency of the seas to push the bows away from the wind.

*Rainbow* was launched in 1845 and on her second voyage sailed from New York to Canton and back in six months and 14 days. By the standards of the day, this was sensational sailing and there were no more 'inside-out' remarks about her.

Smith and Dimon started work almost immediately on a second clipper, the *Sea Witch*. She was bigger at 907 tons and finer-ended than *Rainbow*. She also had the rather daring deadrise of 16 degrees which was generally considered too much as she proved tender and had to carry a lot of ballast. However, she proved an exceptional vessel and made a number of outstanding passages both to the west coast and China and attracted a lot of favourable attention.

Other American builders now began to get in on the act, the best known being Donald Mackay of Boston. During the next ten years this stern-faced expatriate Scot built a series of the most spectacular and successful sailing ships of all time. They were all built of native timber at hectic pace and none of them lasted long. The log of *Flying Cloud* on her record breaking passage to San Francisco is one long recitation of broken yards, sprung masts, torn sails and lost gear, for to achieve high speed these ships had to be driven with reckless determination. The softwood hulls could not stand up to it for very long and most of the Mackay clippers were reduced to leaky, soggy hulks within a remarkably short time. However, this did not matter when the name of the game was quick profit and five years was considered a reasonable life for a ship.

Mackay built increasingly large and daring ships as time went on and owners demanded more speed. Stability is a function of length as well as of beam so Mackay was able to increase the length-to-beam ratio as the size of the ships increased. Before long his clippers had over 6 beams to the length which is slim by any standard. His first clipper, *Staghound*, had an extreme deadrise, like *Sea Witch*, but she was too tender and later Mackay ships had a relatively full midship section. They were stiff but needed correspondingly harder driving to achieve the same speed.

The other great American builder was William Webb who built some of the most beautiful clippers, including the superb *Young America*, but

*Donald Mackay's famous* Staghound, *a ship that exemplifies the brief, hectic American clipper era. The enormous demand for shipping space from East to West coasts during the California gold rush meant that the fastest ships could charge astronomical rates and both owners and designers were willing to take big risks in the search for speed* (National Maritime Museum)

he was also a very astute businessman and changed over to building steam ships in 1853. Mackay, on the other hand, went stubbornly on building larger and more extreme clippers even when the writing was clearly on the wall.

Mackay wanted to build a 'super-clipper' and, unable to find backing at a time of falling freight rates, built with his own money. His *Great Republic* was 335ft (102·1m) long with a tonnage of 4,555 which would have made her far the biggest fine-lined sailing ship ever built and hence probably the fastest, but she never sailed as she was destroyed by fire in her fitting-out berth. Mackay was practically ruined and would have been except for a run of orders from the Liverpool shipowner James Baines whose famous 'Black Ball Line' had a big share of the ever growing traffic from Britain to Australia. Because of the vast distance – still far outside the range of early steamships – this remained a profitable

27

route for sail long after the tea trade had declined. Hearing of the legendary speed of the Mackay ships, Baines chartered his *Sovereign of the Seas* and sent her to Australia and back in 1853. He was sufficiently impressed with her performance that the following year he ordered four ships from Mackay, *Champion of the Seas*, *Donald Mackay*, *James Baines*, and *Lightning*. The last two named of these were over 2,500 net registered tons and were certainly among the fastest sailing ships of all time. Unfortunately some controversy surrounds the runs that have been claimed for them but their performances certainly rank with the best.

It is all too easy to come out with some neat and straightforward chronology of design development – for instance that the Baltimore clippers led to the Mackay and Webb clippers which in turn influenced British builders who then built their tea clippers. But, in the words of the song 'It ain't neccesarily so'. For instance the *Cutty Sark*, one of the most famous of all the clippers, had quite a different background. Her owner John Willis bought a strange old ship named *Tweed*, originally built in Bombay in 1854 as a paddle frigate named *Punjaub*. Her designer Oliver Lang was said to have modelled her on the lines of an old French Napoleonic war frigate which lay in Bombay. Willis bought *Punjaub* as a job lot with another ship, threw out the engines and had her

4. Lightning. *The Mackay clipper* Lightning *shows the American school of sailing ship design at its most exciting and elegant. Notice that being cargo carriers the clippers had a full mid-ship section and were totally different from the 'Baltimore clippers' in this respect. However the bluff bow had gone for ever, replaced by the lean, knife-like clipper bow with its characteristic hollow in the forward waterlines*

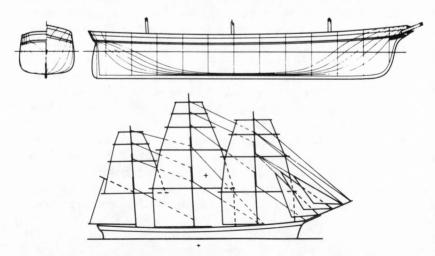

lengthened and then rigged as a sailing ship. Much to everyone's amazement she was extremely successful in her second career and made a number of fast passages to the Far East and Australia. Even after conversion she retained the big square frigate stern and was much drier and safer in following seas than the very fine lined clippers. Willis had the lines taken off the *Tweed* and presented them to Hercules Linton when he ordered *Cutty Sark*. When Linton's masterpiece appeared she was considerably more powerful than the usual tea clipper form, particularly in the stern which is full and buoyant above the waterline.

French naval architects were among the first to try to place ship design on a scientific basis in the 18th century and Basil Lubbock in his book *The China Clippers* even suggests that the Baltimore clippers owed a good deal to the French republican privateers that had been seen in American waters during the War of Independence. They in turn had no doubt been influenced by fast Mediterranean galleys, Xebecs and the like, and so the threads of design twist, turn, disappear and then surface again like the colours in a tapestry.

Tea clippers of the 1860s were beautiful but also tricky, delicate ships that required constant skilful handling by large and very skilled crews. They were too narrow and heavily sparred to stand up without ballast, even loaded. Typical clippers carried around 1,000 tons of tea which, being a light cargo, was simply loaded until every crevice of the holds was full. In addition they generally carried around 100 tons of permanent iron ballast and took on something like 200 tons of shingle ballast before starting to load cargo. In spite of this they were fairly tender, and unlike a modern yacht with a fixed ballast keel, there was no guarantee that a sailing ship would right herself if she got knocked down. For instance, it was conventional practice in a square rigged ship to bear away and bring the wind aft if caught in a squall. In a clipper this was considered too dangerous because if she took the full force on the beam she was liable to be laid flat, as in fact happened to several ships, so instead the clipper had to be very carefully luffed through squalls. If, on the other hand, the ship was luffed too sharply, there was the risk of being taken aback which almost always led to some degree of damage to the rig, if not actual dismasting. Running before the wind in heavy conditions was equally tricky. The lean, knife-like bow of the clipper would bury deeply into the back of a sea while the stern was lifted by the following one. A moment's lack of concentration by the helmsman could result in broaching-to when the stern would sweep uncontrollably round until the vessel lay broadside on in the trough of the wave, completely at the mercy of the wind and sea.

*Faster! Faster!*

With their fine ends, the clippers were just as trim-sensitive as a modern yacht and a badly loaded ship might prove impossible to steer. In the famous 1866 tea race, Captain Keay of the *Ariel* went to immense trouble to get her trim exactly right, constantly moving spare gear around the deck until he was satisfied. He was so dedicated that he had his own cabin filled with cable and hawsers when he wanted to bring more weight aft. Apparently this was no great hardship as he hardly ever went below during the three month passage to England except to eat or navigate! Keay had his carpenter build a large wooden box into which some weighty items such as kedge anchors and chain were placed, topped up with coal. These items were normally stowed under the fo'c's'le head so Keay obviously understood the importance of getting weight out of the ends. This box was then dragged around the deck as moveable ballast – there being no 'racing rules' to prevent this. Of course this was an instance of a top skipper pulling out all the stops in an effort to get ahead of his rivals, but it is very interesting to find that the clippers were trim-sensitive in a way that a modern yachtsman would understand.

*Ariel under sail. Commercial pressures led to these ships being raced with a dedication that would seem remarkable even today. The size of the figures indicate how small the tea clippers were partly as a result of the need for good light-airs performance in the China Sea (National Maritime Museum)*

An intriguing fact about the tea clippers is that they were so small. The Aberdeen-built *Chrysolite* which was one of the first successful British tea clippers was only 471 tons, and *Cutty Sark* which came right at the end of the clipper era 921 tons. Of course this is not displacement tonnage but net registered, a formula which expresses the internal volume of the hull with deductions for crew and working spaces. The way tonnage was measured actually had an important influence on the design of ships. Prior to 1854 British ships were measured (and taxed) by an antiquated formula that was basically just length times breadth. Not surprisingly, this led to short, deep vessels. After this date, Moorson's 'Registered Tonnage' was introduced, which measured volume in a way that did not penalize any particular dimension.

*Cutty Sark* has a 200ft (61m) waterline length and displaces perhaps 2,000 tons loaded to her marks: hardly the size of a decent coaster in modern terms, yet she is big compared to most tea clippers. The reasons seem to be two-fold. The only way that builders could get a reasonable light-airs performance in those days was to give the ships a very high sail area/displacement ratio and the materials of the day simply were not adequate to put a sufficient sail area on a big ship. *Cutty Sark* was ultra-modern when built and had brace-winches, but prior to this the only power available for hoisting and setting sail was human muscle heaving on rope tackles. Although the clippers had big crews, the essence of their success was that they had to be sailed hard with incessant trimming and changing of sails so the rig had to be reasonably handy. The American clippers were considerably bigger but they were not so heavily canvassed in proportion to their size as the British tea clippers and, in fact, did not achieve better sailing times over the same routes. Sailing conditions were the other big influence on size. The spring departure from the Chinese tea ports meant that the first part of the passage, down through the South China Sea to Anjer, would normally be sailed against light headwinds and as there are numerous islands and reefs to be negotiated (using very indifferent charts) it was a matter of constant short tacking. A small, manoeuvrable ship with plenty of sail was a must for this part of the passage which could take up to a month in a bad year. After clearing Sunda Strait the next stage of the passage was right across the Indian Ocean to Mauritius. They normally had a favourable SE trade for this but it was not a strong wind and on this very long stretch the ships would be dressed up with every possible stitch of canvas for which human ingenuity could find a place. The clippers all set stun'sails on light spars that extended beyond the ends of the normal yards and there was even a sail called Jamie Green that hung down under the jib-boom. It was only after passing the latitude of Mauritius that the clippers were likely to meet sustained periods of strong winds. Light-wind passages obviously breed small, heavily canvassed ships.

# Rigs of clipper ships

An awful lot of nonsense is talked about the efficiency or lack of it of square rig. In fact there is nothing that inherently prevents a square sail from being efficient and unlike a Bermudian sail, it represents a good compromise between windward and off-the-wind sailing. With the wind abaft the beam, a square rigged ship presents her sails more-or-less square to the wind but as the wind draws further ahead, the wind flows across the sail from luff to leach just as it does with a fore-and-aft sail except that the square sail does not have the aerodynamic drawback of a spar on the luff. In ideal conditions, therefore, a square sail should be of comparable efficiency to the jib on a modern Bermudian rig, except that it was difficult to keep the luff tight enough. The drawbacks to square rig are almost all concerned with the difficulties of setting the sails efficiently.

When one looks at a sailing battleship such as HMS *Victory*, it is hardly surprising that this type of ship lacked windward performance. The masts are the size of large trees and they are supported by an absolute jungle of thick, hemp rigging. If one added up the frontal area of all the masts, spars and rigging, it might come to about one third of the total sail area. The result is, enormous drag and hence an exceptionally poor lift-to-drag ratio. The sails themselves were made of flax canvas which is a thick, hairy cloth that had an inherently poor lift-to-drag performance and also held its shape poorly. Being very beamy, the lower shrouds have a wide spread and the yards cannot be turned or 'braced up' very far before they foul the backstays.

The rig of the clipper ship showed big improvements over *Victory*'s but they are improvements of degree not of kind. There was a big step forward when steel wire rope started to be used for standing rigging: this permitted much taller rigs and narrower rigging angles. Until metal masts were introduced, the heights of masts was limited to the length of trees available to be made into spars. To get the height needed, the technique is basically to stand one spar on top of another with an overlap to give strength. Metal masts were just beginning to be tried at the end of the clipper era but a late clipper such as *Cutty Sark* still had the traditional arrangement of three spars stepped above each other. The designers naturally made these spars as slim as they dared and the

*Reproduction of the 17th-century brig,* Nonsuch. *It is not difficult to see why such a vessel was barely able to sail to windward* (Brian G. Long)

engineering of rigging improved tremendously, but there was still an awful lot of standing rigging required to support these intricate spar plans and an awful lot of running rigging to set and sheet the sails. The sail material improved a lot as a result of the American introduction of cotton rather than flax.

The top clippers were raced so keenly that they used to slack off the rigging on the lee side in order to brace their yards up sharply when going to windward, which sounds a most hair-raising procedure in view of their 200ft (61m) high rigs! This enabled them to point about six points off the wind ($67\frac{1}{2}$ degrees) and was in fact not much improvement over the ships that sailed in the Armada but there was a very big difference in leeway angle, the angle between the ship's heading and her track. Medieval ships went sideways almost as much as forwards and were thus hardly capable, if at all, of making to windward. The sharp lined clippers on the other hand made between 5 and 10 degrees of leeway depending on speed, sea, condition of bottom and so on. The captain of *Ariel* claimed that she could make 11 knots hard on the wind with about 5 degrees leeway. However, an effective 77 degrees off the true wind leaves a great deal to be desired in windward performance. By comparison a modern racing yacht gets to within 40–45 degrees of the true wind.

In any case, windward performance of the clippers is slightly academic because they always recorded their best speeds with the wind abaft the beam. Wind dead aft was no use to them as the sails blanketed each other so the favourite point of sailing was the quartering reach when all sails could be made to draw.

# Speeds of the clippers

Elsewhere in this book we convince ourselves that speeds under sail never get very interesting unless the vessel is capable of exceeding the wind speed. However, this is only achieved by modern planing dinghies, catamarans, hydrofoils or other special high speed craft and the clippers could not even remotely approach this kind of performance. They were firmly rooted in the 'displacement zone' of hull types and their rigs were simply too draggy to allow them to draw the apparent wind ahead in the way that a modern yacht does. We are therefore looking at speeds achieved in strong winds and quartering reaches. In big seas such as those experienced in the 'roaring forties', even a laden ship should get a good shove forward from the waves and produce bursts of speed above the theoretical hull maximum. However, these tend to be balanced out by the time spent wallowing in the trough and the net effect of a good following sea could hardly be more than to increase the theoretical maximum from 1·3 to 1·5 times the square root of the waterline length. Therefore, in the case of a ship such as *Cutty Sark* with an effective waterline of about 200ft (61m), one is looking at a theoretical hull maximum of just a fraction over 21 knots. Any claims for a higher speed by ships of similar size can be instantly dismissed as nonsense while speeds even approaching this figure, accurately measured and achieved over a period, have to be seen as remarkable achievements.

The first question we must ask is how were speeds measured in the mid-19th century? The oldest method of measuring speed at sea was by the 'chip-log' which was still carried by most ships in the clipper period. This consisted of a reel of light line with a kind of wooden drogue on the end. The drogue was cast into the wake and the line allowed to run out freely for a measured time, usually a minute, after which it was stopped and the number of knots that had run out were counted. This was not a very accurate method, as can be imagined, and we can only accept its evidence to within the nearest two knots or so. Its other drawback is that it only 'sampled' the speed over a short period and it was a matter of judgement as to whether the average speed was higher or lower than that given by the chip-log.

From about 1850 onwards, the 'patent log' began to appear and as clippers were equipped without regard to expense most of them had one. The patent log is a spinner on the end of a line which trails astern of the ship. A system of gears counts the number of revolutions it makes and this is normally calibrated in nautical miles. As many a cruising yachtsman can testify, the 'Walker' log, when properly calibrated and maintained, is a remarkably accurate instrument which is rarely more than 5 per cent in error. Modern logs have the gearing part of the instrument mounted on board, operated by the twisting of the line to the spinner. However, the early ones had the gears built into the spinner itself so that the whole thing had to be pulled back on board to be read. This was normally done either daily to read 'day's run' or at noon and again in the evening or following forenoon to find the difference between two sextant sights.

Although it is a slight diversion it is worth mentioning how ships of this period were navigated, or rather how they fixed their position. The problem of how to find longitude at sea having been solved in the mid-18th century, every qualified ship's officer was competent in celestial navigation, and every foreign-going ship carried the necessary instruments and tables. Although there were none of the modern aids, such as short method sight reduction tables and radio time checks, celestial navigation in 1850 was capable of producing perfectly accurate results given:

(a) good instruments,
(b) good officers, and
(c) clear weather.

The normal method, still extensively used by yachtsmen today, consists of taking an altitude of the sun during the morning, meridian altitude at noon and a third sun-sight in the afternoon. Each of these sights produces a single line of position and these have to be combined into a 'running fix' by using the dead-reckoning course and distance run by log. If all goes well, this is a moderately accurate fix which can produce results to within about two miles. However, there are a lot of potential sources of error: in observation, in the instruments, in the tables and the use of them or in disturbance caused by currents or tidal streams. Star-sights, in which three or more stars are observed nearly simultaneously, are far more accurate but were not much used during this period. Lunar sights, which are hardly ever used nowadays, were quite popular in the 19th century but the moon is not that good as a navigational reference because it moves quickly, and because its outline is often hazy at the times when you can also see the horizon.

Because of the way in which the clippers were navigated, the speeds claimed for them are almost always based on the distance run from noon to noon. Even if the sights are accepted as accurate, things are still not straightforward because unless the ship is heading due north or south the length of time between zenith observations will be somewhat more or less than 24 hours and so an adjustment of the distance has to be made. Furthermore, difference of longitude and latitude have to be translated into nautical miles by a formula, adding yet one more source of error.

It must be fairly clear from the above that although the navigational methods of the period were *capable* of giving accurate results, there were a great many sources of possible error. In addition to these, we must in all fairness consider the possibility of deliberate exaggeration either by masters or owners or hyperbole on the part of subsequent historians. There was so much pride, loyalty and outright competitiveness involved that it would hardly be surprising if some of the claims made for clipper ships have not benefited from a degree of exaggeration. In his book on *Cutty Sark*, the late Alan Villiers recalls talking to a man who had served on her, who told him that 'she was never passed at sea by any other ship!' He adds drily that if a jet aircraft had come along the man simply would not have seen it!

The greatest day's run *claimed* for a sailing ship is 465 miles by the Mackay clipper *Champion of the Seas* on her maiden voyage to Australia in 1856. However this claim is viewed with considerable scepticism by experts on the period. In an article which appeared in *The Mariner's Mirror* in 1957 the late Captain James Learmont argued pretty convincingly that claims for day's runs of an average of more than 15·5 knots are likely to be apocryphal. In a way the Mackay-built Black Ball Line clippers *ought* to have been the fastest. They were considerably bigger than tea clippers and were designed to carry a mixture of passengers and general cargo. Hence they were not deep-loaded and should have been capable of being driven harder. But it was not the *Champion of the Seas* or any of the other Black Ball Line ships that held the record for the passage out to Melbourne, but the *Thermopylae* with her maiden voyage passage of 60 days. The considerably larger *James Baines* sailed from London to Melbourne in 63½ days and claimed to have reached a speed of 21 knots on the way. *Thermopylae* never claimed anything like this, her best day's run being recorded as 358 miles (14·9 knots). Of course it is quite possible that *Champion of the Seas* had some unfavourable weather which knocked her average for the voyage back, but it is obviously easier to believe record speeds if they form part of a record passage.

Another Mackay clipper, *Flying Cloud*, set the record for the fastest time from New York to San Francisco: 89 days 21 hours. On the 58th day of this passage she logged a day's run of 374 miles (15·58 knots). A fully detailed log of this passage survives, including the navigational calculations which were carried out by the captain's wife. Since she did not need to go on deck, Mrs Cressy had time to do an excellent job. She had three chronometers, Bowditch's five-figure log tables and a Dent sextant, and no one, including her husband, could fault her work. Because of the circumstances, and because of the believable nature of the claim, and because it did form part of a record passage, *Flying Cloud's* 374 miles is perhaps the most convincing claim made for a clipper ship. She was running up from Cape Horn into the Pacific on a north-westerly heading and her corrected day from observed noon to observed noon was 24 hours 19 minutes and 4 seconds. If the run is adjusted back to exactly 24 hours it becomes 369 miles (15·4 knots). It will be apparent to every yachtsman who has ever taken part in a race that in order to *average* 15 knots over a 24 hour period, the ship must have been sailing a good deal faster than that for long periods of time. As we have seen, the crew had no accurate method of measuring speed instantaneously but Captain Cressy used the chip-log from time to time and notes in his log for the day in question: 'During the squalls, 18 knots of line were not sufficient to measure the rate of speed.'

*Flying Cloud* was 225ft (68·5m) overall and 208ft (63·3m) on the keel, giving an effective sailing length of perhaps 215ft (65·5m). Square root of waterline multiplied by 1·3 gives her a hull speed of 19 knots. She was a brand new ship on her first voyage with a clean bottom and the best sails and equipment so her performance is perfectly believable.

Most experts seem to agree that the fastest British sailing ships were the two rivals *Thermopylae* and *Cutty Sark*. They were very similar in size and sail area, both being 212ft (65·5m) overall. *Cutty Sark* claimed to have sailed a day's run of 363 miles and *Thermopylae* 358 miles. In neither case does the evidence seem to be so strong as in the case of *Flying Cloud*. What no one can take away from these ships is their excellent passage times which are a matter of hard fact. *Thermopylae*'s 60 days from London to Melbourne shows that she was perhaps the best balanced clipper design of all because she kept up an excellent average in a variety of weather conditions. For instance, she could easily beat any of the Mackay clippers in light airs.

*Cutty Sark* had the reputation of being slightly superior to *Thermopylae* in heavy weather due no doubt to her more powerful lines plan. She achieved her best performances with her second career in the Australian wool trade. In the 'roaring forties' she once ran 3,737 miles in 13 consecutive days (11·9 knots) and 2,180 miles in 7 days (12·9 knots). It is these wonderful sustained averages that are her great glory rather than any slightly dubious claims of having sailed at 17½ knots.

When one looks at these performances in the light of modern experience, it is tempting to see them as disappointing. After all, a modern maxi ocean racer of 65ft (22·9m) waterline can easily rival the maximum speeds of the clippers and would leave them for dead in a race to windward. Big offshore multihulls of the type that have been built for races such as the two-handed transatlantic would be far quicker on all points of sail. However, this comparison is quite unfair. Every performance has to be viewed in its correct context. First, although the clippers are spoken of as 'racers' they were really fast freighters. *Cutty Sark* was carrying 1,200 tons of coal when she ran over 2,000 miles a week, more than her own light displacement. If your maxi racer had to carry her own weight again in cargo, the performance would be different indeed. Or, to look at things from the other viewpoint, if *Cutty Sark* could be re-rigged with aluminium spars, stainless steel wire rigging and Terylene sails, her performance would be vastly improved, especially to windward. She would probably get another knot all round just by having modern antifouling paint instead of Muntz metal sheathing. If her captains had had modern charts and navigational aids they could have sailed better and shorter passages and if her crew had had anything like decent waterproof clothing they would have had a far easier time, and so on.

For these and hundreds of other reasons, it is quite unfair to compare the clippers with modern yachts. You have to compare them with typical merchant ships of their own era, and by this standard they were flyers indeed.

# 3
# Dinghies and catamarans

Racing dinghies developed gradually from various types of small working boats. The basic definition of a dinghy is of a small open boat with no fixed keel which can be conveniently hauled out of the water when not in use or carried on board a larger vessel. One imagines that the first 'dinghy racers' were naval crews holding inter-ship races in the pulling and sailing whale-boats that were carried by warships. Today, one would hardly consider a Montague whaler to be a dinghy yet this type of craft is probably the direct ancestor of today's lightweight racing craft.

Very early in the history of the dinghy (mid-19th century) it was found advantageous to fit a drop keel or centre-plate to stop the thing from going sideways. For a long time, centre-plates had the dual function of providing lateral resistance and stability and were therefore generally made of metal. Although Uffa Fox is credited with having said that 'weight as such is of value only to the designer of a steam-roller' most of his dinghies had heavy metal centre-plates and it is only in the past 20 years or so that the majority of dinghies have been totally unballasted. Although it has always been obvious that sailing boats go better if the crew sit on the windward side, it was not so obvious that it was just as important to reduce the all-up weight of the craft.

One of the most comical of all sailing craft is the Bermuda 'Fitted Dinghy'. An open boat of only 14ft 1in (4·2m) overall length, it carries a crew of six and is 'fitted' with a deep, heavy, metal centre-plate. A gigantic sail-plan of up to 1,400 sq ft is used to drive the boat. Five of the crew hike out over the gunwale just as far as they can while the sixth bales like a madman in an effort to keep the thing afloat. Although Fitted Dinghy racing is highly spectacular and amusing, the boats are not particularly fast because they are far too heavy for their length and cannot get onto the plane unless five of the crew jump over the side, which they normally do after rounding the windward mark for the last time (they sail windward-leeward courses so that the final leg is a run). Of course the Bermudians understand this very well and the 'Fitteds' are lovingly maintained as a piece of maritime history rather than a contemporary racing craft. The Fitted Dinghy traces its origin right back to the 1880s and is a most interesting survival because it shows us a kind of 'snap-shot' of what a small racing boat could have been like in the last century.

The most interesting contrast to the Bermuda Fitted Dinghy is provided by the Sydney Harbour 18ft (5·4m) dinghies, the famous 'Aydeens'. Although bigger, they originally bore a strong resemblance to the Bermuda dinghy in that they were over-weight and over-powered. A crew of six strapping Aussies would fight to control an absolutely vast sail-plan including a spinnaker of up to 500 sq ft! However, it gradually became apparent that the boats went much faster if half the crew stayed ashore and a far smaller but more efficient sail-plan was used. The modern 18 footers therefore sail with a crew of three and with a sail area which is big but nothing like what it used to be. As a result the boats are much lighter and faster. Although all claims for their speed should be reduced by the usual 'Oz-factor' of 50 per cent, they are almost certainly the fastest single-hulled boats of their size in the World.

However, we are running ahead of ourselves! We should drag ourselves back to 1922 when the Yacht Racing Association (forerunner of the RYA) established a set of rules for a 14ft (4·2m) dinghy by amalgamating the features of the West of England, Norfolk and Small Boat Racing Association dinghies. This became the National and later the International 14ft Dinghy Class. The class has had a most interesting influence on design: at some stages being the leader in innovation and at others the staunch upholders of the status quo. They were popular little boats and soon became the premier small-boat racing class, especially after the Oxford and Cambridge University sailing clubs adopted them, thus bringing in the most outstanding young sailors of the generation, such as Peter Scott, John Winter and Stewart Morris. The steam yachts that travelled around the coast to the various big-yacht regattas often used to carry a 14 footer on board, thus creating a travelling circus that was the forerunner of today's 'open meeting' system. If daddy did not own a steam yacht, then you could always travel by train, with the 14 in the guard's van (not many undergraduates owned cars at that time). To cater for this very possibility, the original rules called for the spars to be short enough to stow inside the length of the boat until Uffa Fox devised a Bermudian mast with a 'fishing rod' joint. Eventually it was found that you could just wheedle a one-piece Bermudian mast into the average guard's van and the spar length requirement was dropped!

Each area tended to have its local variation but throughout the twenties the leading designer was the West Country boatbuilder Morgan Giles. Morgan Giles did his best to produce a 'balanced' design that would not gripe uncontrollably when it heeled. This entailed having a very full, 'U' sectioned bow and a fairly narrow and uplifted transom. The crew sat on the weather gunwale, of course, but everyone accepted the fact that the boats would heel 15 or 20 degrees on the wind. Well, not quite everyone! Uffa Fox, the brash, iconoclastic young Cowes boatbuilder had been apprenticed to S. E. Saunders, the remarkable pioneer of fast powerboats, hydroplanes and flying boats. During his time at the Saunders yard, Uffa had learned two lessons especially well: (a) the route to higher speeds was through planing, and (b) weight is only admirable in steam-rollers. Uffa's contribution, which was an enormous one, was to apply these lessons to the sailing dinghy. Although Uffa later liked to claim that he had invented the planing dinghy, this is really an over-simplification. Another outstanding sailor and designer, Tom Thornycroft, had also learned from fast powercraft, having designed among others the 50-knot Coastal Motor Boats of the First World War. He designed a planing 14 footer named *Pintail* which was built by Uffa Fox, whose own boats subsequently showed some Thornycroft influence. Unlike Uffa, however, Tom Thornycroft was too modest a man ever to make any dramatic claims on his own behalf.

The very first Uffa Fox 14 footer, *Avenger*, hit the class like a bombshell. In 1928 she won the Prince of Wales Cup at Lowestoft and from a total of 57 races had a record of 52 firsts, 2 seconds and 3 thirds. For the 1929 POW at Plymouth he had a new boat, *Daring*, and he won again, just beating *Pintail* which had a knock-down on the final leg. These boats were the first really effective planing dinghies and they introduced not merely a new shape of hull but a new style of sailing. The most obvious change in the hull shape was from a basically U-shaped to a basically V-shaped section, especially in the bow. In his own book, Uffa rather naïvely describes this as being 'broadly the only difference' between *Avenger* and the older Giles designs such as *Snark*. In fact they are profoundly different. As well as the strongly veed bow, *Avenger*'s lines show that the point of maximum depth has been moved well forward, giving the characteristic 'deep-chested' Uffa Fox shape. Just as important, from the point of maximum depth, just about under the

*The International 14ft dinghies* Daring *and* Pintail *off Cowes. Uffa Fox received much of the credit for developing the planing dinghy, but* Pintail *designed by Tom Thornycroft was probably just as influential* (Beken)

mast, both the centre-line and the quarter-beam buttock are virtually straight compared to the graceful even rocker of the Giles boat. The straight lines aft were to prevent the boat tucking down or 'squatting' as the speed increased and the deep chest was to give an angle of attack in the forebody in order to create lift.

The drawback to the new shape was that it is unbalanced and therefore sailed very badly if allowed to heel. Moral: don't allow it to heel! Uffa soon realized that *Avenger* would only plane if kept substantially upright and that a completely new style of sailing was necessary to achieve this. Firstly, it was essential to hang out over the side with renewed vigour and dedication and secondly, as soon as the boat started to heel, the sheet should be eased. Uffa himself described it like this:

'The playing of her mainsheet won her many races, for often she would leave other dinghies standing with her mainsail eased off and flying out to leeward like a flag, while they had theirs full of wind, the difference being that they were heeled over and lifeless while *Avenger* was upright and footing fast.' Curiously, Uffa retained the usual heavy bronze centre-board for *Avenger*. The class minimum weight of 225lbs (102kg) does not include the centre-board so a dramatic reduction in all-up weight could be achieved by changing to a wood or aluminium board. It was Peter Scott who hit on this in 1937 when he fitted a wooden board to *Thunder*, meanwhile disguising the change by painting it bronze-colour and going through a charade of making it look heavy whenever it had to be picked up in public. It took a surprisingly long time for people to realize that in a dinghy designed to be sailed upright, there was no point in a ballasted centre-board. In order to keep the boats upright, toe-straps were introduced and crews had to accustom themselves to the modern style of sitting out in which only the legs from the knees downward remain inside the boat.

When the trapeze, that simple invention that could have put a stop to all this agonizing sitting out was introduced, the class, or rather the YRA, roundly rejected it. It was an unruly young American, Beecher Moore, who first hit on this brilliant idea while sailing his Thames Rater *Vagabond*. The Raters are a fascinating survival from the Edwardian era when yachts were 'rated' according to the formula:

$$R = \frac{waterline\ length \times sail\ area}{5000}$$

with no restrictions on either structural weight, beam or overall length. Hence they have wide beam, long overhangs and very light hulls. These intriguing boats are carefully preserved and still sail on the river at the Thames Sailing Club at Surbiton where some new ones have recently been added to the small fleet. Beecher had the idea of attaching a line to the hounds and having his crew Bill Milestone hang onto it so that when sailing to windward he could not merely sit but *stand* out from the windward side. This proved to be extremely effective in keeping the boat upright especially because, as the third person in the crew, Milestone did not have to handle the jib and on tacking could simply walk across in front of the mast to the other side. As the photograph shows, there was no harness of any kind: Milestone just hung onto a knotted 'bell-rope'. This was not as ridiculous as it sounds because racing at Surbiton consisted of endless short tacking, although Beecher did later fit sliding seats to *Vagabond* – initially three, later reduced to one – which he found both more comfortable and more effective. The interesting part is that

*When Beecher Moore fitted a 'bell rope' to the mast of his Thames Rater* Vagabond *he hit on the idea that developed into the modern trapeze. But when Peter Scott used it on his International 14, the device was immediately banned!* (Daily Mirror)

no one ever protested against Beecher's sitting out aids on the Rater because they sailed under the Small Boat Association which had no rules on the subject.

Beecher was such an aggressive skipper that he found he had a mini-mutiny on his hands during Bourne End Week 1934 when his crew of Bill Milestone and Bessie Ellison declined to sail. Not a whit abashed, Beecher invited Peter Scott and John Winter to crew for the day and they were entranced by the 'bell-rope' idea. Four years later, they decided to try it out on the International 14, but first they had to devise a harness because it was obviously not possible to just hang on during a long race at sea. The trapeze proper was therefore unveiled during the 1938 POW at Falmouth which Scott and Winter won, sailing *Thunder and Lightning*. Charles Currey and Phil Gick sailing *Thunder* also had a trapeze but they capsized. Unlike the SBA, however, the YRA had a rule which banned projections beyond the gunwale which the trapeze was held to contravene, so this immensely important development was stillborn as far as the International 14 was concerned. The most extraordinary part of the whole story is that the Class managed to maintain this farcical ban on the trapeze for a further thirty years, long after other dinghies had been using it for ages.

As well as the International 14, Uffa Fox interested himself in another type of small boat, the sailing canoe, which had no restrictions on sitting-out aids because it came under yet another organization, the Canoe Club. These long, light, fully-decked boats were the result of a completely different line of development from dinghies, having evolved from paddling canoes which had to be light enough to carry. An undergraduate friend of Uffa's, Roger de Quincey, decided he would like to have a crack at the International Canoe Trophy, which had been held in the United States for the previous 48 years. Uffa had already designed, built and successfully raced a canoe built to the English rules and so it was decided that he should build a pair of new canoes which would fit both the English and American rules.

This was quite tricky because the American canoes were 3ins (76mm) narrower and 40lbs (18·1kg) lighter and were fitted with sliding seats. They were also supposed to be yawls with unstayed masts but Uffa got round this in an ingenious, not to say Foxy manner, by stepping the mizzen right up in the bow and using it as a spar forestay. The lines of the two canoes, which were named *Valiant* and *East Anglian*, looked something like a stretched-out *Daring*, except that there was less deadrise and an attractive pointed stern. The rudder fitted through a slot in the hull on a removeable frame, a device he used again on the Flying

Fifteen keelboat. The American canoe was permitted the useful sail area of 111 sq ft (10·3 sq metres) which would have laid it flat in all but the lightest of breezes were it not for the sliding seat. This consisted of a plank of wood that could be pushed out to one side of the hull enabling the helmsman to sit well outboard with his feet resting on the gunwale. Later in the development of the canoe, the plank became longer so that bodyweight was even further outboard, but not in Uffa Fox's day.

These light, narrow, heavily-canvassed single-handers are among the fastest yet trickiest of boats to sail, a fact which only increased their appeal to Uffa Fox. To cut a long story short, he and Roger de Quincey took their two canoes to the United States in 1933 and came back loaded with every trophy available to them, including the prestigious International Canoe Trophy. Their visit had a further and very beneficial effect because it was afterwards decided to amalgamate the English and American canoe rules, thus giving birth to the International 10 sq metre Canoe. Uffa designed and built one of the first of the International Canoes; named *Gallant*, it became one of his favourite boats and the well-known Beken photograph of him sailing her was his especial pride.

Uffa was so entranced by *Gallant* that he was determined to prove that she was indeed the fastest small boat afloat and this is very fortunate because it provides us with one of the very few pre-war measured speeds, albeit one that can only be accepted with reservation because Uffa apparently did the timing himself, while sailing on the sliding seat. He spent more than four months attempting to get a perfect run over a $\frac{1}{2}$-mile measured distance in the River Medina, upstream from Cowes. This course was far from ideal as it seldom gets a steady wind and Uffa admitted being physically exhausted by a run in a strong, gusty wind. However he finally achieved 16·3 knots, a speed far in excess of anything achieved by any contemporary dinghy, and a remarkable performance by a boat of only 17ft (5·18m) LOA. Indeed, until we get to lightweight catamarans, there is no faster small boat than the 10 sq metre canoe.

This fact was brought home to me quite dramatically in 1969 when the International Yacht Racing Union decided to run a competition for a new single-handed dinghy for use in the Olympics. All sorts of top dinghy designers and sailors built special new boats for these trials which were run at Weymouth. However it was the 10 sq metre canoe, sailed by Alan Emus, which not merely won every race but generally finished a whole leg of the course ahead of the next fastest boat. The IYRU loftily declared that the canoe 'was not the kind of boat they were looking for' and subsequently chose the Contender which was not the kind of boat

*Uffa Fox's wildest boat was his double sliding seat canoe* Brynhild. *Her influence extended beyond her actual achievement because she provided the inspiration for the first* Crossbow (Beken)

that anyone was looking for and has never become either popular or Olympic. But we digress!

Uffa Fox's mind worked in a highly original way: he always liked to maintain a pose of being 'a cruising man at heart' – especially when racing. He somehow came to the conclusion that a sailing canoe would make a good cruising boat but he did at least recognize that the single-handed 10 sq metre canoe was too tiring for this purpose. He therefore designed the 20ft (6·09m) LOA, twin sliding seat canoe *Brynhild*, in which he hoped to be able to nip over to Cherbourg for lunch and return in time for supper. Rather surprisingly, *Brynhild* never bettered the speed achieved in *Gallant*, but Uffa and his crew Bill Waight did go on a cruise to Brittany in her. Nowadays, when people cross the Atlantic on sailboards, this might not seem very remarkable but in 1936 it was quite extraordinary. *Brynhild* was light enough for two people to pick up and carry up a beach so the idea of coastwise cruising was not so silly. Incidentally, Uffa later used the hull of *Brynhild* as the prototype of his well-known airborne lifeboats (ABL) which were dropped from aircraft to ditched aircrew. The early ABLs were even built with blanked-off centre-board and rudder trunkings so that they could be converted back to canoes on cessation of hostilities!

*Brynhild* had an influence beyond her actual achievements because she clearly demonstrated how faster speeds under sail could be achieved. High power, high stability and low weight are the key factors and it is significant that when Tim Colman first sat down to think about a World Speed Record boat, *Brynhild* was his starting point. In fact, *Crossbow I* can be seen as a kind of super-*Brynhild*, an enormous canoe with very long sliding seats.

The Second World War put a stop to Uffa Fox's wilder experiments and his post-war dinghies such as the Firefly, Albacore and Swordfish were more or less variations on the *Avenger* theme. Although there is a very respectable retired naval officer who believes that he sailed at 30 knots in a Fairey Fox, Uffa's fastest dinghy was probably the 18ft (5·4m) Jollyboat, a rather narrow dinghy with a trapeze. When the first ever speed trials were held over a measured mile in the Solent in 1954, the Jollyboat, sailed by Peter Scott, had the best average of two runs in opposite directions, recording 10·227 knots. A much more impressive performance was that of the Hornet which was second fastest dinghy including a capsize! The Hornet, which was sailed by Beecher Moore with Brian Walker on the sliding seat, was 2ft (610mm) shorter than the Jollyboat and a more efficient boat in almost every way.

The success of the Hornet showed that leadership in the dinghy field had passed to the Putney boatbuilder Jack Holt who went into partnership with Beecher Moore shortly after the war. The combination of Jack's design ability and Beecher's pushiness and love of innovation proved to be uniquely successful and was the powerhouse behind the great surge in the popularity of small-boat sailing in the early post-war period. Their first project was *Merlin*, a 14ft (4·26m) dinghy that had to be cheap, simple to build and a 'wizard' performer. As originally built, *Merlin* was a low-freeboard dinghy with rules that allowed a self-draining cockpit, though this was not actually fitted to the first boat. She had a very advanced rig with a high aspect-ratio mainsail set on a 25ft (7·61m) high, streamlined, rotating mast. She was sponsored by *Yachting World* whose editor Teddy Haylock played a large part in the popularization of dinghy sailing in post-war Britain by sponsoring a series of designs by Jack Holt for amateur construction. After a couple of years the Class

Association decided that it would be useful to get the design adopted as a National class. Unfortunately, this enabled the RYA Dinghy Committee to get in on the act; being mostly International 14 men, they did their best to impose the worst features of the older class on the new one. Thus, *Merlin* lost 2ft 6in (761mm) off the mast, the freeboard was increased and worst of all the self-draining cockpit was deleted for the incredible reason that it was felt that 'it would tend to encourage an unseamanlike attitude to capsizing'. Even after this, it proved to be nearly as fast a boat as the International 14 and about half as expensive.

Holt's greatest successes were with plywood boats which he understood better than anyone. The fastest was, and is, the Hornet, a really exciting yet simple and cheap plywood boat that anyone with basic handyman skills could build at home. It brought high-performance sailing to a wider public, and being designed from the outset with a sliding seat was particularly suitable for a man and woman crew. After the Hornet appeared with its seat, other dinghy classes had to respond by allowing sitting-out aids and there was a sudden rush of new trapeze dinghies including the Flying Dutchman, the Coronet (which later developed into the 5-0-5) and the Jollyboat.

The Fairey dinghies introduced hot-moulded wood construction, a method which has hardly been improved upon in 30 years. The pre-war canoes had been very lightly built from two 1/8th inch (3mm) mahogany veneers with oiled silk between layers, laid over tiny steam-bent frames. This intricate construction could only be done by craftsmen and was very expensive. However, one of the most important spin-offs from war-time aircraft production was the development of reliable waterproof wood glues. Aero Research Ltd. of Duxford (ancestor of the present-day CIBA) designed the first urea-formaldehyde glues for the De Havilland Flamingo airliner just before the war which were used as the basis of the wooden construction system for the famous Mosquito fighter-bomber. This was built, rather like the Uffa Fox canoes, by building up several thin layers of wood over a former or mould. But instead of oiled silk, there was Aerolite glue between the laminates. Curved laminates built in this way have a built-in stress and hold their shape permanently so that much less internal framing is required. Hot moulding is a further refinement in which thermosetting glues are used and the final 'fixing' of the shell takes place under heat and pressure in a kind of pressure-cooker called an autoclave.

Not many boatbuilders could afford an autoclave and this method of boatbuilding more or less died out when Faireys stopped building wooden boats but 'cold moulding', which is the same system, without the final heat and pressure setting, has become a popular method of boatbuilding which can be used by any small boatbuilder or even the amateur. It produces, light, stiff, smooth shells and can only be improved upon, if at all, by advanced composite plastics. Ordinary glass fibre construction, as practised by most production boatbuilders, is markedly inferior in everything except price.

The 1954 speed trials saw a selection of fast, lightweight planing dinghies with trapezes or sliding seats. The years since then have seen a steady, gradual improvement, particularly of gear and sails, but there has been no real leap forward to compare with the breakthrough to the planing dinghy. A second set of speed trials the following year showed how things were going to develop when Ken Pearce's catamaran *Endeavour* proved considerably faster than the dinghies.

The Sydney Harbour 18 footer (5·4m) is almost certainly the fastest and most highly developed of dinghies. The class is fortunate in having very few rules so that there is a strong impetus towards lighter construction and more efficient rigs. A modern 18 footer can be built with an amazing low hull-weight thanks to advanced composite construction, and rigs can be changed according to weather conditions. With the crew of three all on trapezes, this certainly results in sparkling, not to say startling performances. Exactly how fast the 18 footers sail is hard to say since their performances in measured speed trials have usually been disappointing. Although their crews, like those of the *Cutty Sark*, would never admit to being passed by a jet plane, they are, for example, not as fast as a Tornado catamaran. We know that the Tornado peaks at around 20 knots, so to credit the 'Aydeen' with aydeen knots would probably be to err on the side of generosity.

## Cats can

To sail faster than the planing dinghy requires more stability without more weight. The dinghy gets crew weight as far outboard as possible on the trapeze and the only way to improve on this is to have a long sitting-out plank like the modern 10 sq metre canoe but this results in a very tippy boat. How about splitting the boat in two along its centre-line and then separating the two halves?

In fact, the Pacific Islands multihulls came about, not through the need for speed but for shallow draught, because they were built on reef islands. The basic boat is a hollowed out tree-trunk which has no stability and is therefore only suitable for paddling. But if you place two such log canoes side by side and connect them together by lashing tree-branches across them, then you create something much more interesting: a craft that is only slightly heavier than the sum of the two canoes and has no more draught but masses of stability. Furthermore, the individual hulls are long and slim and slip through the water nicely. It is incredible that European boat-builders never hit on this amazingly simple idea but except for some isolated experiments they didn't. When Captain James Cook first reached Tahiti, he and his shipmates were amazed by these 'double canoes' as they called them. Although they were so simple and crude, these native craft romped around the lumbering European ship like puppies playing with a tortoise.

Thanks to the 'not invented here' rule (nothing that was not invented here can possibly be any good), it was not until the middle of the 20th century that anyone took very serious note of what Captain Cook had observed two hundred years previously. In the early 1950s there were experimenters such as 'Bee' MacKinnon, Ken Pearce and the former Spitfire test-pilot Don Robertson. The Prout Brothers of Canvey Island then brought out the first catamaran offered for sale, the Shearwater, just ahead of Bill O'Brien with his Jumpahead. These boats offered a standard of performance that was startling compared to the conventional planing dinghy, particularly off the wind. Strangely enough, catamarans were never accepted with open arms by the yachting fraternity, indeed they seemed to represent some kind of threat to the established order of things and for a long time, cat sailors were generally cold-shouldered by yacht clubs. In spite of this, the Shearwater IV did eventually become popular and was adopted as a national class. There was a similar level of interest in Australia where Lindsay Cunningham was the pioneer. Oddly enough, catamarans never achieved any real degree of popularity until the early seventies when the Californian Hobie Alter brought out the Hobiecat, a strange banana-shaped craft that most catamaran designers view with a mixture of envy and distaste.

Popularity, however, is not a good measure of performance. On the other hand a very strong impetus towards better performance was provided by the imaginative conception of the International Catamaran Challenge Trophy. In 1959 the American magazine *Yachting* staged a 'One of a kind' regatta in which the oustanding catamaran and fastest boat overall proved to be *Tigercat* designed by Bob Harris. This led to the magazine describing *Tigercat* as 'the fastest small boat in the World', a remark which was irksome to the British cat designer Roderick Macalpine-Downie, designer of the successful Thai Mk IV cat, then the most potent performer on this side of the Atlantic. He decided to issue a challenge to the Eastern Multihull Association of USA for a series of match races, to be sailed in catamarans measuring to 'C' Class under the newly-established IYRU catamaran rules. He first asked his own club, the Royal Highland Yacht Club, to make a challenge but they were not smitten with the idea so Macalpine-Downie decided to team up with John Fisk, a Southend-on-Sea cat enthusiast who sailed a Thai. Fisk then made the challenge through the Chapman Sands Sailing Club, of which he was a flag officer. This was accepted and the organization of the first races entrusted to the Seacliff Yacht Club of Long Island, New York which generously donated a beautiful trophy, the International Catamaran Challenge Trophy, popularly known as the Little America's Cup because the competition is organized along similar lines to that most famous of yachting events.

'C' Class, which was the one chosen for the competition, has very nice, simple rules: maximum length of boat 25ft (7·61m), maximum beam 14ft (4·2m) and maximum sail area 300 sq ft. As usual with new departures in sailing, Beecher Moore was involved and he was responsible for the very important idea of measuring the 'actual' sail area including spars. It was this that made it possible to introduce wing masts since the rule makes no distinction between soft and hard sail area. The very first boat ever built to this rule was the famous *Hellcat*, certainly one of the most influential of post-war small boats. With this design, Macalpine-Downie established the basic theme that has been used for the vast majority of high-performance multihulls ever since. The basically 'U' shaped hulls were drawn out to a long, fine raking bow that incorporated a spray-board above the waterline to prevent diving. No attempt was made to go for a planing hull as Macalpine-Downie believed that such light, slim hulls are able to exceed 'hull speed' without planing. A planing hull-form would involve extra wetted surface and furthermore long, slim hulls make bad planing shapes because of their poor aspect-ratio. Like his Thai cat, there were generous-sized centre-boards to optimize windward performance, which previously seemed to be the weak point of catamarans. A major innovation was that instead of a solid bridge deck, the hulls were connected only by three light beams, to the after two of which a sailcloth 'trampoline' was laced in order to enable the crew to cross from one hull to the other. The mast was stepped on the centre of the main cross-beam, a wooden box structure which in later boats was replaced by an aluminium spar with a wire-braced strut or 'dolphin-striker' underneath to take the downward thrust of the rig. This layout made it possible to build *Hellcat* to the maximum permitted beam without undue weight penalty. The new boat was cold-moulded from two layers of specially-made ⅛ inch (3mm) Obeche two-ply, laid up at 90

Hellcat I, *first of the famous series of Macalpine-Downie designed C-Class catamarans*

degrees. The rig was a high aspect-ratio sloop with a large, fully-battened mainsail and small jib.

After playing with this exciting new boat for a few months, Fisk and Macalpine-Downie decided to incorporate the lesson into a second boat with glass fibre hulls. This was *Hellcat II*, which was the boat actually taken to America for the first challenge in 1961. The Americans meanwhile had held a trial series and chosen as their defender *Wildcat*, a somewhat banana-shaped craft from California, a bit like a prototype Hobiecat, which had a rather low rig with an enormous amount of roach in the mainsail. When it came to the test, *Hellcat II* sailed by Fisk and Macalpine-Downie, proved to have a marked superiority to windward and won the series by four races to one. *Hellcat II* was then sold in the United States to cover expenses, and the International Catamaran Challenge Trophy crossed the Atlantic to reside at the Chapman Sands Sailing Club for the next eight years.

During those eight years, the Trophy was defended annually, on every occasion but the last in boats designed by Macalpine-Downie, and the technology of sailing took some remarkable forward strides. This was largely due to a successful team effort which included Macalpine-Downie as overall designer, Austin Farrar as rig-designer/sailmaker and Reg White of Sailcraft as builder and helmsman. From *Hellcat I* onwards, hull design was more or less a matter of gradual refinement, but rig design took two giant steps forward.

The first was the *Emma Hamilton* sloop rig of 1964. Farrar was nearly unique among sailmakers in that he actually knew something about aerodynamics. He had also done a considerable amount of work with General Parham, an amateur experimenter, who was particularly interested in the concept of a twist-free sail. Parham had a little catamaran with a mast whose tip curved to windward which showed considerable promise. He argued that since it is impossible to have an absolutely straight leech in one plane with the straight mast, the answer was to curve the mast to the same shape as the leech, much as in a gull's wing. In recent years it has become clearer that the real villain of the piece was not so much twist in the sail as openness of leech, in other words sails that were incapable of maintaining their camber if permitted to twist. It has only really become possible to achieve sails that maintain correct camber even though twisted, with the most modern sailcloths and sailmaking methods.

In *Emma Hamilton*, the rig was increased in height by a full 2ft (610mm) compared to the previous year's boat but without raising the height of the shrouds. As well as improving the aspect-ratio of the rig, it was found possible to make the tip of the mast hook over to windward under the influence of leech tension. To give the leech the power to do this, there was a wire running up through the ends of the battens, controlled by a winch on the boom. The sail was so tall and slim that the luff and leech were parallel for about three-quarters of its height, and was fully battened. The mast rotated, the degree of rotation being controlled by a 'spanner' adjustably linked to the boom. It had been found advantageous to over-rotate the mast so that the spar and sail formed a continuous, smooth curve on the lee side (see diagram, p. 57). This over-rotation of the mast pulls the sail forward and this would not be possible if it were attached to the boom in the conventional way. Instead, the sail was 'loose-footed' and only connected to the boom at the clew where it was shackled to a traveller on top. If this starts to sound familiar, it is because this rig system was later adapted for use on the Tornado catamaran and subsequently on numerous other production multihulls.

*Emma Hamilton* defended the trophy for two years, first against *Sealion* from USA in 1964 and the following year against *Quest II* from Australia. Reg White, who sailed her on the latter occasion says that she was the nicest of all the 'C' Class boats to handle. She exhibited a marked superiority to windward yet was a safe boat to sail on the reach because the rig could always be 'de-powered' if necessary by freeing off the leech. The whole rig was powerful, controllable and yet reasonably light and is in use on thousands of boats around the world today.

The next step was to *Lady Helmsman* and her famous wing mast. Austin Farrar had believed for years that a greatly improved lift/drag ratio could be obtained by using something like a slow-speed glider wing standing on end. The difficulty was that aircraft wings are asymmetrical – like a sail that is permanently fixed on one tack! To be capable of sailing on either tack, a wing has to be in some way deformable. This can be achieved by some system of moving flaps or slats but this tends to be complex, heavy and expensive. The idea of the wing mast was not new – a number of people including Lord Brabazon and the Norwegian, Finn Utne had played around with it – but Farrar's solution to the tacking problem was innovative. He decided to use a composite sail which was partly solid and partly soft.

After a series of wind-tunnel tests at Southampton University it was decided to use a ratio of 40 per cent wing and 60 per cent sail. It was hoped that this would be an effective compromise between the efficiency of the solid wing and the ability of the soft sail to tack to the same camber on either tack. The camber itself was not adjustable and had to be a compromise: more would have been welcome in light winds and less in heavy. The only way to de-power the rig, if over-powered, was to let the boom rise and twist off the head of the sail. This was not the original intention; the *Lady H* first sailed with a wishbone boom arrangement that thrust down on the clew from part way up the mast (like *Crossbow II*) and power was adjusted by turning the whole rig like a barn-door.

This proved to be too drastic, as the power was all or nothing and so the wishbone was replaced by a normal loose-foot boom and out-haul traveller plus a dual mainsheet arrangement. One very powerful purchase from the end of the boom to the traveller on the radiused track was operated by the crew and acted as the vang, while a less powerful purchase led to a fixed position and was used by the helmsman to control the angle of the rig to the centreline. The wing was built by Sail Craft during the winter of 1965, using an ⅛ inch (3mm) ply skin over ply and polystyrene frames with spruce stringers. The completed mast weighed 92lbs (41·7kg) and was probably somewhat over-built as it survived three seasons of tough sailing without any structural problems. The section used was one of the old German Göttingen glider-wing sections (Gö. No. 652) with a very rounded leading edge and a camber ratio of 7. The mast itself was symmetrical but together with the sail it formed the characteristic 'tadpole' shape of the Göttingen section. Those who expected to see something like a modern, high-speed wing section hadn't done their sums correctly because even in the case of a boat as fast as a 'C' Class cat, the maximum apparent wind will be in the region of 50 knots, which is about the stalling speed of a modern light aircraft below which its wing is useless.

A special feature of this wing was its curved trailing edge, whose purpose was to eliminate twist in the sail. It is a little difficult to vizualize the geometry involved but when the mast turned to leeward (actually it turned itself, controlled by the spanner), the convex trailing edge put a leeward bow into the luff of the sail that corresponded to the curve of the leech – as with General Parham's curved mast. Also, the join between

*A Göttingen glider wing section compared to* Lady Helmsman*'s wing-mast plus sail* (Austin Farrar)

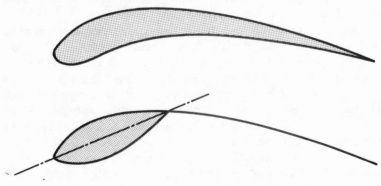

mast and sail being curved ensured that the sail faired into the section of the wing mast, eliminating the angle or 'knuckle' that is unavoidable if a wing mast is made with a straight trailing edge.

The *Hellcat* hull form really needed a complete re-think to match it to this powerful yet heavy sail-plan but there was insufficient time and money to go back to the drawing board. As a stop-gap solution, a knuckle was worked into the bow above the waterline to give additional reserve buoyancy. This was just as well because the boat's Achilles' heel proved to be her inability to shed power on the down-wind legs. Indeed, Reg White had to develop a special tactic for getting down-wind: this consisted of trapping his opponent on his weather quarter and then sailing backwards and forwards on a series of close reaches.

To windward, *Lady Helmsman* proved to have a devastating performance advantage. In trials, she proved capable of pointing nearly 10 degrees higher than the sloop-rigged boats without loss of speed or sailing 10 per cent faster on their heading. She was also quite easy to sail to windward; the rounded leading edge is very stall-tolerant and the boat could be feathered up-wind just like a conventional sloop. On a dead run she was actually slower than a conventional sloop because of her extra weight but as fast cats virtually never sail on a dead run this was not important. On a broad reach in a fresh breeze she was terrifying and showed a marked desire to cartwheel over the lee bow. Reg White describes it as being like driving down a mountain road with the accelerator stuck fully down! The power and weight of the rig imposed a fearful strain on the boat. During her three-year racing career she suffered a long string of damage, such as, centre-boards, rudders, and beams. In spite of this, her superior windward performance proved decisive, as usual in racing, and she successfully defended the Little America's Cup three times. This very important boat, which marked one of the really big steps forward in sailing technology, can be seen at the National Maritime Museum, Greenwich.

One of the more dubious achievements *Lady Helmsman* was to be credited with was being 'the fastest sailing boat in the World', by no less an authority than the *Guinness Book of Records*, with a speed of 30 knots. It turned out that the method of measurement was by pacing her with a car along the Southend-on-Sea seafront – hardly a scientific method. The fact that this 'trial' was organized by the public relations company acting for the paint company that sponsored the boat might also give us a clue as to the kind of weight that could be placed on it. The Speed Trials at Weymouth were conceived partly as a response to this kind of unsubstantiated claim, so perhaps it did some good!

Lady Helmsman *(K31) was not the first yacht to use a wing mast but the first to conclusively prove that it was a practical, race-winning device. To windward is* Quest II *in the Little America's Cup race on 4 September 1967* (Associated Press)

This might be an appropriate place to ask why, if wing masts are so clever, more boats are not fitted with them? The answer is that except for special events such as the Little America's Cup, they are too expensive and impractical. For instance, even boats as stable as the 'C' Class cats have to be de-rigged after sailing otherwise they are liable to wreck themselves. One owner found this out to his cost when his boat disappeared from the Catamaran Yacht Club at Sheppey during the night and was never seen again!

Britain lost the International Catamaran Challenge Trophy to Denmark in 1969, mainly because *Lady Helmsman* was no longer in a fit state to defend it for a fourth time, having been left in the open without attention since the previous year. Reg White cobbled together a defence using *Lady H*'s rig on *Ocelot*, a rather unsuccessful boat he had designed himself. *Ocelot* was beaten by Denmark's *Opus* which in turn lost to *Quest III* from Australia (previously beaten by *Lady Helmsman*), since when the Trophy has been held either by Australia or the USA.

In the years since *Lady Helmsman* became a museum-piece, the hulls of 'C' Class cats have not changed greatly although they have become lighter thanks to more exotic materials. Development of rigs, on the other hand, has continued apace. There was a particularly interesting trials series for the Australian defence of 1972 in which *Quest III*, using a very sophisticated and adjustable version of the *Lady Helmsman* rig, was opposed by *Miss Nylex* which had a fully-solid wing rig with adjustable trailing-edge flaps. *Miss Nylex* was both faster and closer-winded on the windward legs but the lack of camber control made her a dull and erratic performer downwind. *Quest* was chosen as defender and went on to trounce the US challenger *Weathercock* four-nil. Since then, the trophy has been won both by a solid wing-rigged boat *and* by a fully soft-sailed boat which turned the tables by being so fast down-wind that it could give away windward performance.

The main drift of development has been to produce a fully-solid wing rig that embodied both camber control and twist control. It is probably a good moment to emphasize why twist is important. Apparent wind is the result of the true wind velocity and direction, and the boat's velocity and direction. The faster the boat, the greater the angle between true and apparent winds, until in the case of a really fast boat such as a 'C' Class, the rig is in a fully close-hauled attitude although the boat is sailing on a broad reach. Now there is considerable difference in wind-speed between water-level and 30ft (9·14m) above it – due to friction between the moving air and the sea surface. The angle between true and apparent wind also depends on the wind velocity so if there is more wind at the masthead than at the deck, there will also be different apparent wind direction. Furthermore, the faster the boat, the more marked will be this effect. It is also worth pointing out that Austin Farrar feels that the emphasis on 'twistability' in modern wing rigs has gone too far. Many years ago, he and General Parham conducted a classic experiment which showed that wind twist on a 20ft (6m) mast was virtually undetectable. They set up a Swordfish dinghy with no sails but streamers at 1ft (304mm) intervals up the mast. The boat was then towed at a speed and angle to represent windward sailing and the streamers were filmed from below, showing no evidence of twist. General Parham's theory was that although wind speed is undoubtedly less at sea-level, the air has to speed up when it passes over a boat and that this cancels out the expected twist effect.

A team in the United States led by Dave Hubbard and Tony Di Mauro have built a series of *Patient Ladys* and wing rigs in an effort to achieve camber and twist control. *Patient Lady III* came very close to it in 1974 with a solid wing mast with three slotted flaps on its trailing edge. Control arms introduced twist into the wing by allowing the middle and upper sections to bend off to varying degrees. They perfected the rig with *Patient Lady IV* whose flaps and slots all automatically tack to the same value of camber and twist and they managed to do this with an all-up weight of 550lbs (249·4kg). The whole wing looks a little like the trailing edge of a Boeing 747, where instead of one big flap, a series of slotted ones come out on a curved track so that the overall effect is of a smooth curve. *Patient Lady IV* defended the Little America's Cup in 1978 without losing a race.

Farrar would nowadays like to try a really deformable wing rig using a 'D' section mast with two fully-battened sails. This approach was used by an Italian team which made two very convincing challenges for the Little America's Cup. On the first occasion they came within one race of winning, sailing against the fully wing-sailed *Patient Lady*. There is reason to believe that a deformable wing with really effective camber control could be extremely effective down-wind.

Experience with a 'C' Class boat named *Thunder* led Rodney March and Peter Shaw to develop what they called the 'tortured ply' method of construction. Briefly, this consists of forcing plywood into a limited degree of double-curvature which creates stiffness with a minimal amount of internal framing. March, a Post Office engineer, then used this system to design the Tornado catamaran which in 1967 won the IYRU's competition for 'B' Class catamarans. For once the IYRU chose wisely for the Tornado rapidly became popular and was used in the Olympics from 1976 onwards, when Reg White won the first Gold Medal at Kingston, Ontario. At the original selection trials organized by the Catamaran Y.C. at Sheppey, two prototype Tornadoes appeared, one with a wing mast and one with a sloop based on the *Emma Hamilton* system. The selectors wisely chose the latter which has proved to be one of the most powerful, practical, tunable rigs ever mounted on a one-design. Its good qualities can be seen from the fact that people working on experimental rigs for speed trials have repeatedly chosen the Tornado rig as an 'off the shelf' powerplant which is hard to improve upon, except by the great expense of a wing rig.

In this brief canter through the development of the dinghy and

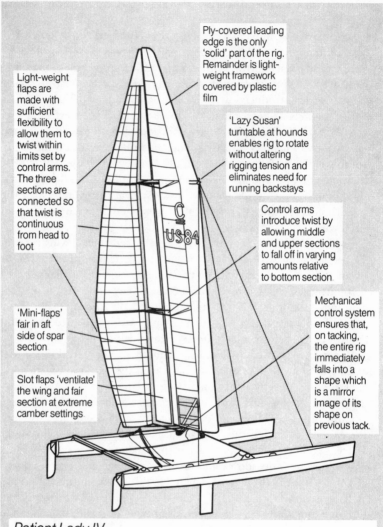

Light-weight flaps are made with sufficient flexibility to allow them to twist within limits set by control arms. The three sections are connected so that twist is continuous from head to foot

Ply-covered leading edge is the only 'solid' part of the rig. Remainder is light-weight framework covered by plastic film

'Lazy Susan' turntable at hounds enables rig to rotate without altering rigging tension and eliminates need for running backstays

Control arms introduce twist by allowing middle and upper sections to fall off in varying amounts relative to bottom section.

Mechanical control system ensures that, on tacking, the entire rig immediately falls into a shape which is a mirror image of its shape on previous tack.

'Mini-flaps' fair in aft side of spar section

Slot flaps 'ventilate' the wing and fair section at extreme camber settings.

*Patient Lady IV*

*A fully-developed wing rig as used on* Patient Lady IV *when she retained the Catamaran Challenge Trophy in 1978. This very sophisticated construction is necessary in order to combine the efficiency of the solid wing with the adjustability of the soft sail. Devising a practical way of inducing a controlled degree of twist was the most difficult problem and brought one of the biggest improvements in performance*
Yacht Racing/Cruising. January 1979

*The Tornado catamaran was the first multihull to sail in the Olympics and is the fastest class racing dayboat* (Guy Gurney)

catamaran, thousands of fast boats have not even been mentioned because the intention has been to trace the path towards higher top speed rather than write a monograph on the history of small boats. I see the process in terms of a limited number of key developments: in dinghies, planing, lightweight construction and added stability resulting from trapeze or sliding seat. In multihulls, the important steps were those of the lightweight 'trampoline' construction of the Hellcats, the *Emma Hamilton* rig and the wing or semi-wing mast. The next step forward – hydrofoils – is described in another chapter.

# 4
# Offshore yachts

The sport of ocean racing is relatively young when compared to yachting in general. Apart from various one-off events, it was not until the 1920s that some of the major events such as the Fastnet and Bermuda races came along to provide the impetus to get things underway. In the early years of ocean racing, the yachts were conservative in design and came under the heading of what would today be called a 'cruiser racer'. As Uffa Fox put it in his *Second Book*, 'Ocean racers are cruisers developed by racing men'.

A typical example of a cruiser developed by racing men might be the famous Sparkman and Stephens yawl *Dorade* which was the outstanding offshore boat of 1930. She won, among other events, the Bermuda, Fastnet and Transatlantic races. Measuring 52ft (15·8m) LOA, 37ft 3in (11·35m) LWL, she was considered rather daringly small and light with a displacement of 14·75 tons. Today, this would class as a very heavy displacement and *Dorade* achieved her speed by virtue of a long waterline and slim, easy lines. As an inevitable consequence she was firmly bound by the laws of displacement hulls having a maximum hull speed (1·5 times square root of WL) of about 8½ knots. This is borne out by the fact that her best recorded day's run was a fraction over 200 miles, an average of 8·3 knots.

Of course it has to be understood from the outset that in conventional offshore racing yachts are designed, not for outright speed but for good performance relative to *rating*. This is not the place for an exhaustive discussion of the various types of rating rule but what they all have in common (all modern measurement rules) is that they try to provide a mathematical model of the things that make a boat go fast. There is a formula in which the basic physical properties of length, beam, sail area and displacement are given certain values. One might think that this could be done in a completely dispassionate, scientific manner but unfortunately this has never proved to be so. In fact, the weight that the rule-makers place on the various factors in the formula tends to reflect their mental picture of an 'ideal yacht'. For instance if displacement were only a small factor in the formula, it is clear that the result would be an immediate trend towards very light displacement yachts. When this happens, as it does from time to time, the rule-makers say to themselves 'very light displacement boats are dangerous and ought to be discouraged'. They then alter the rule so that light displacement is more highly taxed. The same applies to any other dimension and therefore, at any given moment, the rating rule tends to point towards what the rule-makers view to be a 'healthy' type of boat.

Nowadays, rule-making committees are well aware of this tendency and constantly try to avoid imposing a certain view of design through their rules, yet they cannot avoid the fact that rules tend to dictate what are considered typical values for sail area, displacement and so on. They also have to block off extreme features that might be dangerous, such as yachts which are not inherently capable of self-righting.

The existence of rating rules, and in particular those of the Royal Ocean Racing Club in Britain and the Cruising Club of America and Storm Trysail Club in the USA, tended for many years to encourage conservatism in offshore design and to maintain the ideal of a racing boat that would have an extended life as a cruiser after its racing days were over. One of the main results of this trend was that the great majority of offshore yachts were of moderate displacement and thus limited by waterline length in the speeds that they could achieve.

In recent years, this picture has changed somewhat and it is a change which appears to be accelerating. Several factors seem to be at work, all of them tending to produce lighter and faster yachts. On the one hand there has been a certain impatience with the idea of the rating rule and a new breed of yachts has grown up designed mainly for 'line honours'. These are yachts which race within the established pattern of offshore events but with a general philosophy of 'hang the handicap result – let's be first over the finishing line'. A prime example of this is the current breed of 'maxis', yachts built to the maximum rating allowed under IOR. They operate as a kind of monster level rating class, not often winning races overall, but getting round the course very quickly.

Another influence has been that of the increasing number of sponsored spectaculars such as the various transatlantic or round-the-world races. With one or two exceptions, such as the Whitbread Round the World Race, these have been conducted without the benefit of rating rules or with very simplified ones, such as a maximum overall length only. These have naturally enabled designers to be much bolder and the availability of sponsors' money has made it possible for some very extreme vessels to be built. The result has been that passage speeds have been pushed up dramatically and there is every sign that they will continue to be.

Even in conventional offshore fleets, boats now sail considerably faster than they did twenty years ago. The steady improvement of design and materials have made it possible to build boats with much higher sail area/displacement ratios and as this type of boat has proved itself to be reasonably seaworthy, so rule-makers have pulled back the borderline of what is considered 'extreme'. The net result is that a boat such as a competitive half-tonner today will have an enormously greater sail area/displacement ratio than yachts of the same rating only ten years ago and they are correspondingly much faster through the water. The light, beamy, flat-floored ocean racer of today is perfectly capable of planing in the right circumstances and thus escaping from the limitations of waterline length. Thus even quite small boats such as half-tonners can romp along downwind at around 10 knots in a good breeze, while the 80ft (24·3m), maxis can, under ideal conditions, average speeds of 18–20 knots.

Prior to the First World War there were occasional transatlantic races but not sailed in anything that we would recognize today as an 'offshore racer'. These forays were made in the large schooners or cutters which were the seagoing gentleman's yachts of the day. One of the first races was in 1870 when the English yacht *Cambria*, later to be the first of many challengers for the America's Cup, raced across the Atlantic East to West in competition with the American schooner *Dauntless*. *Cambria* was the winner with the time of a little over 23 days from Daunt Rock (Southern Ireland) to Sandy Hook, an average of approximately 128 miles per day or a little less than 5½ knots. This was hardly a brilliant performance for a vessel of 108ft (32·9m) overall but it must be remembered that this crossing was by the northern or windward route on which a schooner with flax sails could not be expected to excel.

The 1905 Transatlantic Race was a very different affair and resulted in a record which stood until 1980. During that period, the Kaiser Wilhelm II was very envious of British sea-power and was keen to outdo 'Perfidious Albion' in every way possible including yachting. He kept buying up well-known racing yachts in the hope of sweeping the field at Cowes, but with little success. He also promoted Kiel Regatta as a rival to Cowes and among other things gave the 'Emperor's Cup' for a transatlantic race in order to tempt the cream of American yachts over to Kiel.

For the 1905 race, the lovely 185ft (56·3m), William Gardner designed three-masted schooner *Atlantic* was commanded by the famous professional skipper Charlie Barr who had already sent various America's Cup challengers back home disappointed. This tough Scots-born American was the leading skipper of his era and at the height of his power and reputation when Wilson Marshall engaged him to race *Atlantic* over to the Baltic. Marshall came along for the trip with a party of guests, but in the fashion of the day took little or no part in the handling of the yacht. Apparently they would retire to their bunks after a good dinner, leaving Barr to do his worst. Now Barr was a real driver in the sense that a modern offshore skipper would understand and he couldn't care less if the owner and his friends felt sea-sick or if seawater was spoiling the saloon carpets. His aim was to keep the yacht sailing at her absolute maximum every minute of the day and night. In an era when practically all yachting took place during daylight, this was more or less unheard of.

*The mighty schooner* Atlantic *whose record for the Atlantic crossing, West to East, stood unbroken for more than 70 years* (Rosenfeld)

*Atlantic* was a gigantic yacht, with about 160ft (48·7m) effective sailing length once she got her ends into the water. Her three-masted topsail schooner rig was well-suited to heavy-weather down-wind sailing because it developed lots of power low down. Barr was lucky in that a series of deep depressions kept him supplied with westerly gales for most of the way across. *Atlantic*'s time for this epic passage was 12 days, 4 hours and 1 minute from Sandy Hook to the Lizard, which is approximately 248 miles per day or 10·3 knots. Her best day's run was 341 miles or 14·2 knots.

In many ways it is hardly surprising that this performance remained unsurpassed for over 70 years because yachting on such an enormous scale more or less died out with the First World War. Even the monsters of the 'J' Class that raced for the America's Cup in the thirties were nothing like as big, and anyway were dayboats. If they had to cross the Atlantic they did it very gently under reduced rigs or were towed. Therefore, it was not until the present generation of maxi-yachts and offshore multihulls came long that anyone stood much chance of bettering *Atlantic*'s time. In recent years, a number of yachts have made serious attempts on this record and found it an extremely hard nut to crack. Huey Long's *Ondine III* made a well-planned attempt in 1979 which included a great deal of outside assistance that was not available to Charlie Barr, such as satellite weather reports. *Ondine* actually stayed ahead of *Atlantic*'s time for most of the way across but ran out of wind off Southern Ireland. The same sort of thing happend to Chay Blyth in his big trimaran *Brittany Ferries GB*, but success eventually came to Eric Tabarly and two crew sailing his hydrofoil-stabilized trimaran *Paul Ricard*. This time the wind stayed with them all the way and they were able to knock a whopping 46 hours off *Atlantic*'s old record with a passage of 10 days, 5 hours and 14 minutes, representing an average of 286 miles per day or 11·92 knots. This new record remained in force only a year, after which Marc Pajot in *Elf Aquitaine* bettered it with the amazing time of 9 days, 10 hours 6 minutes or approximately 320 miles per day. During this tremendous passage, *Elf Aquitaine* recorded a day's run of 360 miles (15 knots). Thus, it was not until the development of the light-weight ocean-going multihull that it was possible to find an alternative to *Atlantic*'s enormous waterline length. Her 1905 time remains the record for a single-hulled vessel and could well stand as such after another 70 years.

One of the reasons that *Atlantic*'s record stood for so long was that offshore racing was not really the 'done thing' in the Edwardian period. There were plenty of big and fast yachts about but they were used mainly

*The royal cutter* Britannia *under her original gaff rig. In this form she raced across the Channel and back in record time. In general, however, the big racing yachts of this era did not race over long distances* (Beken)

for day-racing. In retrospect it is extraordinary to think of huge yachts such as *Britannia* and *Satanita* being used almost exclusively for short coastal races. It was not that they were unseaworthy or lacked accommodation – indeed the permanent crew lived aboard throughout the season and the afterguard had quarters of great splendour – it was simply that the idea of racing after dark was not attractive to the owners of these yachts. When big racing yachts needed to move from one regatta to another, say Cowes to Kiel, they were either towed or sailed under easy canvas by the permanent crew. The owner, if attending the regatta, would travel in comfort and arrive in time for the racing.

There were occasional exceptions to this rule. In 1893, the year that G. L. Watson's masterpiece, the royal cutter *Britannia*, came out, she was challenged to a race across the Channel and back by the American cutter *Navahoe*. The Prince of Wales accepted the challenge and the Royal Yacht Squadron arranged a race from the Needles to Cherbourg and back. There was a strong easterly wind which gave the two yachts a thundering reach both ways. Both of the yachts were rigged as gaff cutters which is a reasonably effective rig for off-wind sailing. The distance from the Needles to Cherbourg is about 60 nautical miles and *Britannia* sailed the double distance in 10 hours, 37 minutes and 35 seconds, crossing the line only 57 seconds ahead of *Navahoe* which, incidentally, was declared the winner on handicap after a row because Squadron officials had moved the finishing line. This represents an average of 11·3 knots.

*Britannia* was 122ft (37·1m) LOA, 87ft (26·5m) LWL, displaced 153·5 tons and could set 10,797 sq ft of sail on her original rig. Her 'hull maximum' was about 14 knots and she must have sailed well up to this in order to average 11·3. This was confirmed much later in her career by her well-known helmsman Major Philip Hunloke. Following a race off Harwich in which he pressed her to the limit, sailing with the lee skylights in the water, he said that she had done 14 knots through the water and that this was about her limit.

It was sad that this famous dash across the Channel was never repeated. One reason, pointed out by Uffa Fox, is that the rigs of the big racing yachts became so specialized that they did not care to venture out in more than about Force 6. As she was finally re-rigged in 1930, *Britannia* qualified for the 'J' Class, then in use for the America's Cup. Most of the yachts built to this rule were strictly day-time butterflies which could not have risked a sea passage under their racing rigs.

One problem when talking about the speeds of the big yachts of this era is that no one was making any special effort to measure them accurately. After all, the objective of a yacht race is to reach the finish in front of the others so the actual speeds achieved are of no more than passing interest, even if someone took the trouble to record them. Another speed that is quoted as a record is that of the racing cutter *Satanita* which is alleged to have been timed at 17 knots between two points on the Clyde. She was even longer than *Britannia*, being 93ft 6in (28·4m) LWL, but it is difficult to know whether to believe this speed since it represents a performance of better than 1·7 times square root of waterline length and, as we have seen, heavy keelboats are hardly ever able to exceed 1·5 times root WL. Heckstall-Smith in his book *Britannia and her Contemporaries* says that she was the fastest of the big cutters on a reach but gives her best performance as 12·25 knots over a 45 mile reaching course in the Solent in 1893.

# *America's Cup*

Although the America's Cup is not strictly an 'offshore' event, it is sailed on the open sea. Some absolutely vast yachts were built for this contest, particularly in the early stages. The largest of all was the 1903 defender *Reliance* which was 144 feet (43·8m) LOA, 90ft (27·4m) LWL. These measurements indicate that she had immensely long overhanging ends which were not taken into account by the measurement rule then in force. As soon as she heeled these long ends became immersed and added at least another 20ft (6m) to her effective sailing length. Built of bronze alloy, *Reliance* was a very innovative design by the great American designer Nathanael Herreshoff and could set a staggering 16,000 sq ft of canvas on her hollow steel mast. Like many of the big American yachts of the period she was very beamy with a 'champagne glass' midship section. British yachtsmen referred to them deprecatingly as 'skimming dishes' apparently not having the wit to see that if you got some of your stability by beam rather than ballast ratio, you could keep the displacement down and hence improve the sail/area displacement ratio. It is ironic that this lesson had to be learned all over again in the fifties and sixties when British designers persisted in the belief that 'nothing stops a boat like beam' (Charles E. Nicholson) and as a result offered little competition to US designers such as Stephens and Carter.

*Reliance* and the other America's Cup monsters were no doubt fast but we don't know with any accuracy just how fast. With an effective sailing length of perhaps 120ft (36·5m), *Reliance* must certainly have been capable of speeds in the region of 16–17 knots.

Following the *Shamrock III* versus *Reliance* match of 1903, America's Cup yachts began to shrink a little but at the same time design and materials were improving so the speed potential was probably about the same. From 1930, the Cup was raced in yachts measuring to 'J' Class of the Universal Rule. Stripped to its essentials, this rule was 'Eighteen percent of waterline length in feet, multiplied by square root of sail area in square feet divided by cube root of displacement in cubic feet equals 76'. Effectively, this means that if you want more length you have to pay for it with more displacement or less sail area. Yachts also had to be built to Lloyds scantling rules so that freakishly light construction was not possible. This was a situation much closer to that which governs offshore racing today, in which efforts to build faster yachts are curbed by a measurement rule which estimates the speed producing factors and lays down minimum standards of construction and equipment.

## Faster! Faster!

There is no doubt that the fastest of the mighty 'J's' was the final American defender *Ranger*, designed by Starling Burgess for the 1937 challenge. The young Olin Stephens was working for Burgess at the time and many people have supposed that the lines of *Ranger* were his but Stephens himself denies this. *Ranger* was 135ft 3in (41·2m) LOA, 87ft (26·5m) LWL, 21ft (6·4m) beam, 15ft (4·5m) draught and set 7,546 sq ft of sail on a 165ft (50·2 m) mast. Improved rig efficiency was

Ranger, *the ultimate 'J-class'. Her rig, which included one of the first light alloy masts, was very efficient for the period and she set new standards of windward performance* (Rosenfeld)

one of her key features. Her gigantic spar was one of the first to be made from aluminium alloy although it was built up from numerous riveted sections rather than extruded. This much lighter, smoother mast, combined with an efficient 'slutter' sail plan, combined to give her a spectacular windward performance compared to the old gaff cutters such as *Reliance*.

In the fifth race of the 1937 defence, *Ranger* set a record which is believed to stand to this day. She sailed from the starting line to the first mark, 15 miles dead to windward, in 2 hours, 3 minutes and 45 seconds. Needless to say, this was considerably faster than the challenger, *Endeavour II*.

1937 was the last America's Cup contest before the Second World War and when the competition was revived in 1958 it was in the much smaller 12-metre class, so we must begin to look elsewhere for fast seagoing performances.

## *Modern offshore yachts*

When offshore racing got under way again in the fifties, there was a new breed of tough, open-minded yachtsmen and a fresh supply of designers ready to try out new ideas. Although yachts initially had a pre-war appearance, there was a willingness to innovate. People like Col. 'Blondie' Hasler were ready to challenge the notion that light-displacement yachts were not safe for sailing offshore. He did this by entering for RORC events in *Tre-Sang*, an ultra-light Scandinavian day-racer of the 30 square metre class. Of course 'safe' was a relative term for a man who had gone to war in a kayak but he did win the Class III season's points in 1946 with *Tre-Sang* without any major mishap. However, few men had more influence during this early post-war period than Captain John Illingworth RN. For fifteen years he dominated British ocean racing and was instrumental in getting the sport started in both France and Australia.

I once had the privilege of sailing with Illingworth when he was nearly at the end of his racing career and I was at the beginning of mine. We did the Dinard Race in a newly-built 'Maica' type constructed to his design in Cherbourg. For a young man just graduating from dinghies it was a salutary experience. Prior to the race and during it, Illingworth was crisp and authoritative to a degree. You were told exactly what little kit you could bring on board, what you should eat and drink, what you should do and not do. He gave orders and expected them to be carried out without discussion.

It was a moderately tough race and I was soon found to be doubly useless through ignorance and sea-sickness whereas Illingworth spent the race methodically checking the boat over and noting things that could be changed or improved. The yacht was fitted with a new type of French-made WC in which the pump handle stuck out in front. 'The Captain' sat down on it briefly before loudly declaring that: 'No normally-constructed human male could be expected to submit himself to this contraption.'

Although the yacht was new, it was not all that cleverly built and by the time we weathered the Casquets she was leaking copiously through the mast-step. In spite of this, the French owners seemed to think themselves uniquely privileged to have the master on board their very own boat – never mind that he was doing his level best to break it up.

After the finish, Illingworth was a changed man. In just a few minutes the tough skipper was replaced by the genial, back-slapping 'Captain John', pink gin in hand, beaming benignly from under salt-encrusted bushy eyebrows and greeting all and sundry in his famous gravelly drawl.

Although he became a designer in his own right, Illingworth did not design his most famous yacht, *Myth of Malham*. He contributed a great deal to the design but the plans were drawn by Jack Laurent Giles and Colin Mudie, who was a Giles draughtsman at the time. Illingworth had a no-nonsense engineer's approach to design and one of his key remarks was 'You'll never believe the things you can do without – until you have to.' The prime thing he wanted to do without was unnecessary weight. His ideas about design were unclouded by any fog of traditional ideas about what a boat should look like. He was not searching for a graceful sheer and well-balanced ends but for improvements in the basic speed-producing factors, such as sail area/displacement ratio, ballast ratio and displacement/wetted surface ratio. He was also one of the first people to really study the Rating Rule with a view to squeezing the maximum advantage out of it. It is strange to say that today when 'optimization' is one of the most important of the designer's jobs but at that time, designers were content to draw their boat first and find out what it rated afterwards.

Illingworth regarded long ends as useless appendages waving around in the air so *Myth of Malham* had brutally short overhangs. The underwater profile was cut away ruthlessly to reduce wetted area and the keel was a short fin of aerofoil section – one of the first yachts to embody this feature. Neither Illingworth nor Giles had yet made the breakthrough to wider beam: *Myth*'s overall dimensions were LOA

*John Illingworth's famous* Myth of Malham *broke right away from the idea that an offshore racing yacht should be a slightly souped-up cruiser* (Beken)

37ft 9in (11·5m), LWL 33ft 6in (10·2m), beam 9ft 4in (2·8m), draught 7ft (2·1m) and for this reason ballast ratio (the ratio of ballast weight to total weight) was especially important. The interior of the yacht was therefore kept as light and simple as possible with no cabins, compartments or any other kind of nonessential furniture or fittings. In his book *Offshore* Illingworth points out that a simple, basic but well thought-out interior is the one that works best at sea. To illustrate this he published a photograph of *Myth*'s interior taken within hours of finishing (and winning) the 1947 Fastnet Race, looking just as clean and tidy as when she started. There is no sign of the usual shambles of spilled gear, discarded clothing and unwashed dishes to be seen; evidence both of a well-designed interior and a well-disciplined crew.

Illingworth's personal speciality was the rig – hull lines he normally left to others. He clearly saw that headsails were more efficient than mainsails because of the cleaner airflow they experienced and also that because the rule measured the area of the fore-triangle rather than the actual sails set, that 'free' area could be obtained from overlapping headsails. He therefore moved the mast well back in the boat to give more room for headsails and developed his particular form of 'slutter' rig (a phrase he coined meaning a yacht that could sail as either a sloop or a cutter). In the older form of cutter rig, both inner and outer forestays came to the same point on the mast at the 'hounds' so that the headsails converged at the top. Illingworth moved his outer forestay to the masthead and kept it tensioned by a standing backstay. The inner forestay went to the former hounds position and was tensioned by running backstays. Thus the luffs of the two headsails were parallel and did not interfere with each other.

Sailcloth in the late forties was nothing like as good as today so a '150 per cent' overlapping genoa could only be used in light winds. In a breeze, *Myth* would change down to her cutter rig consisting of a yankee jib set over a low, chunky staysail. The theory is that the tall, narrow yankee is efficient because of its high aspect ratio and that the staysail gives power to punch through waves but without generating too much heeling force because its area is concentrated low down. It is an excellent heavy-weather rig and the fact that it is not used so much today has more to do with improvements in sailcloth than any inherent lack of efficiency.

*Myth of Malham* was immediately and devastatingly effective, taking a long string of successes from 1947 onwards including two Fastnet Race victories. Of course there were critics who said that *Myth* was stripped out, 'a machine' and so on – all the traditional carping noises that people make when someone has gone one better – but success is a powerful argument and *Myth*'s string of victories were instrumental in establishing Illingworth as the ocean racing guru of the sixties. Presently he established his own design office: at first John Illingworth and Partners and later Illingworth and Primrose. Angus Primrose took over as hull specialist while Illingworth continued to concentrate on rigs and ratings. Between them they designed some quite radical boats during the sixties, such as *Outlaw* for Sir Max Aitken.

This rather sinister-looking craft (Uffa Fox, no admirer of Illingworth, described her as looking like 'a great turd lying on the water') epitomized the Ill. and Prim. design ideas. She was very beamy (Primrose was not afraid of beam), very light, had a high ballast ratio, an efficient sail-plan and minimum keel area. Her odd appearance was the result of reverse sheer which was intended to reduce surplus weight and windage in the ends. There was also a whole family of 'mini-Outlaws' in various sizes such as *Midnight*, *Blue Charm*, and others.

Max Aitken said of *Outlaw* that she was exceptional to windward but nothing special down-wind. Part of the reason was that Primrose kept shortening the keel to reduce wetted surface but never made the breakthrough of separating the rudder from the keel and moving it aft. Therefore, as the keel got shorter, so did the steering couple. I recall sailing on one of the Blue Charm class and thinking it a frightful boat. A kind of dagger-board was provided that one was supposed to push down through a slot in the cockpit floor to steady her in difficult conditions in spite of which she was still dreadfully wild in following seas.

The idea of separating the rudder from the keel was not new. Dinghies were always built this way and so were a number of small racing keelboats designed around the turn of the century such as the 'one-raters' and 'half-raters' of Sibbick, Linton Hope and Herreshof. However, separated rudders were not considered strong enough to be seaworthy, so for offshore yachts the rudder remained firmly attached to the aft end of the keel. This was always a moderately poor arrangement because the rudder is almost bound to be operating inside a thick band of attached or turbulent flow, with the result that it has to be turned through a considerable angle before anything happens. This is why traditional keelboats feel so soggy compared to the crisp steering of a racing dinghy or modern keelboat.

The first man to put a separate rudder on an offshore yacht was the Dutch naval architect E. G. Van de Stadt. In the fifties and sixties, 'Ricus' Van de Stadt made a number of bold and innovative steps forward in design. Like Illingworth he favoured light displacement and was a pioneer of hard-chine plywood construction for offshore yachts. Right from the start, his designs featured fin keels and separate spade rudders at the extreme aft end of the waterline. People said they would break off or get clogged with seaweed, but they didn't. Some of the early Van de Stadt boats such as *Zeevalk* and *Black Soo* were fairly extreme and failed

*Van de Stadt designed the planing offshore racer* Black Soo *which was one of the first to feature a fin keel and separate spade rudder* (Beken)

to achieve the success hoped for. Perhaps they were ahead of their time or perhaps they did not have the right people sailing them.

Van de Stadt had the idea that an offshore boat could be made to plane. He was correct, and his boats did plane, given suitable conditions, but the shape that enabled them to do this tends to be a slow one in light airs due to its over-high prismatic and wetted surface. Therefore, although these boats might go tearing away on a breezy broad reach, they did not find these conditions often enough to be consistent winners. Offshore races are won by designs which offer an effective compromise between outright speed, good performance in light airs, and low rating, which is a pity for the purposes of this book which is more interested in actual speed. Except for a few special races such as the 'TransPac' which nearly always enjoys fresh following winds, it is hardly ever worthwhile going for flat-out speed in a yacht designed to win races under IOR.

Van de Stadt was also one of the first people to experiment with Glass Reinforced Plastics (GRP) as a material for building yachts. His appropriately-named *Pionier* was a cheap basic offshore yacht in the days when the RORC's minimum size was a 24ft (7·3m) waterline, and many people had their first experience of offshore racing in one. Many of Van de Stadt's designs were built by Southern Ocean Shipyard in Poole, a company which made maximum use of the technique of racing their own boats as hard as possible as a method of both developing and selling them. One of the most successful was *Excalibur* with which Alan Bourdon won the 1963 Class II points championships.

The stories of Van de Stadt and Illingworth come together in *Stormvogel*, a most important and influential boat that was effectively the first of the maxi-raters. When the Dutch-South African timber magnate Cornelis De Bruynzeel decided to build a super-boat, he made up a design team by calling on the leading specialists in each field. Thus, hull design was by Van de Stadt, construction by Laurent Giles and rig by Illingworth.

*Stormvogel's* measurements are 74ft (22·5m) LOA, 69ft (21m) LWL, and displacement 33 tons. Such dimensions do not sound exceptional today but no one had previously dared to design such a large yacht with such light displacement. Instead of the deep, slack bilges blending gracefully into the ballast keel that was the norm for this size of boat, Van de Stadt gave *Stormvogel* a 'canoe body' with deep fin keel sticking straight out from the underside like the centre-board on a racing dinghy. The rudder was his customary semi-balanced spade at the extreme aft end of the waterline, mounted on a massive stainless steel stock. As the dimensions indicate, she is very short-ended with a dinghy-like bow and upright transom stern. Many commentators referred to her as a 'giant dinghy' which seemed quite an apt description at the time. In fact, no dinghy was ever so slim in proportion to her length so it might be more accurate to call her a slightly plump International 10 sq metre canoe. Another of Van de Stadt's trademarks was very straight lines in the afterbody which he considered essential to give the boat a really good surfing performance in strong following winds.

To hold this big, light boat together required special construction. Although Van de Stadt was an enthusiast for glass construction, there was no real attraction in making a mould for what was expected to be a one-off boat and anyway De Bruynzeel wanted wood because that was his business. Laurent Giles designed her construction as an adaptation of the methods they had developed for wartime high-speed craft. Built in South Africa, she was triple-planked over light, close-spaced bent frames

*Stormvogel, jointly designed by Van de Stadt, Laurent Giles and Illingworth, is the real ancestor of today's maxi-raters. She was the first really light, big boat* (Beken)

and multiple stringers. Giles himself described this as 'basket-work' and it also has obvious similarities to aircraft construction. The result was a wonderfully light yet stiff shell though it is a *very* expensive way of building a large yacht.

Although Illingworth might have liked to rig *Stormvogel* as a cutter, the technology was not yet available to handle such large sails. Instead, he made her a ketch with the mizzen taller than usual and well separated from the mainsail so that the mizzen would not be permanently back-winded by the main. The main-mast was rigged exactly like a larger version of *Myth of Malham*, with a cutter fore-triangle with parallel forestays. The two masts were rigged completely independently so that one could fall down without affecting the other.

Throughout the sixties, *Stormvogel* ranged around the globe, taking part in all the great offshore events. She was nearly always the first to finish though not as often the winner because it was difficult for her to sail up to her rating in light airs. However, as well as being tremendously influential as a design, she also helped give birth to the 'maxi' philosophy that winning overall was not so much fun as being first home. Other big, light boats started to be built such as *Windward Passage* designed by Alan Gurney, *Kialoa* by Sparkman and Stephens and *Infidel* by John Spencer. These were all big, fast exciting boats that broke right away from the tradition of the tubby, conservative, medium-displacement cruiser-racer.

Today's maxi-racers are much more developed than *Stormvogel*, but recognizably the same type of boat: maximum rating, light-displacement yachts designed to be first home. They are not really extreme in design because they have to compete in a variety of conditions in different parts of the world so they cannot afford to be over-specialized. On the other hand if an owner demands a boat to win one particular race, then the designer can go a lot further out on a limb. This was the case with the so-called 'Ultra Light Displacement Boats' designed in the first instance for the TransPac Race. Because this race is normally one long down-hill spinnaker ride, the yachts can be specialized for running conditions. Beamy, planing-type hulls with the absolute minimum ballast required by the rule are the result. In 1977, the ULDB *Merlin* designed by Bill King, completed the TransPac course in 8 days, 11 hours, 1 minute, 45 seconds, a staggering 11 knots average and the record for the course. The design of these ULDBs became so extreme that the rule makers had to place new minimum limits on righting moment.

Of the various trans-ocean spectacular races that have sprung up in recent years, some are run under IOR but most with no recognizable rating at all. An example of the former is the Whitbread Round the World Race where the most recent winner *Flyer*, designed by Frers, is recognizable as an IOR maxi with specialized rig and deck-layout. Very much an all-round design, it is interesting that she proved superior to the more specialized down-wind planers such as *Ceramco* and *Disque d'Or*. *Flyer*'s 120 day circumnavigation in the 1981/2 Whitbread race is easily the best time for any kind of sailing vessel and represents an average of 9·5 knots for the entire distance of 27,430 miles. This remarkable achievement illustrates as well as any the very high state of development reached by the IOR maxis.

The opposite state of affairs is illustrated by an event such as the Single-handed Transatlantic Race in which, originally, the sole restriction was that only one person could be on board. This event, and others of its kind, soon turned into a battle between monohulls and multihulls, which has now been won so decisively by the latter that no more big monohulls are likely to be built for such races. While the issue was in doubt, yachts just got longer, lighter and slimmer, the funds available being the sole limiting factor. A British yacht, *Strongbow*, started this progression off and was leap-frogged by the Dutch *Bestevaer* in the next race. Although extreme, *Bestevaer* was a nice boat and at 55ft (16·7m) LOA not really a monster but it was clear that things were getting out of hand when the 128ft (39m) schooner *Vendredi Treize* was entered for the 1972 race. Even this was not the ultimate for in the following OSTAR (1976) Alain Colas entered the 236ft (71·9m) schooner *Club Med*. That she was not the winner was partly due to the fact that Colas had seriously injured his foot but also because the designer, Auzepy-Brenneur, had been forced to make compromises in the rig to enable her to be sailed by one man. Fully-crewed and with more sail, *Club Med* could be an enormously fast sailing ship but as there are no longer any events open to her, we shall probably not find out how fast. Following the notorious 1976 race, which attracted widespread criticism, the Royal Western Y.C. placed a top limit of 60ft (18·3m) LOA on entries for the OSTAR which made it even more certain that it would be won by a multihull which is almost certain to be faster length for length.

The idea of a rating-free race is attractive because it gives designers a free hand but combining this freedom with the single-handed ˙or short-handed concept just makes the boats slower and more dangerous. If only a big sponsor would have the sense to create a trans-ocean spectacular for fully-crewed yachts without rating, then we should *really* see some speed!

# 5
# Offshore multihulls

It is conventional to ascribe the origin of multihulled craft to the Pacific Islanders, particularly the Polynesians and Micronesians but in fact outrigger craft were always much more widely distributed around the coasts and islands of the Pacific and Indian Oceans. Outrigger craft were developed in many different areas as a way of giving stability to a basic dugout or log boat. The word 'catamaran', which we use for a boat with two similar hulls, is derived from a Tamil expression which just means 'tied trees'. Fishermen working from a shelving beach or a reef island needed boats of shallow draught and light weight and a dugout canoe balanced by an outrigger is a simple and cheap way of achieving this.

What is certainly true is that the Pacific Islanders improved the design of such craft above the level of the merely practical, and they established the main features of the seagoing multihull as it exists today. These island races were (and are) intelligent, resourceful and highly dependent on the sea. Indeed, if you believe Thor Heyerdahl, they reached their island homes in the first place as a result of trans-Pacific voyages of emigration from South America aboard *Kon-Tiki*-type rafts. They needed boats in their daily lives for fishing, inter-island transport and war-like expeditions. A very important point is that the Pacific Island civilizations had no metals until European explorers introduced them and this severely limited the size and type of boats that they could build.

The outrigger canoe or proa could be used in a variety of sizes, either as a paddling or sailing boat. The main hull was normally made of a single tree-trunk, hollowed out with infinite care with stone tools and bent to give it rocker by filling it with water and hot stones and this limited length to a maximum of 50–60ft (15–18m). Extra freeboard could be obtained by lashing a gunwale strake to the hull on boats designed mainly for sailing rather than paddling. The outrigger would normally be a solid log of light wood, lashed to the ends of two or more tough, springy branches. These cross-beams could be given extra clearance above the water by attaching them to pegs driven into the outrigger rather than directly to the log. Simple materials and narrow hulls limited the height of the rig which generally consisted of matting sails of a basically sprit-sail or lug-sail form. Although built from crude materials, boats of this type became quite sophisticated and the native 'master builders' had a great fund of rules-of-thumb concerning length-to-beam ratio, rocker, sail area and so forth. The outriggers were naturally fine in form because of their tree-trunk origin and were correspondingly easily driven. Provided they were kept light, outriggers were speedy and seaworthy and the flexible nature of their construction was an advantage in avoiding structural failure.

The big drawback to the outrigger canoe is that it is a very poor load carrier. This is why the early European explorers such as Cook did not take them too seriously, because they were interested in ships that could carry a heavy weight of stores, guns, and cargo, so the speedy native craft were little more than amusing. The islanders needed weight carriers but did not have the means to build them. The best they could achieve was the double canoe which we call a catamaran. As well as having double the displacement of an outrigger, the double canoe offered the possibility of having a superstructure built up on the connecting bridge between the two hulls. In the Polynesian islands, some very imposing double canoes of up to 100ft (30·5m) in length were built as vessels of war or royal transports. They could carry a fair load and retained the essential shallow draught but were not nearly as speedy as the outriggers.

As far as we know, native builders never developed the symmetrical outrigger or trimaran whose big advantage is that it can tack like a normal boat. Outriggers were built to carry their 'ama' on the same side all the time (normally to leeward) and to change direction had to stop and reverse. This is fine if you are on a 100 mile reach to the next island but hopeless for beating up an estuary against the tide – another reason why such a boat would find no favour in European conditions. The credit for both the symmetrical outrigger and the name 'trimaran' is normally given to Victor Tchetchet who built a day-boat of this form in 1945. Nowadays, we see the main advantage of the multihull as being a boat that achieves stability without ballast or an excessively beamy hull-form. The native builders achieved this quite by accident but it is rather remarkable that it took so long for others to realize that an unballasted multihull could be both fast and seaworthy.

Prior to 1945 there were no more than isolated experiments with multihulls in Europe and America. In 1661 Sir William Petty of Dublin built a double-hulled craft with two 15ft (4·5m) cylinders set 4ft 6in (1·3m) apart and connected by a hinged bridge structure so that the hulls could pitch independently. Record exists of a race involving Sir William's novel craft in which he won handily. There is also a hint of a larger catamaran built during the reign of Charles II which is supposed to have been lost in the Bay of Biscay. Lack of information prevents the crew of this vessel from being given proper credit as pioneer multihull martyrs.

Nathanael Herreshoff, the great American designer whose creations defended the America's Cup on a number of occasions, definitely did build a 30ft (9·1m) catamaran in 1870. The hulls had 1ft 6in (457mm) beam and were 15ft (4·5m) apart and like Petty he allowed the hulls movement on the ends of the crossbeams. A certain amount of legend surrounds this craft: it is alleged that it was so successful in racing that other yachtsmen asked Herreshoff not to compete with it. It seems more likely that in an era when rating was calculated purely from length and sail area, the catamaran was seen as a 'rule cheater' and barred for that

*This painting of the yachts* Jessie *and* Valkyrie *racing off the American East Coast in 1883 appears to show the mysterious Herreshoff catamaran that was allegedly so fast that he was asked not to enter it for races. Herreshoff 'the wizard of Bristol', was one of the greatest of all yacht designers and his catamaran appears to have been about 80 years ahead of its time* (National Maritime Museum)

reason. This is certainly true of the catamaran *Dominion* designed by the Canadian G. Herrick Duggan for the Seawanhaka Cup in 1898. Because of the lack of beam measurement in the rating rule, the tendency was to build wide scows so Duggan put a hollow in the middle to reduce wetted surface. There's always been a tendency for yachtsmen to regard multihulls as not really cricket or hitting below the belt and the reason is that they don't fit into existing measurement systems. Therefore, when a multihull wins a yacht race by an enormous margin over conventional yachts, the first reaction of other yachtsmen is not so much 'how marvellous' as 'that's cheating'.

The first modern ocean voyage in a multihull seems to have been that of the 38ft (11·5m) catamaran *Kamiloa* in 1937/8. The two Frenchmen Eric de Bisschop and Joseph Tatiboet built the boat in Hawaii and sailed it home to Cannes. It is obviously significant that this passage started in an area where ocean-going multihulls were traditional and it is to Hawaii that we must look for the background to the postwar beginning of offshore multihulled yachts.

If you go to Honolulu as a tourist, the outing not to be missed is a catamaran trip, rather in the same way that Edwardian visitors to the English sea-side resorts would go for a 'sixpenny sick' trip in a beach lugger. These trips round the Honolulu bay were begun shortly after the Second World War with a series of 'Manu Kai' (Sea Bird) cats built by Woody Brown and Alfred Kumalae. The essential features of these boats were, and still are, that they must be shallow enough to come in over the reef and onto the beach near the Queen Capiolani Hotel, so that the tourists can just climb up some steps to get aboard, and that there should be plenty of deck space for them to sit down. For this reason they had shallow hulls without keels and a solid bridge structure to give a large amount of deck space. Then in 1955 a new company consisting of Warren Seaman, Alfred Kumalae, and Rudy Choy, built their first real seagoing cat, the 40ft (12·1m) *Waikiki Surf*. She was an odd-looking boat with rather full bows and very narrow sterns. Because they felt they must avoid a tall mast, she was cutter rigged and had two bow-sprits. She was sailed to Santa Monica, California to join the 1955 TransPac Race and sailed back to Hawaii in 10½ days, being beaten over the line by four large Class A yachts of 75ft (22·8m) LOA or more. This was a good performance, but she had a number of faults as an offshore yacht including lack of under-bridge clearance and insufficiently strong construction.

*Waikiki Surf* attracted the attention of Ken Murphy of Hawaii and Los Angeles who ordered a real racing catamaran from Rudy Choy. The result was the 46ft (14m) *Aikane* which established the C/S/K style of design and was one of the most successful offshore multihulls of all time. Choy gave her plenty of freeboard so as to reduce pounding under the bridge and an unusual hull section that is basically flat on the inboard face of the hull and curved on the outboard face. This was because Choy had observed that if a catamaran had hulls with a conventional section, the bow waves would meet and clash between the hulls and create extra resistance. He therefore sought to achieve a hull-form in which all the wave-making was on the outboard faces. To put it another way, his hull section was like a conventional hull that had been sliced in two along its centreline. If he had started with slimmer hulls set further apart he would not have needed this odd section which certainly has more resistance than a semi-circular one. *Aikane* has no keels or centreboards so the hulls were well rockered to give her some grip on the water amidships. Perhaps the biggest change from *Waikiki Surf* was that *Aikane* had a tall, modern sloop rig exactly like the conventional offshore racers of the period.

She 'paced' the TransPac Race (there being no class for multihulls) in 1957 and 1959. On the first occasion she crossed the line at Diamond Head having taken 10 days and 10 hours for the 2,500 mile course, beating the 84ft (25·6m) *Barlovento* by 26 hours. Two years later, with more experience and rather better weather, she did even better, finishing after 9 days 22 hours and beating the 161ft (49m) schooner *Goodwill* by 17 hours. She averaged 10 knots for the whole distance. At the time, this was a staggering performance for a 46ft (14m) yacht and one that was widely disbelieved in Europe. In 1961 *Aikane* was taken on a 10,000 mile cruise through the South Pacific during which she sailed 306 miles in 24 hours and 122 miles in 8 hours. Strangely enough, other people credited *Aikane* with even better day's runs than either her owner or designer ever claimed. For instance, when Eric Tabarly sailed his 70ft (21·3m) tri *Pen Duick IV* across the Atlantic in 10 days, 12 hours in 1968, he believed he was trying to beat a day's run record of 315 miles by *Aikane* in the 1955 San Francisco to Honolulu Race. In fact she was not even built in 1955 and never claimed 315 miles per day!

There were two reasons why European yachtsmen viewed reports of *Aikane*'s performances with scepticism. One was that at around the same time, the Californian Arthur Piver was making the most ludicrously inflated claims on behalf of his trimaran designs. People who built these heavily advertised boats in England were almost always disappointed by their performance and so Rudy Choy was wrongly suspected of being another Californian braggart. Very few C/S/K boats were seen in

European waters but those were also rather disappointing. The Australian single-handed yachtsman Bill Howell built the 40ft (12·1m) *Golden Cockerel* in 1967 and she proved to be quite a dull performer, especially to windward when she earned the nick-name 'Golden Rocking-Horse'. She capsized shortly after the start of the 1967 Crystal Trophy Race, in spite of which Bill Howell went on doggedly sailing her for a number of years. *Cockerel* was overweight and ketch-rigged, but a really race-oriented C/S/K boat, the 35ft (10·6m) *Polynesian Concept*, came over for the 1969 Crystal Trophy. She was fast enough down wind but not very impressive at all to windward in a Channel chop. Beating from the Wolf Rock to Plymouth in a force 5/6, she was no faster than the 30ft (9·1m) Iroquois *Wardance*. However there is no doubting *Aikane*'s performance in the TransPac so the explanation has to be that it was sailed in ideal conditions for which the boat was particularly designed. The TransPac is known as a 'downhill' slide in which competitors are disappointed if they cannot carry a spinnaker for 90 per cent of the distance. *Aikane* was probably a rotten performer to windward, but she did sail from Santa Barbara to Diamond Head in 9 days 22 hours!

Offshore catamarans started to be built in Europe slightly later than in California/Hawaii but quite independently. One of the first was a 35ft (10.6m) bi-plane rigged cat named *Eb and Flo* which was around at the time of the 1955 Solent Speed Trials, but she was not too successful. It was the former test-pilot Don Robertson who commissioned, in 1960, one of the first successful offshore cats from the Prouts of Canvey Island, who were already building their own Shearwater cats very successfully. The 36ft (10·9m) *Snowgoose* was very different in concept to the C/S/K designs. She was beamier and her hulls were very slim and round-bottomed. She had deep centre-boards for windward performance and an Illingworth style cutter rig. *Snowgoose* performed well for a number of years: she sailed in practically every race open to her including two Round Britain Races. Her only real faults were that her hulls were a bit too narrow so that she was a poor weight carrier and that, partly as a result, she had too little under-bridge clearance and tended to slam badly when going to windward in choppy conditions. *Snowgoose* started the Prouts off building cruising catamarans which they have continued to do ever since, one of the few firms to stay in this business through thick and thin for twenty years. The biggest boat built by the Prouts was the 77ft (23·4m) catamaran *Tsulamaran* but she was a luxury cruiser rather than a racer.

Roderick Macalpine-Downie, whose name we have met before, designed, for John Fisk, a sporty little 'camping cat' named the *Dolphin*.

*One of the first catamarans to race offshore in Europe was* Snowgoose
*built by the Prout brothers for Don Robertson* (Beken)

She was a bit too small and light to be safe offshore: she won everything
at Burnham Week and then capsized on the way back to Brightlingsea!
However, she led Reg White's company Sail Craft to commission the
30ft (9·1m) Iroquois from the same designer. This turned out to be one
of the most successful cruiser/racer multihulls so far. More than 300 were
built in various marks and the basic design stayed in production for 15
years. Compared to a typical 30ft (9·1m) cruising yacht of the period, the
Iroquois was at least twice as fast and had four times as much room
inside. Although the great majority of Iroquois owners used their boats
mainly for cruising, there were a few racing enthusiasts and when
multihull racing was started in this country, the Iroquois was the
mainstay of the fleet and often the handicap winner as well. Like any

89

unballasted multihull, the Iroquois was not immune from the possibility of capsize and a number of them have gone over at one time or another though, to my knowledge, only once with loss of life.

A multihull feat that should not be forgotten was Dr David Lewis's *Rehu Moana* which was the first to circumnavigate the globe. Designed by Colin Mudie she was actually built in 1963 to satisfy one of David Lewis's masochistic efforts to sail to the North or South Pole. In this he did not succeed though he was the first to send a photograph by radio from a yacht while at sea!

*The Ellison brothers setting an improvised jib topsail on* Iroquois, *the stock cruising catamaran in which they won the first Round Britain Race* (Beken)

Mirrorcat, *designed by Macalpine-Downie, showed that it was possible to sail offshore in a really light multihull with no decking between the hulls* (Beken)

Offshore multihull sailing received a boost in 1967 when the Round Britain Race was initiated. Being a two-handed race it offered a greater prospect of success for multihulls than the Single-handed Transatlantic Race because of the great difficulty of sailing a light, fast, capsizeable boat single-handed. Two very influential boats were built for the Round Britain: the 40ft (12·1m) catamaran *Mirrorcat* and the 42ft (12·8m) trimaran *Toria*. Designed by Macalpine-Downie, *Mirrorcat* was an exceptionally bold design being more or less a double-sized 'C' Class. Instead of a solid bridge, she just had three connecting spars like a day-racing cat. This made it possible to go for a very wide 20ft (6m) beam while keeping the weight down to only a little over 2 tons. The main drawback to this approach was the difficulty of staying the mast on a basically flexible structure. As originally designed, she had an enlarged day-boat rig: a big fully-battened main and smallish headsails set well inboard. The mast for this rig could be held up with just two shrouds and a forestay, plus diamonds for stiffness, so it did not matter if it waved around a bit. In her first season, however, she proved to be under-canvassed in light winds or under spinnaker. Subsequently various busybodies, including myself, converted her to masthead rig with standing backstays. This gave her the extra sail needed but led to horrendous rigging difficulties as everything kept twanging and tweaking as the boat twisted.

This rigging problem can be avoided by going for a trimaran in which the mast can be solidly stepped in the main hull just as in a conventional yacht. This was the approach used by Derek Kelsall with *Toria* which had a slim, round-bottomed main hull and substantial floats set well outboard on the end of beams. She was built by the foam sandwich method which was new to Britain although it had been used in the United States and described in the AYRS journal. It is not always appreciated that the effective beam of a trimaran is that between the main hull and one of the floats so she needs one and a half times as much beam as a catamaran to achieve the same stability, but by way of compensation, a tri is much simpler structurally than a cat. *Toria* was not a particularly sophisticated boat but strong and simple and her basic layout has been developed by many others since. One of her key features is that her floats are raised so that they do not both touch the water at the same time. This greatly reduces wetted surface and adds to stability because the airborne windward hull can be regarded as ballast on the end of an outrigger.

The expected exciting contest between these two new boats turned out to be a non-event. *Mirrorcat* was dismasted on the way to the start and finally got under way from Plymouth in a disorganized state eight hours after the rest of the fleet. *Toria* meanwhile was speeding away in the direction of Ireland with a lovely reaching breeze. She was remarkably lucky with her weather most of the way round, with a high proportion of reaching breezes, whereas *Mirrorcat* never managed to get into quite the same weather pattern and fell steadily behind. *Toria* completed the 2,000 mile course in an elapsed time of 11 days, 17½ hours, an average of a little over 7 knots. This was good if not startling but far better than any of the monohulls entered. *Snowgoose* was second while third and handicap winner, finishing less than 24 hours after the leader, was the little

*Iroquois XIII* sailed by the Ellison brothers. This triple result confounded those who said that the multis would never hold together in strong winds, couldn't go to windward etc., and struck a powerful blow for the type.

The following year, the Toria design was considerably improved by Major-General Ralph Farrant's *Trifle*, also built by Derek Kelsall. She had slimmer, better-shaped hull and floats, more overall beam and a much better rig with fully-battened main and rotating mast. She turned out to be fast, reliable, trouble-free and in many ways the first really successful offshore trimaran. She was also the first multihull to fly the Royal Yacht Squadron's white ensign at her stern, to the consternation of some of the crustier members and greatly to the amusement of the General.

In 1967 BP presented the Crystal Trophy for a 300 mile offshore race for multihulls over a course Cowes-Nab-CH1-Wolf Rock-Plymouth. The idea of this was to provide some worthwhile annual challenge for offshore multihulls and create a proper racing fleet such as had existed for many years for conventional yachts under the RORC banner. The sad fact is that this sensible initiative has really been a failure and the main reason has been the problems of rating a variety of multihulls successfully. For the first couple of years, an RYA rating devised by Michael Henderson was used. This was a simple formula of length, beam and sail area but because it did not take weight into consideration it gave every advantage to the sportier craft like an Iroquois over a pure cruiser such as a Bobcat. It was apparent that in an unballasted multihull, which is not strictly limited in speed by its waterline length, weight is crucial. If you took two Iroquois rating the same under the RYA formula and removed 500lbs (226·7kg) of stores and equipment from one of them, it would win a race by a large margin. The answer had to be a more sophisticated rating rule and this appeared in the form of a totally new formula devised by Dr Vic Stern from California. This was extremely scientific in its basis and required the boat to be physically weighed ashore under carefully-controlled conditions with specified lists of equipment on board. It was also a computer-based rule which was virtually impossible to calculate manually.

The Stern Rule was eventually adopted by the International Yacht Racing Union as the International Offshore Multihull Rating (IOMR) but it was all too much and too soon for the British fleet. The organizing club, MOCRA, was neither big enough or strong enough to get measurement of boats properly organized along RORC lines, and there was also strong opposition to the concept of a complex and fairly expensive measurement from a section of members. The introduction of IOMR therefore flopped in Britain and a MOCRA Committee including Robin Chaworth-Musters and myself rather lamely set about organizing handicapping on a Portsmouth Yardstick basis. With so few boats in the fleet, this was not much better than inspired guesswork and did little to enhance the standing of multihull racing in British waters. Eventually, MOCRA wrote its own rule, but in spite of this has never managed to build up a really solid basis of regular offshore multihull racing.

The same thing applies world-wide apart from pockets of IOMR racing in California and Australia. The big surge in racing multihulls has therefore come mainly as a result of the big spectacular events such as the various transatlantics. This is all a great shame because in the late 60s and early 70s it looked as if multihull racing could get properly established. One of the most unfortunate factors affecting offshore multihull racing in recent years has been the unhealthy emphasis on single or two-handed racing as opposed to fully-crewed. When we first started racing offshore in the mid-60s with boats such as *Toria*, *Mirrorcat*, the Sail Craft and Prout boats and later with Musters and Simpson-Wild designs, it was immediately apparent that these boats were less safe than conventional offshore boats and needed to be raced more like cars with constant attention from helmsman and sheet-hand. Although undoubtedly more 'hairy' than keelboat sailing, this could still be a perfectly valid sport with acceptable risks at the same sort of level as, for instance, car rallying. But racing big, fast multihulls single-handed is really madness because it involves an unacceptably high level of risk not only to the occupant but to other seafarers who may be unlucky enough to get in the way. Furthermore, these are not just fears; sadly there have been a number of fatal accidents involving single-handed multihull sailors such as Brian Cooke, Alain Colas, Mike McMullen and others. It has to be said that the organizers of these single-handed races bear a heavy responsibility.

Since about 1970 therefore, the story is of larger and larger multihulls being built for the various 'spectacular' races. Because these are normally single-handed or two-handed, the boats have become increasingly specialized so that they are impractical for almost any other purpose. But even if one feels uneasy about the advisability of these specialized craft, they are undoubtedly the fastest sailing boats ever to cross oceans and record after record has tumbled before them.

Eric Tabarly started the process by building the 67ft (20·4m) trimaran *Pen Duick IV* for the 1968 Single-handed Transatlantic Race. This inelegant but effective boat was built in aluminium with sharply-curved crossbeams to increase clearance under them. She was originally built with semi-wing masts but these were too troublesome and she was converted to a conventional ketch. The boat's greatest virtue was her strength of construction which meant that she could be kept smashing through heavy seas without knocking herself to bits. Her first outing was a disaster and a vivid illustration of the dangers involved. On the first night out of the OSTAR, *Pen Duick* sailed slap into the side of a trawler and was forced to retire. The following year, Tabarly, with Alain Colas as crew, took her across the Atlantic setting a new time of 10 days, 12 hours from Teneriffe to Martinique. This was an average of 10·47 knots – slightly faster than the speed of the schooner *Atlantic* though over a different course and distance. They then went through the Panama Canal into the Pacific and entered a multihull TransPac race from Los Angeles to Honolulu, completing the course in 8 days, 13 hours (260.5 miles per day or 10·854 knots).

Tabarly then went on to Pen Duicks new while his friend and erstwhile crew Colas took over the trimaran for the 1972 OSTAR which he won in a new record time of 21 days, 13 hours – more than four days less than the previous best by Geoffrey Williams in *Sir Thomas Lipton*. Colas' greatest feat, however, was his single-handed circumnavigation in *Pen Duick IV* in 1973/4. Since multihulls were not admitted to the Whitbread Round the World Race, he decided to 'pace' the fleet but, like Sir Francis Chichester, stopping only once, at Sydney. His elapsed time for the circumnavigation was 168 days and he broke some other records along the way: best day's run by a singlehander (326 miles), and 4,000 miles in 20 days which Chichester had attempted but failed. Colas unfortunately became a somewhat embittered personality following a serious injury during the run-up to the 1976 OSTAR. In spite of the disabling foot injury he insisted on sailing in the race on the monstrous 236ft (80·1m) schooner *Club Med*. This ludicrous boat finally managed to persuade the organizers of the folly of allowing a completely unrestricted entry and class limits were introduced. To the joy of all, *Club Med* did not win the race. In 1978, back at the helm of *Pen Duick IV* now renamed *Manureva*, sadly Colas disappeared in yet another single-handed transatlantic race, the Route du Rhum.

The 1968 OSTAR was very nearly won by the attractive little proa *Cheers*. Designed by Dick Newick, this marked a return to the original concept of the light, simple Polynesian outrigger. The 40ft (12·1m) main hull was only just wide enough for the helmsman Tom Follett to squeeze into and was surmounted by a low and simple 340 sq ft schooner rig on unstayed masts that rotated when the boat reversed direction. Follett took the southern, tradewind route and finished third, less than two days after the winner, *Sir Thomas Lipton*, in a remarkable 27 days. Weighing a mere 1·34 tons, this boat seemed exactly in the spirit envisaged by the race's originator Col. Hasler, in sharp contrast to monstrosities like *Vendredi Treize* and *Club Med*. For long-distance, short-handed racing,

Colt Cars GB (*below*) and Livery Dole (*right*) *are examples of the big, light multihulls which have been developed for the various sponsored ocean races. Boats such as these are the fastest things afloat offshore and have broken many long-standing records*

the proa layout seems attractive: it has less weight and wetted surface than a cat, more effective beam than a tri and most of the weight is concentrated where it is wanted – to windward. But there are considerable difficulties. A proa must be reversible and hence double-ended and this involves compromises both in the rig and the centre-board and rudder layout. Since the rig is inevitably stepped in the weather hull and must be reversible it almost has to be an unstayed una rig because of the difficulty of fitting a forestay for headsails. The result is that it seems difficult to build an efficient large proa. Various designers including Kelsall and Daniel Charles have tried but without much success.

The favoured layout for offshore racing boats in recent years has definitely been the trimaran mainly because of its advantages of simple, conventional rigging, reasonable wetted surface and relatively simple structure. In order to get sufficient stability it is necessary to go for very wide beam but if sailing in a race in which the only restriction is overall length, there is nothing to stop the designer making the boat as wide as she is long – other than structural worries. Derek Kelsall has remained in the forefront of trimaran design and construction, with boats such as Chay Blyth's 80ft (24·3m) *Great Britain III* and the even larger *William Saurin* which at 82ft (24·9m) LOA was the largest tri around at the time of writing. Kelsall is an effective but at times inelegant designer and more attractive shapes have come from the drawing-board of his former draughtsman John Shuttleworth whose *Brittany Ferries GB* was one of the best boats of 1982.

The other really successful trimaran designer is Dick Newick, especially in the series of boats commissioned for Phil Weld. This amazing sailor only took up serious competitive yachting after retiring as a newspaper publisher at the age of 60. Since then he has competed in the OSTAR twice and the Round Britain three times, his greatest victory being his overall win of the 1980 OSTAR in the 51ft (15·5m) *Moxie*. His previous Newick tri *Gulfstreamer* was lost in a mid-Atlantic capsize in 1976 (later salvaged by the Russians) which was important for proving that this type of accident was survivable. After the capsize, the crew were able to continue living in the inverted hull for several days until they attracted the attention of a ship. The important thing is that the cabin should be planned for this possibility with enough airspace for the crew to be able to keep out of the water. If this is done, remaining in the upturned boat can prove a better bet than getting into a liferaft. In contrast, when Alain Gliksman capsized the 55ft (16·7m) *RTL Timex* (ex *Three Legs of Mann II*) he and his crew were suffering acutely after only a few days in an overcrowded liferaft.

Newick's tris are unusual in that he normally uses solid side-decks rather than the commoner open cross-beams. This makes the boats prettier, drier and easier to handle because of the large amount of deck-space and also simpler to build in timber. There is always the fear however than when beating to windward, the wind will get underneath the raised, windward 'wing' and help to capsize the boat. All Newick's designs, from the little 25ft (7·6m) Vals up to the largest are all rather elegant, well-designed boats in sharp contrast to the French tradition of trimaran designs by Allegre, Joubert and others which tend to resemble the working parts of an oil-rig.

Catamarans have been relatively less successful (or at least less numerous) offshore although they now seem to be making a comeback. The first really serious, big offshore cat was *British Oxygen*, built in 1974 for the Round Britain Race. Designed by Macalpine-Downie she was 70ft (21·3m) LOA by 30ft (9·1m) beam and had the unusual feature of a central 'pod' which contained the working cockpit and the accommodation. The enormous hulls were not used at all, except for sail storage. A gigantic 90ft (27·4m) mast was stepped on a steel crossbeam and she had aluminium centre-boards made by British Aerospace which were raised and lowered hydraulically. There were tremendous engineering problems in getting a cat as big as this to hold together but with *Mirrorcat* behind him, at least the designer knew where to expect them. *BO* as she was known, was sailed in the Round Britain by Robin Knox-Johnston and Jerry Boxall who had put up a very spirited performance in the previous race in the Iroquois *Minitaree*. Their main rival was Mike McMullen's 50ft (15·2m) Newick tri *Three Cheers*. Although much smaller, this was a fast and well sorted-out boat compared to the newly-launched cat. On the first two legs, *BO* maintained a small lead over *Three Cheers* but then after losing a halyard and peeling off her mainsheet track, dropped behind on the third to Barra in the Outer Hebrides. The only time she really showed her mettle was on the long fourth leg from Barra to Lowestoft, when they enjoyed good reaching breezes. Starting two hours after *Three Cheers*, they finished 12 hours ahead after a truly epic passage down the North Sea at an average 12 knots. The final leg was sailed in light airs.

That autumn, Robin Knox-Johnston took her to the Portland Speed Week where she recorded a speed of 24·26 knots under conditions which were cramping for such a large boat. Robin had planned to sail the boat in the next year's OSTAR but regrettably she had to be sold due to lack of funds. The purchaser was Jean-Yves Terlain who also entered her for the OSTAR but unfortunately she broke up in heavy seas and he abandoned her. There appeared to be two main reasons for the failure: she was somewhat over-rigged and tended to plunge heavily into a head sea and Terlain had very unwisely replaced the screw-down metal fore-hatches with light plywood ones because it was easier to haul sails through them. It seems very likely that she took water forward through these hatches, which made her plunge even worse until she finally stuck her nose right through a big sea and carried away the fore-beam.

Anyway, that was the end of the very short career of *British Oxygen*. But not quite, for her moulds were used again in 1980 to build *Sea Falcon* for Robin Knox-Johnston. Since then he has sailed in several big races but without particularly good luck or good results. The new boat had a lower, lighter rig and handled much better in a seaway. She was undoubtedly one of the fastest offshore boats in the world, but was unfortunately written off as a result of a collision in the 1983 Vilamoura Race. Never a man to take adversity lying down, Knox-Johnston then managed to obtain the backing of British Airways for a new 60ft Macalpine-Downie catamaran. This was intended as an entry for the 1984 OSTAR race but it proved impossible to get her completed in time so the debut of this exciting new boat was expected to be in the Quebec-to-St-Malo Race.

A catamaran of similar size and layout to *BO/Sea Falcon* is Patrick Morvan's 60ft (18m) *Jet Services* which became the new holder of the

*The handsome* Sea Falcon *was the second of the 'British Oxygen' class.
She was badly damaged in 1983 when a ship ran her down off the coast
of Spain* (Patrick Roach)

Atlantic record in 1984 when she crossed from Sandy Hook to the Lizard
in 8 days 16 hours 33 minutes 17 seconds at the fantastic average speed of
14·03 knots. It does seem possible that catamarans will have the
advantage over tris especially in fresh following winds: they have the
edge in stability, steer better and have less tendency to broach. This certainly seemed to be the lesson of the 1982 Route du Rhum Race. Marc
Pajot was first in *Elf Aquitaine* 62ft (18·2m) while the handicap winner
by a very large margin was Mike Birch sailing the 50ft (15·2m) cat *Vital*.
This interesting boat was designed and built by Nigel Irens who was a
member of the *Clifton Flasher* syndicate.

If you wanted to go faster offshore (in races with no rating rules) it
would seem sensible to look at the results of the Portland Speed Week
competitions to see what kind of boats have done well there. 'What about
hydrofoils?' I hear you cry! Oddly enough, there already has been a
successful offshore hydrofoil which attracted remarkably little attention

and has never been copied. The 31ft (9·4m) trimaran *Williwaw*, designed and built by Californian Dave Keiper, first flew on foils in 1968 and sailed many thousands of miles without major problems. The main hull had a large foil forward and a diamond-shaped steering foil aft while each of the floats had ladder-foil arrangements built up from an 8in (20·5mm) chord extruded aluminium section welded onto vertical struts. This is a rather draggy arrangement but safe because it is both strong and unlikely to all ventilate at the same moment. *Williwaw* would start to lift clear at around 10 knots and had a top speed of 18–20 knots. She was a fairly unsophisticated boat with a very ordinary rig in spite of which she put up some good cruising passages. Keiper would leave the foils down even if sailing in a big seaway when flying was impossible because he found that the foils stabilized the boat. He seems to have been ahead of his time because no-one has built a Keiper-type boat since.

There is of course a half-way house: foil stabilization. The 'foiler' that sailed at Portland for several years was like a trimaran except that the floats were replaced by foils which were not expected to lift the main hull

*One of the few offshore hydrofoils,* Williwaw *has never been copied although she was apparently quite successful and made several long ocean passages*

out of the water. This layout was copied by Eric Tabarly for his 61ft (18·5m) *Paul Ricard* with which he cracked the Atlantic record in 1980 (later being beaten by *Elf Aquitaine*, then *Jet Services*). The long, slim, easily-driven main hull is stabilized by small floats which have deep, angled foils projecting below them. To start with at least, she was not a very successful boat, being beaten in the *Transat en Double* by the conventional Kelsall tri *VSD*. This may have been due to a large overweight of hydraulic machinery designed to make it possible to rotate the main beams in order to vary the angle of incidence of the foils. In her second year she sailed better but at the time of writing has yet to win a major race.

It remains to be seen if anyone will be bold enough to try to build a really big flying hydrofoil. Certainly they are talking about it and I shall be very surprised if a boat of this type does not come out within the next few years. It will be very expensive to build, very tricky to sail, and extremely fast. I cannot say more than that!

# 6
# Hydrofoils:
# what and why?

Hydrofoils can be described as little wings, working under water. Like foils of any type they work by creating a pressure differential between one side and the other which can be used to provide lift. Actually, hydrofoils are nothing new since practically everything that sticks out underneath a sailing boat is a foil of some sort. In conventional boats however, these foils come in the form of keel or rudder and the force they produce is used to prevent the craft sailing sideways or to cause it to turn. What is unusual is to use hydrofoils to lift the hull of the boat up out of the water so that it no longer relies on buoyancy.

The first and most obvious question is: why should one want to do this? In order to find the answer we have to look into the general question of resistance or drag of various types of boat. Taking first the case of the perfectly conventional 'displacement' hull, in which buoyancy is wholly responsible for supporting the weight of the craft, we find that resistance to forward movement rises approximately as the square of speed. This is because at slow speeds, the majority of the resistance experienced by the hull is caused by the frictional resistance of the water.

As speed increases, another form of resistance which begins to come increasingly into prominence is wave-making resistance. All displacement boats display wave-making characteristics and suffer from the consequent drag. Since it has been under more or less continuous investigation since the 1870s, when the English naval architect William Froude first advanced his 'wave-line theory', the question of wave-making resistance is pretty well understood. It is sufficient here to say that length-to-beam ratio (L/B) is the most important factor in determining the degree of wave-making resistance that a boat of given displacement will experience. As speed increases, the wave-form that the hull produces rapidly lengthens until it becomes approximately the same length as the immersed part of the hull. Typically, this occurs when the speed in knots is around 1·5 times the square root of the waterline length in feet ($V = 1·5 \times \sqrt{L}$). If the hull is short, fat and heavy, this point will be reached sooner and if it is long, slim and light it will be delayed to some extent.

When the length of the wave is approximately equal to the length of the craft, she suddenly runs into greatly increased resistance due to the fact that she is having to 'climb up her own wave' in order to go faster. This phenomenon, known as the 'resistance hump', is well known as that awkward moment when a planing boat is desperately trying to clamber up onto the plane, in order to escape the clutches of wave-making resistance. In the life of every displacement craft, therefore, is this 'speed barrier' which crops up when she reaches her own personal 'hump'. To achieve high speeds, a displacement craft has to be as long and slim as possible as in *Crossbow*. The alternative is to find some way of escaping the dreaded hump.

By far the best known method of escaping the 'hump' is planing. When a boat planes, the force of buoyancy is partly, or even wholly, replaced by dynamic lift caused by the hull being forced rapidly across the surface of the water. Some people think that the main advantage of planing is that the boat rises up in the water and consequently reduces the area of wetted surface but in fact this is no more than a useful extra: the main objective is to escape the clutches of wave-making drag.

In order to achieve planing, the hull must be of a suitable shape and although at various times designers have been prepared to lay down the law about this, in fact an extraordinary variety of shapes can be made to plane. For instance, large offshore racing yachts, of apparently totally unsuitable form for planing, do in fact 'surf' vigorously when they have enough wind pushing them and/or a large ocean wave to help them along. However, the two things which seem to be absolutely necessary for true planing are a fore-body which presents an angle of attack to the water flow, so that dynamic lift can be created, and reasonably straight lines in the after-body so that the stern does not 'squat' and create an impossible angle of trim.

The other vital thing that a planing craft needs is sufficient power to overcome the 'hump' and break through into the planing condition. High power/weight ratio is much easier to achieve in small craft than in big ones. We can see this point demonstrated very easily in fast power-boats. If we take a light-weight speedboat weighing only 200lbs (90·7kg), it will be found that an outboard motor of only 20hp is easily enough to give a sparkling planing performance and a speed in excess of 20 knots (P/W = 0·1). At the other extreme, if we take a fast naval patrol-boat of 100ft

(30·4m) length and displacement say 500,000lbs (223,154·5kg), engines developing at least 5,000hp will be required to achieve the same kind of speed because the power/weight ratio is ten times worse (P/W = 0·01). This is because the weight of a boat, or any other structure, rises as approximately the cube of its volume. Small sailing dinghies with light all-up weight and flattish bottoms plane very readily, the Laser and Fireball being examples. With heavier dinghies such as an Albacore or Wayfarer, there is a more noticeable change over from displacement to planing mode, while apart from some slightly freakish craft such as the American inland lake Scows, planing sailing boats of longer than about 6 metres are pretty unusual. This is one reason why the 60ft (18·2m) *Slingshot* was such a bold experiment.

Once a planing boat is 'up' it is free to go on increasing its speed unhampered by wave-making drag. However, it would be a grave mistake to suppose that it was now in a regime in which drag did not increase with speed. For although wave-making has been left behind, the drag due to frictional resistance is still there and still increases as the square of the speed. At this point we can see the added attraction of planing in that it is generally possible to achieve a reduction of wetted surface of perhaps 50 per cent compared to that which is present when in the displacement mode. Another marginal advantage is that planing craft tend to force a certain amount of air under the planing surface so that the boat can be said to be running on a foamy air-water mixture which has a lower coefficient of friction than pure water. There is a whole family of small powerboats which began with the Hickman sea-sled and is now widespread in the Boston Whaler, Dell Quay Dory and thousands of similar imitators with basically 'W' shaped hull sections, that are designed to make use of this 'ram-air' principle.

To sum up, if we take the case of a straightforward planing hull, compared to a displacement hull, it achieves an almost complete freedom from wave-making drag and also a useful reduction in wetted surface. On the other hand it is still fully in contact with the water whose sticky fingers cling to it with the inexorable power of the square law as speed is increased. This leaves aside the question of power, which in dinghies is limited by their relatively low stability.

Where, therefore, lies the road to higher speeds? Ignoring for the moment the question of where the power is going to come from, it is obvious from the foregoing that a substantial reduction in wetted surface must be the aim. Racing powerboats and seaplanes used to achieve this by putting 'steps' in the hull. These had the effect of dividing the planing surface into two or more smaller planing surfaces which at high speed

105

were capable of supporting the remainder of the bottom clear of the water. As an added bonus the planing steps had a more favourable aspect ratio than the whole of the bottom of the hull. Eventually, in the case of really fast boats such as racing hydroplanes or record-breakers, the hull is supported by three minute planing surfaces or 'points' while the rest of the craft is airborne. For a sailing boat, unfortunately, this approach seems to have no future because a 'stepped' or 'three-pointer' hull form has such a horrific resistance at low speed that it is doubtful if sail power would ever be capable of lifting it onto its planing surfaces, and because it only works properly within a narrow range of speeds.

It therefore looks as though we must seek another method of raising the hull out of the water in order to reduce skin-friction drag, and this brings us to hydrofoils. Before beginning to discuss the merits of one type of foil or another let us see what their advantages, or supposed advantages, are.

1. *Wave-making drag*: as a method of avoiding the wave-making resistance of the hull, hydrofoils can be 100 per cent effective, since they can be used to raise the hull completely clear of the water.
2. *Skin friction drag*: skin friction drag of the hull can again be completely eliminated but it is partly replaced by the wetted surface of the foils and their supporting structure. However, a special appeal of foils (or at least of the most usual type of foil) is that as boat speed increases, so wetted area is reduced. Thus with reasonably good luck and good design, drag due to skin friction can remain almost constant as speed increases.

Total elimination of one form of drag and dramatic reduction of another makes hydrofoils seem like magic but of course in dynamics, as in nature, one never gets something for nothing. The very action of providing lift is itself inherently drag-creating, the amount of drag being dependent on the coefficient of drag of the foil section being used, the immersed area of foil and the square of the speed. Now although we are again confronted by a powerful looking $V^2$, the other factors in the equation are quite small so that the actual value of drag caused is encouragingly small.

In theory at least, therefore, hydrofoils do offer a considerable breakthrough. When a craft is fully foil-borne, the hull or hulls can be considered to be totally eliminated apart from the fact that their weight has to be carried and air-drag overcome. Drag associated with the foils themselves is quite small and rises with speed in a manner which is not too alarming. There are no abrupt 'humps' in the curve of resistance, or at least not until one is talking of speeds in the region of 40 knots – still out of the reach of sailing craft.

This rather rosy picture is in reality infested by a whole series of irritating difficulties and drawbacks which nibble away like greenfly at an otherwise perfect bloom. It is not my purpose here to present a complete analysis of hydrofoil design which has already been done much better by others but it should be useful to briefly review the various types and layouts of hydrofoil with comments to their advantages/disadvantages from a practical standpoint.

The top diagram on p. 108 shows a horizontal foil supported on two struts. This deceptively simple arrangement is used by the Russians on their large hydrofoil water buses which plough up and down the river Dnieper. It has an absolutely fundamental drawback which is that unless some form of incidence control is fitted it will gradually rise up in the water as speed increases until it is running just below the surface when there begins to be loss of lift. It is obvious that such an arrangement would be useless except in very smooth water.

The centre diagram shows a 'V' shaped, surface piercing foil of the type often used on sea-going powered hydrofoils., This has the merit of being self-stabilizing both in heel and in height of riding. For any given speed, this foil arrangement will rise up in the water until the area of foil remaining is working as hard as it can and is not able to lift the weight of the boat any higher. Although this layout is nice for a powered craft it does not offer sufficient resistance to heeling on a sailing craft. However, this can be quite simply corrected by, in effect, splitting the boat in half along its centreline and moving the foils outboard (bottom diagram). This is a catamaran with twin angled foils, in fact the arrangement that has been used with considerable success by boats such as *Mayfly* and *Icarus*. It offers good resistance to heeling, adequate lateral resistance and good control of riding height. On the other hand it does have some quite severe drawbacks. All surface piercing foils tend to suffer from an effect known as 'ventilation'. Pressure on the upper side of the foil can drop sufficiently to draw air down from the surface along the foil thus destroying its ability to produce lift. This can be mitigated by fitting 'fences' designed to obstruct the flow of air down the foil but these are not normally completely effective and tend to bring some minor problems of their own. In any case, that part of the foil that actually 'pierces' the water surface produces no useful lift and throws spray which is a form of drag. The fact that the foil is angled away from the horizontal means that only part of the force it produces is useful lift, the remainder being side force. In the case of a 45 per cent dihedral, lift would be reduced to ·707 (cos. 45

*Faster! Faster!*

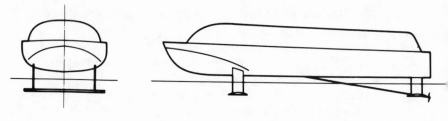

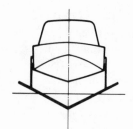

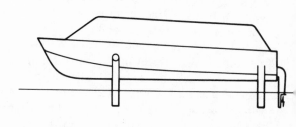

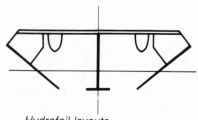

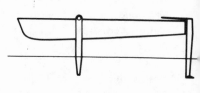

Hydrofoil layouts
Top: a very simple powered hydrofoil of a type only suitable for smooth water
Centre: veed, surface-piercing foils as commonly used on sea-going powered hydrofoils
Bottom: split the above layout vertically and add a central 'inverted T' rudder and you have the layout for a sailing hydrofoil of the Icarus/Mayfly type

degrees) of that obtained from a horizontal foil. In one way, this is no fault, because a large proportion of the force produced by the rig is acting at right angles to the direction of motion of the boat.

The total force produced by the rig has a large proportion of side force and a rather small driving force; therefore any hydrofoil system has to be capable of effectively countering side-force as well as providing lift. This immediately brings us to a difficulty: the value of lift required is easily calculated but the value of side-force is not. The weight of the boat and crew is known and remains constant. It is therefore only necessary to provide a foil which will provide a lifting force equal to the weight of the boat within the speed range envisaged. In the case of surface piercing foils there is in addition the nice self-stabilizing factor that, as speed increases, so foil area decreases and there is no need for fine adjustment of angle of incidence. Side-force on the other hand is something that can change rapidly and grossly, depending upon factors such as wind-speed, boat-speed, apparent wind angle and drag angle of the rig at any given moment. Moreover, there is no way that this rapidly changing force can be accurately countered except by some kind of very sophisticated incidence control system.

In a symmetrically disposed foil system the effect of excessive side-force will be to increase leeway angle. Leeway increases the angle of incidence of the foil on the lee side of the boat and decreases the incidence of the windward foil. In a typical system of the *Icarus* type, the overloaded lee foil will continue to struggle to keep the boat upright, albeit at an increasingly unfavourable lift/drag ratio, but the windward foil will tend to suddenly lose lift as it goes from positive to negative angle of attack. This causes the phenomenon which has been experienced on boats such as *Icarus*, of sudden 'crashes' with the windward side losing lift first.

Logic would bring us to the conclusion that the correct solution for a sailing hydrofoil would be to separate the elements providing lift and resisting side-force and to provide them with separate control systems. This is what John Walker is trying to do with his very sophisticated *Flyer* project. The drawbacks are weight and complexity. The most sophisticated powered hydrofoil boat in the world is probably the Boeing Jetfoil which rides perfectly steadily as it cruises at 50 knots a few metres above a rough sea thanks to its electronically controlled incidence control system. Yet it is sobering to realize that what the sailing hydrofoil is trying to do is inherently trickier.

Instead of being powered by a steady thrust acting in the line of motion, the sailing boat is powered by a constantly changing thrust whose centre of effort is half-way up the mast and whose greatest force is to the side. The problems of harnessing and controlling these forces are considerable, especially, as in order to be useful at all, the mechanism must be light, simple and cheap!

The performance of sailing hydrofoil boats under measured conditions has so far fallen considerably short of what has been hoped for them. Not only have they failed to capture the outright World Sailing Speed Record but, leaving aside the unauthenticated speeds of *Monitor*, they have only just managed to break through the 25 knot barrier which the first *Crossbow* did in her very first year. Even more shaming, during 1980 a sailboard exceeded the best measured speed by a hydrofoil! Following this achievement, Philip Hansford, the originator of *Mayfly*, told me that he was not sure that there was any point in continuing with development of small hydrofoil boats. Yet it is important to realize that the measured speeds so far achieved have been by amateurs working within severe time and cost restraints. There is no doubt that the potential is there and that it will eventually be achieved. Were a reasonably generously funded effort to be made, 40 knots ought to be a realistic target. To achieve it, good foil design and construction will be required and an efficient wing or semi-wing mast. These things are easily within the range of present knowledge and technology. Above 40 knots, things begin to get much more tricky because foil cavitation starts to appear. No one has so far even attempted to sail on supercavitating foils, let alone succeeded.

Hydrofoils first appeared as a means of lifting boats in the water near the end of the 19th century, but it was not until very much later that a sailing hydrofoil made its first tentative tacks.

The idea of fixing inclined plates or blades to the hull of a boat in order to lift it or correct its trim or stop it from rolling occurred to a number of people in different places and at different times. However, insofar as anyone can be said to have 'invented' the hydrofoil, the Englishman Thomas Moy seems to deserve the credit. He was actually interested in flying and is credited with many important contributions to the science of aerodynamics, but he recognized that it would be safer and easier to conduct some of the basic tests in water. He carried out a series of model towing tests in the Surrey canal during 1861. His model was fitted with three lifting foils which had a proper curved section rather than being merely flat inclined plates, and these lifted the boat out of the water. Moy noted that 'a kind of vacuum' was created on the upper surface of the foil and that the force required to tow the model decreased as speed increased.

Moy carried his 'water flight' experiments no further than the model stage because he was not really interested in boats, but in Paris the Comte de Lambert, assisted by the Englishman Horatio Philips, constructed a full-scale hydrofoil boat which first took to the waters of the River Seine in about 1897. This was a catamaran formed by two skiffs connected by a metal framework to which was attached four athwartships foils, the whole contraption, as the saying goes, being driven by steam. The lifting surfaces appear to have been inclined flat plates rather than real foils so one might say that it was more of a stepped planing boat than a hydrofoil, but in any case it worked and was credited with a speed of 34 miles per hour.

Italy has long been a centre of the development of power driven hydrofoil boats and it was the great Italian engineer Forlanini who appears to have developed the idea of a 'ladder' of small hydrofoils which rise out of the water rung by rung as the speed is increased. The great advantage of this system is that while the wetted area is reduced progressively, the lower rungs remain fully immersed and, therefore, do not suffer from the problems associated with surface piercing foils. Forlanini began playing with hydrofoils around 1898 and by 1906 had quite a sophisticated boat which apparently reached a speed of 38 knots with an engine of only 75hp, drive being via a pair of enormous tandem airscrews of the type that Forlanini was also using on his well-known airship projects. Only a short time later Crocco and Ricaldone had reached a speed of 50 knots with a power of 100hp. Their boat was well ahead of its time having all metal variable incidence foils and also all metal variable pitch airscrews which did not become general in aviation until about 30 years later!

From this point onwards we can say that the principles governing the operation of a powered hydrofoil were reasonably well established and that development was held back mainly by the shortage of applications. Of course, one can also say that the development of sailing hydrofoils was held back by the complete absence of applications, there being no incentive whatever to perfect one other than the satisfaction of the owner.

In asking the question 'Who developed the first sailing hydrofoil?' one has to be a bit more specific and say if one is only concerned with 'flying' hydrofoils or whether hydrofoil stabilization also counts. There is a school of thought that it is, literally, flying in the face of fortune to want to lift the whole boat clear of the water, but that a useful function is to keep a slim hull with very little natural stability on an even keel: in other words a trimaran with foils instead of floats. Eric Tabarly's *Paul Ricard*, in which he claimed the record for crossing the Atlantic West to East, is a boat of this type. The main hull is not expected to lift clear of the water, but foils on the ends of the crossbeams take over the work of keeping the boat upright so that the floats do not touch the water. At high speeds, the main hull displacement is partly carried by the foils. A patent, taken out by Emil Palmblad of Hamburg in 1919, shows the basic arrangement with a central hull having foils on the end of outriggers. Furthermore, it is apparent from the diagram that Palmblad had understood that the centre of lateral resistance of the foil could be made to pass through the centre of effort of the sail so as to achieve a proper compensation of heeling force. Unfortunately, there appears to be no record of this boat having been built.

As far as 'flying' hydrofoils are concerned, the American engineer Robert R. Gilruth appears to deserve the credit for being first in this field. Gilruth, who subsequently became head of the Mercury space project, successfully flew a small catamaran on foils in 1939 but, having done so, did not carry the project any further.

Development took an enormous jump forward during the 1950s with the appearance of Baker's *Monitor*. This boat and its designer have always been shrouded in a certain amount of mystery to the extent that many people asserted that it was literally fabulous or that the speeds claimed for it were grossly exaggerated. *Monitor* certainly did exist and sailed at speeds that would have seemed quite incredible in 1950, but it has not been possible to authenticate her speeds in any really satisfactory way.

The facts are that J. G. Baker of Wisconsin built an interesting little 16ft (4·8m) monohull with large Vee foils disposed in an 'aeroplane' configuration during 1950 and flew it successfully during that year. He developed this boat over a period of three years giving it an improved rig and adding vertical fins to the foils so as to cope better with side-force, and eventually reached a speed in the region of 23 knots.

Now this was a period when the US Navy suddenly became interested in hydrofoils and, casting around for anyone who might might know something about them, alighted on Baker. The British inventor Christopher Hook was another person who got sucked into this sudden burst of military enthusiasm. Anyway, the Navy gave Baker a development contract which enabled him to build *Monitor*. As this was just about the only sailing hydrofoil boat in history to enjoy anything like adequate funding, it is perhaps reasonable that it achieved a level of performance that is only now being approached again by those of more slender means.

*J. G. Baker's first hydrofoil, built in 1950. US Navy interest led to his second, much more ambitious boat* Monitor (Baker Mfg. via James Grogono)

Like the earlier Baker craft, *Monitor* was a monohull but considerably bigger and with, for the date, an efficient fully-battened sloop rig. The main foils, which were in line with the mast, consisted of a pair of tapered ladders of six foil elements each, set at 45 degrees to the horizontal. These ladders were mounted on tubular beams whose rotation controlled the incidence of the foils. Steering and pitch control was taken care of by a two rung V-foil arrangement at the stern. The whole secret of *Monitor*'s success lay in the fact that the incidence of the two main foil sets could be controlled *independently* so that control of roll was achieved. Furthermore, there was an elaborate mechanical linkage system that translated stress in the rig into instructions to the foils so that roll stability was fully automatic.

*Monitor* first flew in August 1955 and was soon achieving speeds around 25 knots. The following year she went considerably faster, reportedly in excess of 30 knots. The problem is that her performance was apparently only measured by accompanying motor boats, a notoriously inaccurate method. From a study of the photographs, and a short piece of film which has recently come to light, a speed of 30 knots seems credible, especially as there does not seem to have been any great strength of wind. In the absence of any real evidence one can only say that *Monitor* was *probably* the fastest hydrofoil boat to date and possibly even the fastest sailing boat of all time. The frustrating thing is that being a military project, there were doubtless masses of reports and technical data which are presumably gathering dust in some long forgotten file in the Navy Department. If only they could be dug out, Baker and his work could perhaps receive the recognition it deserves.

In any case the story of *Monitor* came to an abrupt end when the Navy lost interest and cancelled the project. One might wonder just what they had expected to learn anyway since it is difficult to imagine that they were anticipating fleets of sailing hydrofoil warships. If it was hydrofoils in general that they were interested in, why bother with a sailing boat which, as we have seen, is a totally different kind of animal? *Monitor* could certainly not have taught them much about the main problem in powered hydrofoils: that of power transmission. It is an interesting sideline on history that Christopher Hook's US Navy project met a similar end. He had a contract to develop, of all things, a hydrofoil landing craft. He used the opportunity to develop his 'hydrofin' system, which is a mechanically operated incidence control using a sensor arm to 'feel' the water surface in front of the craft and adjust the incidence of the main foils accordingly. This brilliantly simple and effective way of controlling both roll and riding height can be used on either powered or

Monitor *at speed, showing her ladder foil system which was incidence controlled by a mechanical computer. Sadly, the speed of this very advanced craft was never accurately measured* (Baker Mfg. via James Grogono)

sailing boats. Not surprisingly, the landing craft was cancelled and Hook then wasted years trying to prise his patent out of the US authorities so that he could make some use of it. As the final irony, when the US Navy eventually took up the idea of hydrofoils again, instead of using the cheap and reliable hydrofin system they spent millions developing powered incidence control and sophisticated electronic sensors as used in the Boeing 'Jetfoil'.

Hydrofoils are like aircraft in that the various lifting and control surfaces can be arranged in a variety of ways. The main variable is the position of the rudder which is normally combined with some sort of pitch controlling mechanism. We are used to seeing rudders on the sterns of boats and on the tails of aircraft, but it is equally possible to arrange things the other way around and steer from the front, as in a car or a bicycle. The normal arrangement of an aircraft, with the control surfaces at the rear, is so familiar that it is worth remembering that this was not in fact the arrangement favoured by some pioneers of aviation, such as the Wright brothers, who placed the elevators in front of the main lifting surfaces. Interestingly, there is now a tendency to return to this 'canard' layout – for instance in the efficient light aircraft designed by Bert Rutan in the USA.

Anyway, the 'canard' layout was the one chosen by the American Don Nigg for his series of hydrofoil boats. After Baker, Nigg appears to have been the first person to experiment with sailing hydrofoils in any serious way. Unlike Baker, he was a pure amateur who did all the work in his garage in his spare time, although he is an engineer by profession. Nigg built his first boat in 1963 and from the start adopted an 'ice-boat' layout with three-point suspension. A main beam at the rear carried two well spread dihedralled surface piercing foils while steering was carried out by a double Vee foil set well ahead of the mast on the end of a central fore and aft spine. Initially he made up wooden foils of the low drag NACA 66–S209 series. However, this is pretty tricky for the amateur to make having complex curves on both upper and lower surfaces and he later changed over to using the much simpler ogive which has been seen on so many hydrofoil boats since. An ogival section is one which is flat on the lower side and has an arc of circle curve on the upper side. It is theoretically less efficient but has many practical advantages, not the least being ease of construction. Incidentally, the Anglo-French Concorde has ogival wings so the section cannot be too bad.

Like a lot of hydrofoil experimenters, Nigg was initially more interested in getting the boat off the water and demonstrating the feasibility of the layout than in achieving an amazing speed. Thus he provided a more than adequate lifting area whose effect was to give 'lift-off' at the very low speed of 6·5 knots. However, this was necessary because the 'floating' part of the boat was somewhat rudimentary consisting of three rather boxy little floats. Nigg soon realized that it was neither necessary or desirable to get up onto foils at such low speed and so his second and third designs tended to be more seaworthy and capable of greater hull speed. A basic feature of the canard layout is that the front foil supports a fairly small proportion of the total load – only 18 per cent in the case of Nigg's first boat. He has described the unique and rather diverting sequence of events that occur at 'take-off'. The boat starts off sailing gently along on its floats until the front foil is developing sufficient lift to carry its modest load. It starts to gently lift the bow and as it does so the angle of attack increases and so does the coefficient of lift. This is a regenerative process so the bow foil suddenly pops up out of the water leaving the craft with a pronounced bow-up attitude. It continues like this until the main foil gradually accepts its load and trims the boat back into a more sensible looking angle. At full speed, the boat is in more or less level trim.

Nigg's first boat fell to pieces when he tried to tack her on foils and he built a second one that had a 'space-frame' arrangement of light girders supported on three small floats and with the same layout of foils as before. This boat was quite successful and demonstrated the feasibility and stability of the canard layout although she was not a very seamanlike contraption. Nigg's best known boat was his third, *Flying Fish*, for which he published plans; several examples were built in different parts of the world. In place of the spidery arrangement of girders, there was a sealed, cylinder-like main hull and a large tubular crossbeam which also provided buoyancy when the boat was not moving. The *Flying Fish* design was intended to make use of various standard sail plans which owners might have lying around their garage; the original being fitted with a 'Y-Flyer' sail of 124 sq ft. The foils were basically similar to the previous two boats but were now employing the ogival section. *Flying Fish* flew well and reliably and did a lot to interest people in the idea of hydrofoil sailing. As far as is known, Nigg never entered *Flying Fish* for any kind of speed trials, probably because there were none available, and did not measure his speed in any rigorous fashion. However, he writes of having sailed at speeds approaching 30 knots so it is really a shame that this was never verified. *Flying Fish* was launched in the spring of 1968 and her plans were published later that year.

It is not the purpose here to write a history of hydrofoil development except insofar as it has led to faster sailing. There have been a number of other experiments made, with different layouts and varying degrees of success. In several cases the same feeling of frustration is occasioned as with Nigg in that exciting speeds are mentioned or even claimed but without any verification. This does not imply any kind of dishonesty on the part of the people concerned, but merely that the means or the incentive for accurate speed measurement were not present at the time.

One of the more interesting boats was that built by Howard Apollonio while a student at the University of Michigan in 1966. He was one of those people fired with enthusiasm after having seen a photograph of *Monitor*, which was apparently his only prior knowledge of the subject. Armed with this scanty knowledge he designed and built a very sensible and apparently quite successful catamaran with tandem surface piercing foils. A point of interest is that all the foils were fixed and that steering was by trailing edge flaps on the aft set; the only instance I know of this being used on a sailing boat. The boat was quite heavy and robust but as the photograph shows she had a reasonably efficient sail plan of 160 sq ft. Because of the weight, Apollonio found he needed at least 15 knots of wind 'to fly', but on the other hand the boat was stable and fast in

*Don Nigg's canard layout* Flying Fish. *Plans were available for this boat and several were built in different countries* (Nigg, via James Grogono)

*Howard Apollonio's* Flying Feline *was a crude but apparently quite successful hydrofoil catamaran with an unusual veed ladder foil arrangement* (Anon, via James Grogono)

a strong breeze and, because of her high riding level, not much affected by waves. Apollonio claimed to have reached speeds around 30 knots in gusts which from the photographs seems within the bounds of possibility. He concluded that the boat was too heavy and that the foils had more area than needed. In spite of the very considerable success of his boat, Apollonio apparently did not carry things any further.

# 7
# Hydrofoil record breakers

The whole story of sailing hydrofoils would be of no more than passing interest to us if it were not for the fact that they have actually increased World Record Speeds on a number of occasions. So far, three different hydrofoil boats have held records: *Mayfly*, *Icarus* and *(NF)²*. *Mayfly* and *Icarus* have always been closely associated so it is convenient to tell their stories together. If this turns out to be as much a personal as a technical story I make no apology since boats are no more than an expression of the ideas of people.

The family Grogono are entirely English, in spite of their name. For at least the past two generations, the family has produced a large number of doctors whose hobby is sailing. Until his recent retirement, Dr Bernard Grogono was a general practitioner in Woodford, Essex and a life-long sailing enthusiast. Of his three sons, all are sailors and two are in the medical profession. There are also numerous uncles and cousins who are doctors or sailors or both.

The Grogono who chiefly concerns us is Dr Bernard's second son James who was the first member of the family to become interested in hydrofoils and speed sailing although the entire family and a lot of other people eventually became drawn into the whirlpool of enthusiasm that James generated. In a family of keen sailors, James has been the keenest. As a young man he was an Olympic trialist in the Finn class and at the same time a team-racing enthusiast. Even before this he had shown an interest in the technical side of sailing. While still at school he acquired a simple 4in (102mm) wind tunnel and mounted little models of various types of sail in it. From these experiments he concluded that solid aerofoils had a better lift/drag ratio than cloth sails. With typically grandiose schoolboy enthusiasm, he was thinking about solid wings as sailplans but the tests in the tiny wind-tunnel also led him to the conclusion that 'water wings' would be more efficient than hulls. At the time (mid '50s) James was not aware that anyone else was experimenting with hydrofoils, so we can certainly credit him with a degree of originality even if his ideas were not put into effect until some years afterwards.

James thought about the idea of sailing hydrofoils for some years and came to the conclusion (which he now regards as laughable) that it might have some commercial future and therefore instead of publishing anything he decided to keep quiet until the opportunity arose to put some theories into practice. The next step in the story was not until 1967 when the Tornado catamaran first appeared. James immediately realized that this would be an ideal vehicle for hydrofoil trials. It had a particularly powerful and efficient rig, light weight and a layout which offered plenty of scope for screwing or strapping on extra bits and pieces. However, nothing actually got done until 1969 when a school-friend and Olympic silver medallist oarsman named John James came back to Britain after a period in Australia. His presence provided an extra boost of enthusiasm – and cash – needed to get the 'Icarus' project under way.

During 1969 James Grogono bought a Tornado catamaran and with John James made the first set of foils for it. The boat had been built by Alan Bell of Whitstable with hydrofoil attachment in mind and the rather frail tortured ply construction had been beefed up locally with solid blocks of timber where it was intended to fix the foils. The first set were neither 'canard' nor 'aeroplane' configuration but more of a 'motor car', i.e with a wheel on each corner! The main foils, which were intended to carry 80 per cent of the load, were located in way of the centre-board boxes and had a vertical strut which passed up through the box with the foil itself being set outboard at 45 degrees dihedral. The bow foils, which were placed well forward, were attached with wood screws to the built-in strong points on the hull. Both sets of foils were 9 per cent thickness-to-chord ratio, made up from laminates of Douglas Fir bonded onto ½inch (12mm) Gaboon ply.

Since all four foils were rigidly attached, the boat had to be carried shoulder high into the water by a team of astonishingly dedicated volunteers. To the amazement of all concerned except James, *Icarus* started to lift out on her foils at around 5 knots and came fully clear of the water at around 10 knots. She was reasonably stable on a variety of headings although there was not much evidence of any great improvement in speed. Steering, which was by normal rudders with extended blades, was poor at high speed and non-existent at low speed. *Icarus* sailed in this form for a total of four days until activities were cut short (almost literally) by the failure of a mounting block on one of the forward foils. The foil folded back at speed and nearly succeeded in cutting the bow clean off the hull.

Judged by later achievements, in this first year of sailing *Icarus* was pretty crude but at least it was a start and the sight of the boat sailing along completely clear of the water fuelled the enthusiasm to try again. The whole success of the *Icarus* team long-term has been that they have always been prepared to try, fail and then try again! It's a healthy mixture of theory and empiricism that brings results in the long run.

At the end of 1969, John James returned to Australia and *Icarus* was turned into a syndicate consisting of James Grogono, his father and two brothers and John Fowler, an Essex farmer who possessed the priceless asset of a barn where a large and rather delicate boat could be stored. It was realized that the first layout was: (a) wildly impractical, (b) had too much foil area, (c) could hardly be steered, and (d) was too unsophisticated in every way. The first decision was to make both front foils steerable and the second to make all foils retractable. A kind of tubular extension frame was built on to the sides of the Tornado in order to provide a mounting for the main foils. These were fitted so that they could swing over from the stowed position lying on deck to the running position in which they were actually in contact with the underside of the hull. To accommodate the front foils, blocks incorporating rudder pintles were attached to the hulls on their outboard sides. The boat went afloat with the front foils lying on deck and these were subsequently fitted onto their pintles without too much difficulty like over-sized rudders. The catamaran's normal rudder linking bar and tiller extension was used in order to operate the two front foils in unison.

The foils themselves were smaller as it had been realized that the first set had far more lift than required, leading to lift-off at too low a speed. The front foils were again ogival but the main units were of the low-drag NACA 65410 section, tapering throughout their length. As well as being very tricky to make by hand, these foils proved to have inadequate lift with the result that it was hardly ever possible to get the stern properly clear of the water, even in a good breeze. The steering system, on the other hand, worked quite well and the whole layout seemed reasonably practical so it was decided to press ahead as quickly as possible with completely new foils of NACA 4412 section. These were again made of wood but for the first time were fitted with 'fences' as ventilation had already been experienced with earlier foils.

During the second year of trials, James Grogono had been in contact with the magazine *Yachting World* where I was working at the time, and as well as contributing an article on his project, he suggested that the

Icarus *in her 'Mk III' layout with wooden foils. At this stage she was bow steered with the main foils carried on an outboard framework* (Yachting World)

magazine should organize some kind of time-trial in order to encourage people to take an interest in faster sailing. This was really the first tentative beginning that eventually led to the Portland Speed Trials. A weekend was arranged at Burnham-on-Crouch and advertised through the Amateur Yacht Research Society. *Yachting World* paid Hunting Surveys to set up a half kilometre measured distance in the River Crouch, the distance being chosen mainly because this was the longest that could be easily fitted into the available space.

Judged by the results alone, this weekend was a fairly dismal failure. Various AYRS-type boats appeared and duly fell to pieces, some even before they reached their natural element. *Icarus* performed with her new foils and proved to all and sundry that she could be lifted entirely out of the water but her efforts were somewhat overshadowed by a perfectly standard Tornado which proved considerably faster! However, there were two successes: first it enabled *Yachting World* to take and publish pictures of a boat undeniably sailing on foils. The second result of this meeting was rather more surprising. At about tea-time on the Saturday afternoon, a young man whom no one knew appeared carrying a small model hydrofoil boat. He set the model in the water at the foot of the

Royal Corinthian Y.C.'s launching ramp and pushed it off, whereupon, to the great astonishment of all observers, it rose immediately onto foils and went hurtling off across the river at great speed exhibiting exemplary stability until it hit the mud on the far bank. Someone then went off in a dinghy to collect the model and restore it to its owner whom we discovered was called Philip Hansford. James Grogono then went into the club to change and when he emerged the mysterious Mr Hansford had disappeared.

Luckily for hydrofoil development, James decided that he must try to find out more about Hansford and his model and therefore worked his way through the Hansfords in the London telephone directory, striking gold with the sixth call. He was intrigued to discover that Hansford was building a 15ft (4·5m) hydrofoil catamaran of a similar design to the model. They arranged to meet and swap ideas and this resulted in one of the most successful partnerships in the brief history of speed sailing. The two men were an unlikely combination, like many successful partnerships: James Grogono is a highly extroverted and hyper-active type, constantly bubbling over with new ideas and hardly ever stopping long enough to complete one project before plunging enthusiastically into the next three. He is gregarious and normally to be found at the centre of a group of devoted helpers who have somehow got swept up in his latest project. Philip Hansford is the exact opposite: an extremely reserved and thoughtful man who likes to work quietly away at things on his own. A draughtsman by profession, he was a keen aeromodeller and had been interested in aerodynamics for a number of years.

Hansford had devised a layout which was simple, original and successful. The basis was a 15ft (4·5m) catamaran, a bit like a mini-Tornado. The main foils were mounted on a rotatable tube which plugged directly into the main crossbeam of the boat. They consisted of tapered, 40 degree dihedral foils of 7 per cent thickness-to-chord ratio and ogival section. Their mounting tube could be rotated so that the foils were inverted for launching. Mounted on the transoms were two steerable diamond shaped foils. The whole emphasis was on simplicity and lightness and the little boat, which Philip named *Mayfly*, was built with an aeromodeller's care and attention to detail. Every part of her had been worked out from first principles with proper consideration being given to dynamics and stability. Philip had seen pictures of the Nigg boat and considered it back-to-front. The front foil lifts first and sets a high angle of attack for the main foils which are only able to reduce this by lifting partly out of the water; hence both main and bow foils work at high values of coefficient of lift. Philip preferred an 'aeroplane' configuration in which the main foils lift first and create an angle of attack on the 'tail' foil. As this lifts, it progressively reduces both its own angle of attack and that of the main foils. The theory is that at high speed, all foils should run at reasonable values of coefficient of lift and that there is no danger of the 'tail' lifting out of the water. In addition, the stern foil or foils can be mounted on pintles and used for steering.

Due to the care which he put into every detail, *Mayfly* took a year for Philip Hansford to build. Then when the boat was finally complete, Philip revealed that he had an extra problem: he didn't know how to sail! James Grogono therefore persuaded him to bring the boat down to Aldeburgh in Suffolk where she was put into the water for the first time. This was during 1970. *Mayfly* was an immediate and marked success: flying in an impressively stable manner. She was not only manoeuvrable but actually pleasant to handle as well. From the very first moment she sailed, *Mayfly* has always been the most effectively possible argument in favour of sailing hydrofoils because she looks right and is great fun to sail.

Following her first outings, it appeared that there were possible areas for improvement. The first was that the sail – an old Fireball mainsail – was quite unsuitable and second that the steerable 'tail' foils were

*James Grogono sailing* Mayfly *on the River Crouch on her original wooden foils. This picture shows rather well the fact that foils have their own special wave drag formation plus tip vortex and spray drag* (Yachting World)

running in the turbulence created by the main foils. In discussions with the *Icarus* team, Hansford proposed to change to a single inverted 'T' stern foil mounted centrally, making the layout even more of an 'aeroplane'. He made his first 'T' foil from wood using a symmetrical section that produces zero lift at zero angle of attack, like a rudder blade turned through 90 degrees. This was mounted on a lightweight tubular cross-beam on the extreme aft ends of the hulls and forming, in effect, a false, central transom. With this modification, *Mayfly* was even more successful and she built up a satisfactory number of hours of sailing with this layout during 1971.

From this point onwards, the stories of *Icarus* and *Mayfly* become more closely linked. Due to Hansford's lack of sailing experience, James Grogono became the regular 'pilot' of *Mayfly*, and because of this he realized that Hansford had evolved a first-class layout which could be copied on the larger and more powerful *Icarus*. It was therefore decided to pool resources and have metal foils made up for both boats to a design similar to *Mayfly*'s 1971 wooden foils. (In fact, there was also a third boat, *Hustler*, which dropped out of view when the owner emigrated.)

During the winter of 1971/2 therefore, Allday Aluminium of Gosport were commissioned to make three complete sets of foils in marine grade Dural. They were different in size to suit the different boats but all of similar design. The main foils were of ogival section, completely flat on the underside and with an arc-of-circle upper side. One reason for adopting this section was that it was extremely easy to make up – simply a piece of rolled section welded onto a flat plate. By tapering the foil, it automatically reduced thickness/chord ratio towards the tip. Dihedral angle is 40 degrees and the foil is supported by a single strut about two thirds of the distance from the upper end. These front foils are mounted on an aluminium tube that mates with a larger tube on the boat so that the foils rotate from the stowed to the operating position. The angle of attack is controlled by a wire to the bow of the boat that incorporates an adjusting screw.

The inverted 'T' stern foil is made from a symmetrical vertical strut with a cast aluminium 'T' fixed to the end. There was at one time a plan to steer by a trailing-edge flap, like Apollonio, but this was too expensive to make so the whole strut turns as a rudder. The aft foil is so mounted that its angle of attack can be adjusted to fine limits by a screw-thread. It was originally thought that both the main and stern foils needed a careful setting of angle of attack but on further consideration it was apparent that the only angle that matters is the *relative* angle between the front and rear foil units.

The impetus to spend money on metal foils was provided by the Royal Yachting Association announcing their World Sailing Speed Record Competition in association with the cigarette company John Player (see Chapter Nine). In these first years of the competition, there were substantial cash prizes to be won which offered the prospect of a rolling programme of development, financed by winnings. To start with, there was no idea of *class* prizes, just an overall no-limits competition for the fastest sailing boat in the World. The winner was to receive £1,000 and a further £1,000 was to be distributed among any boats that got within 5 knots of the winner.

It was soon apparent that *Mayfly* was the more successful of the two boats and the most impressive foil boat to appear at the first Speed Week. All of the other foil boats that appeared (including *Icarus*) suffered from some kind of misbehaviour: either they could not stay up on their foils for any length of time or could not be steered or were just slow. *Mayfly* was simple to sail, stable, fast and enormous fun. By this time I had joined the '*Icarus/Mayfly* syndicate' and in fact put up the best recorded time by *Mayfly* that year: 16·4 knots. It was clear that she was capable of much better speeds but only in smooth water. This was because at speeds over 15 knots, only 6 or 9 inches of the main foils remained immersed so that if one encountered an 18in wave, she would be totally airborne as the foils passed through the trough. But not for long! These little jumps were inevitably followed by crashes because once the foils lost their 'grip' they could not regain it instantaneously. Since the measured 500 metre course at Portland is more or less in the middle of the harbour, it was inevitable that in winds of force 5 or over, *Mayfly* was going to be in difficulty with the waves.

Sailing *Mayfly* was an absolute revelation compared to a fast racing dinghy. At around 10 knots she would pop up out of the water and all the wetness and violent motion of the dinghy would disappear. There is this very pleasant feeling of skimming effortlessly along just above the water surface with very little noise and almost no spray. She shows no great tendency to heel so that sitting out is more a matter of habit than necessity. As the speed rises, the steering becomes alarmingly light and effective rather like driving a car backwards at speed. When the waves were too big for peace of mind – as they generally are at Portland – the overall effect is of running fast and effortlessly across a frozen ploughed field with the ever-present feeling that if you once put a foot wrong you will go down on your face – hard! In actual fact these 'crash dives' turned out to be more frightening than dangerous. To begin with one imagined that the boat would be smashed up or that one would be shot off the bows like a torpedo. Although the structure of the boat does take a lot of stress at these moments, *Mayfly* survived hundreds of 'crashes'. After one very severe nose-dive, one of her hulls split along the keel line. It was repaired with adhesive tape which remained in place for a further year!

It soon became apparent that *Mayfly* was a sufficiently safe boat for a variety of people to be allowed to sail her and share that thrill of sailing at close to 20 knots on a 15 ft (4·5m) boat. Both *Mayfly* and the *Icarus* group made a number of friends in this way, and a good deal of favourable publicity. However, it was apparent to the members of the syndicate that *Mayfly* really needed smooth water in order to achieve high speeds.

The situation with *Icarus* was slightly different; because it seemed the obvious thing to do she had been equipped with two inverted 'T' foils mounted on the transoms like conventional rudders. Her main foils were basically similar, though of course bigger, than *Mayfly*'s and mounted well forward on special short tubes secured on top of the Tornado's foredecks. She was considerably more powerful and faster than *Mayfly* but not nearly so easy to sail. The twin steering foils tended to suffer badly from ventilation, in spite of being fenced and if this happened on one foil but not the other, the result was strong, unpredictable helm forces. There was plenty of wind during the first speed week and *Icarus* gave those of us who sailed her some fairly 'hairy' moments. I had the misfortune to be at the helm when the boat decided to take a sudden violent swerve to leeward at about 25 knots. The sudden change in direction had the effect of throwing me backwards over the side so that I pulled hard on the tiller just when I wanted to be pushing on it. The net result was a violent cartwheeling capsize in which Alan Grogono made a dramatic 'grand tour' on the end of the trapeze wire. Interestingly, neither of us was hurt in the least – except in our pride – and the boat suffered from nothing worse than broken sail battens. Later in the week Alan had an even greater fright when one of the steering foils parted company with the boat, taking the transom with it. With admirable presence of mind he dived into the water and just managed to grab the foil before it sank.

It was obvious that *Icarus* was far from right but she did manage to end the week with a speed of 21·6 knots which was second-best after *Crossbow* and 2 knots faster than the best non-hydrofoil Tornado. Equally important, she just managed to be within 5 knots of *Crossbow*, and as no other boat managed this, won £1,000. However, this money was not spent on beer and high living because it exactly paid for the year's ironmongery and running expenses.

Icarus *with aluminium foils mounted forward on special brackets. These foils were eventually moved aft to the main beam* (see jacket photo) (Guy Gurney)

In the years since 1972 both *Mayfly* and *Icarus* improved their performances but *Mayfly* has been consistently the more successful boat. In fact it is extraordinary to reflect that in 1980, when *Icarus* regained her World Record in 'B' Class, it was with a speed of 23·8 knots; hardly a dramatic improvement. In the intervening period she has tried out a series of variations on the basic *Mayfly* theme. From 1973 onwards she has sailed with a single, central 'T' tail and the main foils have gradually moved aft until, in 1980, they were plugged into the ends of the main crossbeam. Extending the beam by fitting the main foils on longer tubes was tried and the Allday foils have soldiered on in spite of being bent and repaired in various ways. By 1980 the only part of the original boat that survived was the crossbeam, everything else having been replaced at some stage. Greatly improved sails would probably alone account for the 2·2 knots increase in speed so one might say that *Icarus* had scarcely progressed. In fact, of course she had tried out and evaluated a whole series of ideas and this in itself must be considered worthwhile. In 1983 she raised her best speed once again to 26·59 knots but in the same week a sailboard reached the much more impressive speed of 30·82 knots.

*Mayfly*, on the other hand, has had a history of steadily improved performance. In 1974, without any changes except greater resolve on the part of the various helmsmen, now happily including Philip Hansford himself, she improved her speed to 19·38 knots. Hansford, however, is not a man to sit back and rest on his laurels. He decided that the next step would be to convert *Mayfly* to fully-submerged, incidence-controlled main foils. These would be inverted 'T' foils like the one at the stern but hinged where they joined the strut and controlled in incidence by a 'Hook-type' feeler arm with little planing floats on the ends. Philip first tried this on the boat in 1974 and quickly decided that the feeler floats were wrong. These were rebuilt and the boat did very briefly sail on her new foils in a light wind. Next, she went out with two aboard as both Philip and Andrew Grogono wanted to see what was going on. Unfortunately, this was too much weight for the boat and one of the foil struts folded over. After this, Philip seemed to lose interest and actually sold *Mayfly* to James Grogono, who sailed her in 1975 putting up her speed fractionally to 19·4 knots.

In 1976 the boat was sold again, this time to Ben Wynne, a young naval architecture student and dinghy sailor who managed to find the right combination of wind and sea and put up a speed of 21·1 knots, a new World Record for 'A' Class. The boat was in virtually the same condition as 1972. For the following year, however, Wynne managed to persuade the Department of Mechanical Engineering, University of Newcastle upon Tyne, to help with the production of new foils. The basic layout remained the same but the main foils were now milled from solid metal using computer-controlled machine tools. Wynne employed a basic series 6 NACA section tapered in both chord and thickness/chord ratio. The section was also twisted in an effort to optimize lift coefficient at various speeds and there were turned-down tips of symmetrical section so as to provide a better resistance to side force at high speed when there is very little foil remaining in the water. The highly-sophisticated piece of engineering was a far cry from the basic arc-of-circle foil made by Alldays. A further improvement was a new, larger sail of maximum area permitted in 'A' class.

Another point working in favour of *Mayfly* was that from 1977 onwards the organizers of Speed Week provided an alternative, smooth-water course. This is a fixed course close to the shore and was intended to be used when there was too much wind for the main course. This new provision gave *Mayfly* what she had been waiting for all along: strong wind and flat water and Ben Wynne was rewarded by a remarkable 23·0 knots which not only gave him a new World Record in 'A' Class, but also placed him clear ahead of every other boat in any class except *Crossbow I* and *II*. Wynne sailed *Mayfly* for two more years without any improvement of speed and she was then stored until 1981 when Wynne was tempted back into action by the big cash prizes at the Brest speed event. Unfortunately she was badly smashed up in a capsize but the intention is that she will be reassembled and exhibited at the Science Museum in London, a fitting place for this influential boat.

*Mayfly*'s speed of 23·0 knots stood as the 'A' Class World Record until 1983 when it was bettered by the two-man sailboard *Black and White* with a speed of 25·39 knots and *Mayfly* remained the fastest small sailing boat in the World until 1980 when she was finally passed by *Icarus* and also by the sailboard sailed by Jaap Van der Rest. The last named took over the position of fastest small sailing boat in the World and record-holder of the 10 sq metre sail area class with the truly remarkable speed of 25·11 knots.

In order to complete the story of hydrofoil record breakers, we must cross the Atlantic to the State University of New York at Stony Brook, where, in the Mechanical Engineering Department, we discover Professor W. F. Bradfield to be the head of the department. For a number of years "Brad' Bradfield had been gently developing his ideas for a hydrofoil sailing craft and had organized a number of speed trials at nearby Port Jefferson.

Compared to the average hydrofoil pioneer sawing and hammering away in a garage or basement, Bradfield's department has magnificent facilities with plenty of space and modern equipment. However, the

Mayfly *in her final form with the metal foils designed by Ben Wynne which enabled him to reach 23 knots* (Yachting World)

*(NF)²* project has never enjoyed more status than that of a student exercise and hence proceeds as and when time, funds and student enthusiasm is available. Bradfield has also chosen quite deliberately to follow paths that are technically interesting or instructive rather than the paths of least resistance and this also means that progress has tended to be slow.

With characteristic dry humour, Bradfield named his boat *(NF)²* in the hope that it would be taken as some arcane formula whereas in fact it is an acronym of 'Neither Fish Nor Fowl'.

According to the Professor it is impossible to describe *(NF)²* because she has never been finished, and probably never will be. However, the main drift of development has been to develop a workable controlled incidence hydrofoil vehicle, in which the 'pilot' is able to directly control pitch, roll and steering via a set of aircraft-like controls. The same thing was attempted rather bravely by the elderly Christopher Hook working with a bunch of schoolboys. However, the complex engineering of *Miss Strand Glass* resulted in an unacceptable weight penalty and she was never a practical vehicle.

*(NF)²* is bow-steered a bit like a Nigg boat but with ladder main foils reminiscent of those on *Monitor* except that they are controlled by hand rather than an automatic mechanism. Bradfield has been a devotee of the idea of trying to eliminate conventional hulls as far possible and hence *(NF)²* is a kind of 'space frame' construction in approximately triangular form. During his 1980 season, at least, he had a couple of rubber dinghy hulls to provide minimal buoyancy prior to take-off. This arrangement says a lot for the designer's confidence in the foil system for not many of us would want to be dependent on a couple of inflated tubes in a crash from 25 knots. Indeed, the *Icarus* team have always found that it is essential to have as a basis a fast and reliable boat, such as the Tornado, both in order to reach a respectable take-off speed and to survive the inevitable mishaps.

*(NF)²* has sported a variety of different rigs at different stages in her career with a Tornado or 'C' Class catamaran mainsail forming the basic units. The most 'serious' season so far appears to have been 1978 when Bradfield went to the trouble and expense of having measured distances set up at Port Jefferson and gathering together the team needed to try for record speeds. They decided to shoot for both the 'B' and 'C' Class World records at the same time. The 'C' Class record has always been rather low as there have been few serious contenders. This was done by the very simple method of making 'B' class runs with a 218 sq ft mainsail and then adding a jib to bring the area up to 298 sq ft for the 'C' Class runs. In a

moderate wind of only Force 4, *(NF)²* achieved best speeds of 23·0 knots in 'B' Class trim and 24·4 in 'C'. Both these speeds were ratified as World Records later that year.

Since 1978, Bradfield and his students have continued to tinker with *(NF)²* without any serious effort to establish new records. By 1981 Bradfield expressed himself reasonably satisfied with the foils and the general layout of the boat, but regarded the rig as being dreadfully crude: no more than a collection of off-the-shelf bits and pieces.

# 8
# Flying surfboards

At the time of writing, a sailboard holds the record for the second fastest sailing vessel on earth (Fred Hayward at 30·83 knots in 1983, second only to *Crossbow II*). This fact mirrors the extraordinarily swift development of this novel type of sailing vessel, which has certainly been the most startling thing to happen to sailing for many years, if not ever.

The sailboard as we know it was developed in California during 1967 by Hoyle Schweitzer and Jim Drake with help from various friends. After their idea had become commercially successful, various other people remembered that they had had the same or similar ideas much earlier, the best known examples being Peter Chilvers in England and Newman Darby in the United States. Schweitzer was not a sailor at all, but a surfing enthusiast who thought that it would be good to be able to enjoy the thrills of surfing on days when there was wind but no surf. Drake is a highly intelligent engineer/designer working for the Rand Corporation and it is perhaps fair to give him much of the credit for the dynamic ideas behind the original Windsurfer. A catamaran enthusiast, Alan Parducci also contributed to the various brainstorming sessions but it was certainly Schweitzer who carried through most of the development work and first saw the commercial possibilities of the thing.

Schweitzer gave up his job as a computer salesman and invested his life savings in setting up a manufacturing plant for the Windsurfer. After participating in the original design process, Jim Drake moved to the east and sold Schweitzer his share in the patents which they had taken out to cover the operation of the Windsurfer, patents which Schweitzer has clung to tenaciously and which have been the cause of much wrangling ever since.

In 1969 the Windsurfer was available commercially and it quickly became apparent that its future lay not as a substitute for wave-surfing but as a new type of sailing. Although beginners spend much of their time falling into the water, more practiced board sailors quickly gained complete control of their mounts and could tack, gybe and manoeuvre with as much facility as a small dinghy. As soon as a reasonable number of sailors became competent, it was inevitable that they should start to race and just as inevitable that this rapidly led to improvement of technique.

Surprisingly, it was not until the Windsurfer became available in Europe that the real boom in board sailing began. In the United States it seems to have been perceived for a long time as a fad among many other fads whereas in Europe it was quickly grasped as a real sport breakthrough, enabling many young people to take part in an exciting, demanding watersport that is not expensive and does not demand a great deal of preparation or a long apprenticeship as for instance in the traditional dinghy racing fleets.

When sailboards began to appear in European waters, most established yachtsmen viewed them at first as a kind of amusing beach toy and certainly did not see them as representing any kind of threat to the established order of things. They soon found out how wrong they were: by about 1975, board sailing was growing faster than any other branch of sailing and although many of the enthusiasts were completely new to sailing, a fair number were culled from the ranks of dinghy sailors or were people who might otherwise have taken up dinghy sailing had they not been captivated by board sailing.

In Europe, the initial monopoly enjoyed by the Windsurfer was soon broken down and new brands of sailboard started appearing faster than pop tunes. The sailboard market quickly became highly lucrative and competitive and, inevitably, speed was one of the most important selling points. The manufacturers looked at various ways of selling speed to the customers: the most popular being to maintain a 'team' of highly trained experts whose job it is to go out and win races, very much along the snow skiing lines. However, victory in a sailboard race can be attributed to many causes, speed being only one of them and a customer of even the meanest intelligence is usually able to understand that the skill of the sailor is just as important as the speed of the board.

It was Fred Ostermann, designer and proprietor of the Windglider range, who first saw the possibility of gaining favourable publicity by entering some of his boards in official speed trials such as the ones at Portland and Kiel. The first time that boards were entered for the Portland Speed Week, the organizing committee, of which the author was one, took a rather condescending attitude to them on the grounds that 'they obviously would not be capable of record speeds'. How wrong

*Derk Thijs astonished the world when he sailed at 19 knots on a Windglider. Notice that he did it without either harness or foot-straps because neither of these things had been developed* (Yachting World)

we were! Ostermann arranged for the outstanding Dutch sailor Derk Thijs to sail a special version of the Windglider board at the 1977 Portland Speed Week. This board was basically just a lightened version of the standard Windglider with a larger than normal rig. To everyone's enormous surprise, he recorded a best speed of 19·1 knots, a performance that was greeted with outright incredulity by a large proportion of the sailing world. It has to be remembered that this speed was only just slower than the best recorded by a standard Tornado catamaran which most sailors know to be a whole order faster than the entire range of fast planing dinghies. So, unless Thijs' performance could be written off as some kind of freak, it appears that sailboards had suddenly leap-frogged over virtually all small monohulls and landed in the middle of the faster cats and hydrofoils.

Those who expected, or even hoped, that this startling effort by Thijs would prove to have been either a mistake or an unrepeatable performance were soon to be disabused when other top board sailors started to make serious efforts to better his performance. Curiously, although Ostermann made the maximum publicity out of Thijs' record,

136

he made almost no serious effort to follow it up in subsequent years. He did not develop any specialized high speed sailboards which might have enabled his sailors to stay abreast of what soon turned into a hectic technical race. Instead, the torch soon passed to the Ten Cate company in Holland, the European licensees for the original Windsurfer.

Seeing the great publicity that Ostermann had received from the performance of the Windglider at Portland, Ten Cate acted in a methodical and entirely logical way. They found an enthusiast, Jaap Van der Rest, and offered to back him with the resources of the factory in return for all his activities being made under the Ten Cate banner. Van der Rest is an outstanding sailor and athlete but probably lacked the technical knowledge, to begin with anyway, to produce anything very startling. But Ten Cate had another priceless asset in the shape of Gary Seaman. Originally a Californian surf-board shaper, Seaman had been involved in the early stages of building the Windsurfer and had then been hired by Ten Cate as designer. Seaman is that rare blend of technician and craftsman that is so important when developing something new and untried. Over the next few years, this combination proved spectacularly successful and apart from one occasion when the Englishman Clive Colenso held the record for a brief period, they consistently led the way forward in sailboard speeds until 1982. In a way this is surprising because there has been such an explosion of talent and activity within the sailboard field that most records do not stand for long. However, not many teams have concentrated on pure speed to the extent to which Seaman and Van der Rest have.

The astonishing speed of 25·11 knots which Van der Rest achieved during 1981 was another leap-frog since it put him ahead of all the catamarans and hydrofoil boats and second only to the two *Crossbows*. During this year, many more people became interested in board sailing for speed and, in particular, the West German Jurgen Honscheid actually bettered Van der Rest's record speed for a short time though not by the 2 per cent required to set a new record.

When Thijs did 19·1 knots in 1977 it was on what would now be regarded as a thoroughly conventional 'flat-board', and the same applies to Clive Colenso and his 'Olympic Gold'. Even in special lightweight versions, these boards weighed more than 33lb (15kg) and followed the basic Windsurfer layout of a dagger-board amidships and a skeg aft. As anyone who has ever tried to sail a board of this rather basic type in a wind of Force 6 or more will testify, a fantastic amount of physical strength is required. To have reached such speeds with such primitive equipment seems heroic in retrospect.

*Faster! Faster!*

Seaman and Van der Rest quickly realized that the whole sailboard concept needed paring down in order to achieve significantly higher speeds. The first essential was to reduce the weight. This is fairly easily achieved both by making the whole thing smaller and by using relatively sophisticated materials such as Kevlar woven cloth, laminated with epoxy resin over a light foam former. This is the reverse of normal sailboard construction which uses a heavy, stiff foam inside a weak envelope of plastics or glass fibre; a system which has been developed for convenience of mass production rather than high strength-to-weight ratio. If a much stiffer shell is used, then the foam can be a much lighter

*The Dutch sailor Jaap Van der Rest has been the most consistently successful record-breaker on sailboards* (the author)

*Jaap Van der Rest* (the author)

type and serves mainly to establish the shape while the shell is being laminated. By this kind of technique, weights have come down steadily and it is now considered quite easy to build a strong speed board of less than 22lb (10kg). With the present state of knowledge, it becomes increasingly difficult to get the weight much below 17lb (8kg). Of course, this refers only to the weight of the hull; the rig typically weighs another 11–13lb (5–6kg).

It was quickly apparent that standard sailboards were much too big for serious speed sailing. Once planing, most of the length of the thing was not merely unnecessary, it was an embarrassment, waving around in the air. An excessive area of bottom made the board bounce over the waves and skitter around uncontrollably, quite apart from the added surface friction drag. Seaman and Van der Rest therefore set about making the board itself progressively smaller and slimmer. They proceeded cautiously along this line of development because each diminution of the board made it more difficult to sail. As most speed sailors have discovered, in order to make successful record attempts, it is essential to be able to make repeated runs in order to catch the best conditions.

Therefore, out-and-out speed has to be balanced to some extent by the necessity for a reasonably seamanlike craft that will not totally exhaust the jockey in the first few minutes of sailing. For this reason, the Van der Rest boards, up to 1981, were 'tuned' to support the total weight of sailor and board, with a little to spare – say 190lb (85kg) displacement. It was left to others such as Jürgen Honscheid and Andy Mason to make the final breakthrough to the 'sinker' type whose displacement is less than the weight of the sailor.

'How', I hear you cry, 'can anyone sail a boat whose displacement is less than the weight it has to carry?' Well, think about a water-ski: it has hardly any buoyancy yet it is possible to ride one with ease as soon as planing speed has been achieved. The trick is, of course, to develop the technique of getting from rest to planing speed. For the water-skier, with a 150hp motor up front, this is no very big deal. The normal technique is to lie on one's back in the water with the ski presented at an enormous angle of attack to the water and then hang on for grim death as the tow boat heaves you up onto the plane. For the board sailor, things are not so easy. On a windy day, there is plenty of power available from the rig but most of it is at right angles to the direction in which you want to travel.

There seem to be two possible techniques for a successful 'water start'. One is that the sailor has to wear some kind of personal buoyancy so that he can lie flat on his back in the water, with his feet already hooked into foot-straps on the board and the rig held up above his head. A water start of this type is a familiar freestyle trick with conventional boards, but to do it in extreme wind conditions with a very tiny, wobbly sailboard requires a great deal of technique. The more practiced water-starters don't even need the buoyancy: they have developed a trick of swimming out to windward and lifting the rig clear of the water with one hand, then as it starts to develop lift, of quickly slipping the back foot into its strap.

The second, or 'Portland' technique involves a kind of hop, skip and jump start from a shallow beach. Here, the sailor stands in water just deep enough to float the board and places his back foot in the strap. Then, suddenly applying power to the rig, he pushes off with his other foot and tries to get it into its strap in time to avoid being hurled violently over the bow. Both these techniques are only possible because at the vital moment a lot of the weight of the sailor is directly supported by the lift of the rig rather than the buoyancy of the board.

It is true to say that most serious speed board sailors are aiming to achieve something like a competition water-ski, a minimal planing surface, tapering to a 'pin-tail' at the stern. As in the water-ski, the idea behind the tapering stern is that as speed increases, the sailor can shift his weight further and further back onto an ever decreasing area of planing surface which continues to offer a degree of 'grip' on the water and to penetrate the small waves rather than bouncing violently over them. At speeds above 20 knots, smoothness of ride becomes increasingly important, not merely because it is very hard to stay in control if there is too much motion but also because bouncing will greatly increase the likelihood of skeg ventilation.

With these very fast sailboards, skeg design has become of paramount importance, a fact that took surprisingly long to get through to some of the sailors. Even now, so called speed boards are built with wobbly little plastic appendages under them which a moment's thought would show to be totally incapable of resisting very high values of side-force. Dagger-boards disappeared some time ago: they produced much too much capsizing moment and at high speeds produced an uncontrollable tendency for the board to luff up. The obvious solution was to place one or more skegs at the extreme aft end of the waterline. Viewed on a drawing, this suggests an absurdly large separation between the centre of effort of the sail and the CLR of the board. The extra factor which makes this odd looking layout correct is that at high speed the sailor is leaning back and to windward just as far as he possibly can, so bringing the CE of the sail above the skeg.

Even with this layout, there is a great danger of the skeg ventilating, resulting in a 'spin-out'. The skeg is being asked to resist a very considerable side-force and consequently working at a high lift coefficient. This results in rather low pressures being created on the windward side and if the board becomes airborne momentarily as it skips through the waves, air will tend to rush down this side of the skeg causing immediate and total loss of lift. This is exactly the same phenomenon that causes hydrofoil boats to 'crash' from time to time. In the case of the sailboard it manifests itself as a sudden and dramatic loss of 'grip' by the skeg so that the board spins round with inevitable loss of control.

Efforts to prevent skeg ventilation can include placing 'fences' on the skeg in the same way as they are used on hydrofoils or fixing some kind of end-plate at the top of the skeg. In a yacht, ventilation of the keel is prevented by the fact that the underside of the hull acts as a large end-plate so that it is very difficult for air to find its way down there. With a sailboard, and especially a pin-tail, it is difficult to arrange an effective end-plate but various little winglets or plates have been tried with varying degrees of success. Another approach is to place the skeg a bit further forward under the hull or to use a rounded 'cruiser' stern but both these alternatives tend to be unattractive for other reasons.

The hulls, if that is the correct term, of the 'Van der Rest type' high speed sailboards tend to resemble little canoes: moderately vee-bottomed for wave penetration, pointed at both ends and with some rocker or lift in the bow. The more recent 'sinkers' tend to be rather more flat-bottomed and Jurgen Honscheid's first sinker was in a fact a small stock surfboard – not a sailboard as such. Sailboarders attach great importance to the form of the 'rails' which an earlier generation of designers would call the chine. The board is normally sailed heeled to windward to some degree so it is important to have rails that áre sufficiently angular to achieve a clean breakaway of the water flow and yet not to dig in so much that they steer the craft in an undesirable direction. Since there is so little of the whole craft in the water at high speeds, the precise form and angle of the rail can be quite important in deciding whether the board will handle well.

So far we have not looked at the rig of the fast sailboard, and for a long time it looked as if the sailors hadn't either. Most advanced board sailors are utterly scathing about the rig of the original Windsurfer yet the improvements that have been made to achieve faster speeds are purely ones of materials and detail. Maka's 27 knot sailboard rig appears at first glance to be hardly different from that of the standard Windsurfer.

Clive Colenso did try to sail with a wing sail in 1977. As expected, the problems were practical ones and even the powerful Colenso exhausted himself just trying to get going with this large and inevitably heavy structure waving around in the air. It is undoubtedly this question of practicality which deters sailors from making great departures from the familiar sailboard rig.

An all-round improvement of stiffness can result in a fairly remarkable improvement of lift/drag ratio. Epoxy-Kevlar or even epoxy-carbon-fibre laminates are used to achieve stiffer masts, though the latter is an expensive option because of its tendency to snap rather than bend under excessive pressure. Aluminium masts are also becoming more common and although rather heavy can be made to any stiffness required. The object of having a stiff mast is to be able to use a sail with stiff cloth. The soft sails used in production sailboards tend to go baggy in strong winds, which is of course a killer if high speed is your aim. The material to make stiff sails has existed for sometime but it is useless if set on bendy spars. However, stiff enough masts are now available to make the use of CYT or film-laminated cloths practical.

The actual shape of the sails is, as usual, the subject of constant debate and not a little fashion. The most important thing from the point of view of the hopeful record breaker seems to be to have a selection of sails available of carefully graded area. For instance, in the classic 'Speed Week' of 1981 when the wind blew in excess of Force 8, everyone was desperately scouring the countryside for a sail small enough to enable them to sail without being instantly blasted into small pieces. On the other hand, later the same year, Van der Rest managed a new World Record partly because he was able to whip out a slightly bigger sail just at the correct moment. Attempts have been made to produce sails of higher aspect–ratio: the so-called 'fat heads' have two or three full length battens in the head to give more area high up. These sails only seem useful for a limited range of wind speeds and so far, records have mostly been achieved with rather small sails of reduced luff length. In theory at least, it would seem to be worth trying to keep to a full length luff and to shorten the boom correspondingly.

A major breakthrough in sailboard rigs occurred in 1983 when the American sailor Fred Haywood introduced a semi-wing rig, somewhat similar in general concept to the one that Austin Farrar had designed many years previously for the 'C' Class cat *Lady Helmsman*. Haywood's rig was designed and built by Dimitri Milovich, a Dutch-born American from Salt Lake City whose background was in land-yachting. He constructed a carbon-fibre wing 15ft 8in (4.8m) high with an average chord of 7in (17cm) on to which sails of various areas could be set using a conventional luff groove. The angle between the 'hard' and 'soft' parts of the sail can be accurately controlled by small control lines between the mast and the wishbone booms (rather like the 'spanner' on a cat rig). A further advantage is that because the usual sleeve luff of the sailboard sail is eliminated, it is possible to attach a trapeze line at about three quarter height which removes much of the bending stress from the mast and makes it possible to consider a reefable sail.

Milovich's mast was complemented by some nice, stiff sails by Barry Spanier made up in laminated Mylar material. Such stiff material cannot easily be used on a conventional sailboard mast which bends a lot but the wing mast on the other hand does not bend at all in the fore-and-aft direction. The mast/sail combination was claimed by its makers to be twenty per cent 'more powerful' (a somewhat imprecise expression). Whether or not this is true, it certainly did seem a considerable improvement over 'soft' sailboard rigs and enabled Fred Haywood to add a full three knots to the existing record.

The new record was achieved on the inshore course at Portland in gale-force winds. On the day in question, a number of different board sailors bettered 25 knots but Haywood had a clear advantage and became the first board sailor ever to exceed 30 knots. Interestingly, as

143

well as being faster, he also appeared to be steadier under these very difficult conditions.

After such a sharp upwards jump in the record for sailboards, it is difficult to believe that Haywood's speed can remain unbeaten for very long. The 1983 sponsors of Speed Week, Johnnie Walker, have offered a prize of £10,000 for the first boardsailor to reach 60 kph (32·4 knots) and I shall be surprised if this remains unclaimed by the end of 1984.

Just why sailboards are so fast remains a bit of a mystery to many people, and it is worth drawing attention to the special qualities of a rig which is capable of being set at any desired angle. The most obvious result of this is that the sail can be heeled to windward whenever there is sufficient wind. This means that the rig develops not merely thrust but also lift and this lift is usefully employed in partly supporting the weight of the sailor. The harder the wind blows, the more the helmsman 'hangs' on his rig and the lighter the whole contraption becomes. As it gets lighter, it can operate on a smaller planing area and reduce wetted surface to the the absolute minimum. As well as heeling to windward, the rig is also raked aft in strong winds. The result of this is to eliminate the forward pitchpoling or bow burying tendency that virtually all sailing boats experience when sailing downwind.

All sailing boats are 'interface vehicles' which in plain English means that they exist at the margin between air and water and exploit the difference in density and kinetic energy between the two media. Compared to other sailing boats, it is easy to see that the sailboard is more of an air vehicle than a water vehicle and often comes perilously close to turning into a full time sailplane. If this is the correct way forward to higher speeds, then perhaps we should be looking even more towards aeronautics – of this more later!

# 9
# Speed trials

Talking about fast sailing is all very fine but it does not mean a great deal unless speeds are actually measured. In this chapter we will therefore look at the various efforts to do so, leading up to the present World Sailing Speed Record system.

As we saw in the chapter on the clippers, the speed of sailing ships was only measured completely reliably in terms of the time taken to sail a particular passage. Some noon-to-noon runs can be accepted with a certain amount of reservation. Instantaneous measurement of speed was no good at all. With modern offshore yachts, the situation is better because position fixing is so much more reliable, using electronic aids such as SATNAV, Loran and Decca. Speed and distance logs have improved out of all recognition too but it is still nearly impossible to verify *top* speeds offshore. Skippers of the big yachts competing in events such as the Round the World race come back with stories of 'surfing continuously at over 20 knots' but how can such a performance be proved? Day's runs of the same yacht will show an average of perhaps half the speed mentioned. Why the big difference? For one thing, every dizzy, headlong rush down a big wave ends eventually with the boat stuck in the trough of the next wave, her bow pointing skyward and speedometer recording a miserable 6 knots. The law of average is a hard taskmaster! For another thing, it is hard to be sure about speedometer readings when a yacht is experiencing surfing conditions. In really big waves the water itself is moving in an orbital pattern and may be causing a false reading.

It soon becomes clear that the only truly reliable way of measuring a yacht's speed is by timing it over a measured distance. For offshore events this is obviously impractical but for small boats it is a different story. With a powered craft, speed measurement is no problem. You simply take the boat to one of the measured ranges, usually 1 nautical mile, which exist around the coasts of virtually every maritime nation, punch the stopwatch and off you go. Runs in each direction will cancel out any tidal effect so it only remains to average the result and 'Bob's your uncle'. Why not do the same thing with a sailing boat? Firstly because measured miles never seem to be in a convenient place where there will be a strong, unobstructed wind from a suitable direction and where observers can be positioned. Also, a nautical mile is quite a long distance for a small sailing craft and it is rare to get a steady sustained gust of wind for long enough to cover this distance. So for a practical measurement of the speed of small boats, it is clear that some kind of specially set up measured distance is needed, preferably of a distance less than 1 nautical mile.

We have heard how Uffa Fox struggled for weeks to get a decent measurement of the speed of his 10 sq metre canoe over a $\frac{1}{2}$ nautical mile up the River Medina. The first measured speed trials for sailing boats that I know about were organized at nearby Stokes Bay during Cowes Week 1954, the late 'Tiny' Mitchell having offered a prize of £50 for the fastest boat. The existing measured mile at Stokes Bay was used, with trials being held on one day only, in a near gale-force south-westerly. Beecher Moore, who sailed the Hornet, recalls that the set-up was far from ideal. They had to sail each way over the measured mile and it turned out that this meant one leg was a broad reach and the other a close fetch. It was very rough and the transits were too far away to be seen properly so they never really knew when they had started or finished. Under these circumstances, the best speed for the average of the two runs, 10·2 knots by the Jollyboat sailed by Peter Scott, was really very creditable. Even today, many straightforward dinghies have failed to do better, sailing one way over the shorter course at Portland.

Be that as it may, a speed of ten knots did not sound all that impressive, and the people concerned felt they ought to be able to do better. Being able to run on the boat's best point of sailing was obviously crucial so the fixed transits in Stokes Bay were abandoned for the following year. Instead, boats were allowed to sail on any heading they wished and speed was measured by the radar of an anchored warship. For the competitors, the set-up was even harder to cope with than the previous year. The distance to be sailed was indicated, approximately, by free-floating marks which were expected to drift down-tide at the same speed. Great emphasis was laid on the accuracy of the Navy's radar but with the benefit of nearly thirty years hindsight, one is bound to take a sceptical view of this. It is very hard to believe that the tracking of a slow-moving target moving obliquely across the radar's field could have been precise,

146

and the lack of a fixed measured distance would in any case rule it out as a serious measurement of speed. No-one disputes that the fastest boat was the 18ft (5·4m) catamaran *Endeavour* sailed by Ken Pearce but the speed of 14·6 knots cannot be regarded as irrefutable.

The experience of these two time trials seems to have left the people concerned with the feeling that it was all a bit impractical. The event was allowed to lapse and no one seems to have made any serious efforts at measurement for the next fifteen years. It was emergence of the hydrofoil and the influence of the Amateur Yacht Research Society that finally got things moving again in 1969. The AYRS formed a 'hydrofoil group' of which perhaps the most active member was James Grogono, and they decided that it would help to encourage the *genre* if a regatta could be held in the form of a time trial. James wrote an article for *Yachting World* and ended up by persuading it to 'sponsor' the weekend.

While the AYRS/*Yachting World* speed trial was still in the early stages of discussion, a conversation that had important results took place between the editor of *Yachting World* Bernard Hayman and Peter Scott when they met for lunch at the IYRU Conference that year. Bernard was a rather forthright opponent of sponsorship in yachting but mentioned a possible 'Speed Sailing' competition as an example of something that would benefit from creative sponsorship. Recalling the rather disorganized 1954/5 trials, Scott was enthusiastic and suggested that they should try to take the matter further.

The first step was for *Yachting World* to organize a 'Forum' discussion on the subject. The guests were Peter Scott, James Grogono, Bob Bond, John Fisk and Beecher Moore, and the resulting article was published in April 1970. This ranged over the whole subject of speed sailing but there was fairly general agreement that it would be worthwhile to set up a new time trial competition, especially if fairly substantial sponsorship could be found. As well as enabling a proper course to be set up, this would make it possible to offer sizeable cash prizes, which it was hoped would encourage people to build new and exciting boats. Bernard Hayman put forward the important idea that there should be internationally agreed technical requirements so that yachtsmen in any part of the world could set up a time trials in such a way that the results would be accepted everywhere.

This was really the first germ of the ideas that led to the establishment of the World Sailing Speed Record. The need for this approach was shown by the fact that some fairly wild claims for speeds were beginning to be made. The *Guinness Book of Records*, which many people accept as authoritative, had already published the claim that *Lady Helmsman* had reached 30 knots, a claim which John Fisk dismissed as a 'fib' at the YW Forum. Meanwhile Steve Dashew, owner of the World's only 'D' Class catamaran *Wildwind*, had gone one better with a claim of 32 knots. Owners of Tornado catamarans were claiming that they frequently sailed at over 20 knots and so on.

The first step in the right direction was the already mentioned time trials at Burnham-on-Crouch. *Yachting World*'s sponsorship consisted of finding, and paying for, a system of measurement. This part was my job and turned out to be easier said than done. In answer to my query, most people replied that 'any surveyor' would be able to set up a measured distance using a baseline and theodolite angles but when actual surveyors were consulted and discovered that the baseline would have to be over muddy saltings at the entrance to the River Roach, they became less than enthusiastic. Measurement using either vertical sextant angle or theodolite and subtense bar were not considered to be sufficiently accurate over the distance of ½ mile that we had in mind. Luckily, my enquiries led me to Hunting Surveys who suggested using a 'Hydradistance' instrument made by the Tellurometer Company. This modern form of surveying instrument is an electro-distance measuring system

*An early version of the Tellurometer distance measuring instrument in use at Burnham. This surveying instrument finally cracked the problem of accurate distance measurement over water* (Yachting World)

and is well known to the World's map-makers. It consists of a pair of special radio transmitter-receivers with small dish aerials mounted in front of them. The two sets are mounted on tripods facing each other and transmit a signal to each other on a series of frequencies whose wavelength is very accurately known. The instrument counts the number of waves between the two sets and the surveyor 'narrows down' the distance by switching through a series of shorter and shorter wave-lengths, the final one being to the nearest centimetre! In addition, the signal carries a speech channel which makes life much easier for the two operators. No one could possibly quibble with the accuracy provided by this system which is the one subsequently used to check the course at Portland.

Proving that the system was feasible was just about the only worthwhile achievement of the first AYRS/*Yachting World* meeting held at Burnham-on-Crouch on 30/31 May 1970. There was barely sufficient wind for *Icarus* to get up onto her foils and certainly no memorable speeds. The exercise was therefore repeated in October but without the expense of the Tellurometer. Instead, we tried a new gadget called a 'Whistler' hand-held radar and an old-fashioned optical rangefinder. The Whistler proved quite useless and the optical rangefinder surprisingly good though of unconfirmed accuracy. We also came reluctantly to the conclusion that Burnham was a fairly hopeless place to run time-trials because of the strong tides and limited length and angles of course available. Both *Icarus* and *Mayfly* sailed and foiled but a standard Tornado proved to be faster! Although nothing very remarkable happened at these two weekends, the reports on them, plus the 'Forum', had the desired effect of stimulating interest and discussion.

It was a further year, however, before things finally began to 'gel' when cigarette-makers John Player and Sons approached the Royal Yachting Association in the hope of finding some major new yachting event to sponsor. The RYA pointed them in the direction of Bernard Hayman who was ready with proposals for a fully-fledged World Sailing Speed Record competition. In true British fashion a committee was formed under the chairmanship of Peter Scott and the new competition was announced at the 1972 Boat Show. It had three distinct elements:

1 a set of rules to enable a record speed to be established under agreed conditions anywhere in the World,

2 a trophy plus an annual prize of £2,000 for the fastest helmsman in the World, and

3 a 'Speed Week' regatta to be organized annually in Britain, also with substantial prizes.

*The author and Bernard Hayman attempting to measure distance accurately on the River Crouch in 1970. Neither method was in the least satisfactory!* (Yachting World)

Speed Week we will come to presently, but first we continue the story of the World Record. The Committee, which was established under the aegis of the RYA, drew up rules which have not been substantially altered since and which are printed in an appendix. The record was 'offered' to the International Yacht Racing Union with the idea of making it really international and they promptly handed it back to the RYA which was henceforth to be regarded as the regulating authority for the World Sailing Speed Record. It was remarked by the IYRU at the time that a time trial was 'not yacht racing in the accepted sense' and therefore did not need to comply with the requirements of the Yacht Racing Rules. The basic correctness of the concept is shown by the fact that every serious speed trials since then has been run under the RYA rules. Trials have been held at various times in Holland, Sweden, Germany, France, USA (including Hawaii), Canada, New Zealand and Australia, resulting in new World Records being set up on three occasions.

The basic parameters of the World Record are that the speed has to be established in a single run over a minimum of 500 metres distance, accurately measured between fixed points. Standards are laid down both for the measurement of the distance and the timing, and various affidavits are called for by any record claimant. In particular the trials have to be witnessed and carefully monitored by an observer approved by the RYA. The committee has done its best to become international over the years by appointing new members from countries where interest exists. They have also maintained the status of the World Record by turning down claims on two occasions: in 1975 it refused to approve the arrangements for trials organized by the Pacific Multihull Association because the method of distance measurement, by vertical sextant observation of a yacht's mast, was not considered accurate, and at the same time rejected Steve Dashew's claim for an Outright World Record with his 'D' Class cat *Beowulf V* because proper details were not forthcoming.

The World Sailing Speed Record Trophy has been held by the same man – Tim Colman – since 1972 and it was partly because of this rather over-stable situation that the committee decided in 1974 to establish class records. Some members of the committee opposed this on the grounds that a World Record should be for the fastest speed and nothing else. It was pointed out in reply that most World Records are in fact divided into classes; generally according to the size of the motor. Since a yacht's motor is its sail, it made sense to set up a series of sail area divisions. On a pratical level, it was clear that if this were not done the competition would be in danger of dying out because no craft was in the same league as the existing record holder. It was therefore decided to establish, in addition to the 'Unlimited' World Record, classes for the three IYRU catamaran sail area divisions 'A', 'B' and 'C' plus 10 sq metres because this had just been established as a new IYRU development class. The wisdom of this move is shown by the fact that in recent years the 'action' has been concentrated at the smaller end of the scale with the 10 sq metre Class proving much the most eventful because it contains all the sailboards.

The John Player sponsorship lasted until 1977 when interest in the competition seemed to be waning. Tim Colman had tightened his grip on the outright record by building the second *Crossbow* and the real explosion of growth in the sailboards had not yet begun. Players had sponsored both the World Record trophy and prize and the Speed Week event at Portland. After their departure, Tim Colman presented a perpetual trophy for the holder of the outright World record (and kept it!) so that this most important trophy is no longer linked to a sponsor's name. Smirnoff, the vodka people, sponsored Speed Week for one week only in 1978 after which the event seemed to go into something of a decline, mainly due to lack of money. After a gap of one year when the event ran without a sponsor, the Windsurfer makers Ten Cate came in for two years, after which it was again left without cash in 1982 before Johnnie Walker whisky came to the rescue in 1983.

Smirnoff, who sponsored for one year only at Portland, ran a speed event for several years at Kiel in Germany. This was mainly for sailboards and the speed was measured by a radar 'gun' of the type used by police for checking the speed of vehicles. It is a fairly inaccurate gadget and only gives speed instantaneously rather than for a given distance. For this reason, no record speeds were ever claimed for the Smirnoff Cup and the event now seems to have died out.

Another speed trial that was unfortunately still-born was that organized by the Pacific Multihull Association at San Diego. One of the reasons for the creation of the Record Rules was that the American Steve Dashew claimed to have sailed at 32 knots in his 'D' Class catamaran *Wildwind*, although it was never made clear who had measured this speed or how. Then in 1974, Dashew wrote to the World Sailing Speed Record Committee claiming an official record of 30·9 knots in his new 'D' Class *Beowulf V*. This would have been the outright World Record, if ratified. The Committee then wrote asking for technical details, which were not forthcoming. Subsequently the PMA itself wrote to the Committee with details of its annual speed event, including the fact that the length of the course was measured by taking a vertical sextant angle of the mast of a yacht. The Committee wrote back to the PMA to say that they did not regard this as a sufficiently accurate measurement and would not be able to ratify any claims for records on such a course. It was never clear whether this was in fact the system used when *Beowulf* did her alleged 30·9 knots because a number of letters to him met with no response and so the whole matter just quietly fizzled out.

It is curious that by 1982 when the RYA Speed Week at Portland had reached its lowest ebb, interest in other countries had finally built up to a really worthwhile level. The Dutch speed trials at Veerse Meer in Holland were in their fourth year and the French trials at Brest had begun with great razzmatazz in 1981. Properly run Speed Weeks were also being held at Karlskrona in Sweden and in New Zealand. In spite of this, it appeared that there was no better site available than Portland Harbour as by the end of 1982 all five World records were held there once more. The standing of the Portland Week was reinforced by the 1983 event where three new World Records were claimed and the Johnnie Walker sponsorship permitted some much-needed improvements in facilities.

# *Measurement*

In 1972, when it was decided to hold a special Speed Week for the first time, the hunt was on for the perfect venue. The requirements were for strong winds and smooth water which initially suggested something like a canal. However this would suffer from the enormous drawback of being suitable for only one wind direction. Thoughts then turned to various circular lakes or reservoirs such as the Oxford Sailing Club's water at Farmoor. Some genius then suggested Portland Harbour. The special feature of Portland is that it is a large area of sheltered water separated from the sea on its windward side by the Chesil Bank causeway. The prevailing south-westerlies sweep in unobstructed over the shingle bank which has been moulded into a smooth, aerodynamic sort of shape by the wind. Portland is a naval harbour but, having been built in the 19th century to accommodate the Grand Fleet, can nowadays accommodate most of the Royal Navy in one small corner. The Queen's Harbourmaster gave permission for the laying of a course in the north-western corner of the harbour, furthest away from the navy base. This part of the harbour was also supposed to have been the site of the RYA's Olympic Yachting Centre, which if built, would have provided an ideal home for the speed event. However, it never has been and the burden of playing 'host' to the RYA Speed Week has always fallen on Castle Cove Sailing Club whose small clubhouse overlooks the harbour from the high ground on the north shore.

The tricky requirement was to create an accurately measured distance which could in some way be turned so that it could be used in various

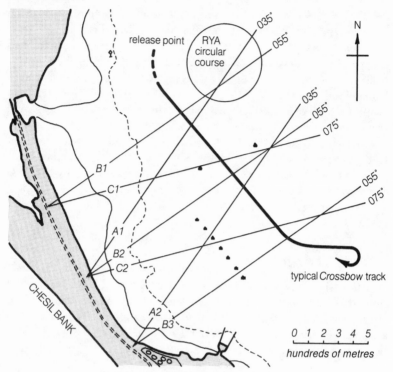

## *Course layout used for* Crossbow II's *record runs*

*The Western shore of Portland Harbour showing the course layout used by* Crossbow II *to establish her World record speed of 36 knots. The course could be swung 25° either way in order to accommodate variations in wind direction and when using the 'B' transits,* Crossbow *could establish two timings on one run. A simplified version of this course, without the third timing post, is used by the RYA for its standard inshore course*

wind directions. Bernard Hayman began doodling with the idea of a circular course but it was his son Alan who came up with the now familiar 'clock face' layout of twelve buoys lying on the circumference of a circle of 250 metres radius. The appeal of this was that any adjacent pair of buoys form a 'gate' and together with the corresponding pair on the opposite side of the circle, a 'lane' of 500m length. This was the theory and it was turned into reality mainly by the ingenuity of a team of divers from Ferrybridge Marine Ltd. The technique used was first to lay a central mooring and to attach one end of a 250m wire to it. Using this as the radius, a 250m circle could be described on the bottom of the harbour, a second wire of 131m length being used to dictate the dropping points for the moorings of the 'clock face' buoys. The twelve sinkers (plus one in the centre) laid in this way are permanent and remain in place from year to year. Any time they are required, the divers go down and attach rope risers with buoys on their upper end. The upper 20ft (6m) of riser consists of elastic cord to accommodate the rise and fall of the tide. The circle was in actual fact made slightly larger than 250m radius so that there would be no danger of the lanes being slightly short as a result of some minor inaccuracy. The precise length of each lane is

*The original circular course layout used in Portland Harbour. Its value lay in the fact that it could be used in any wind direction by choosing the appropriate channel. However, over the years it was found that record speeds were only achieved in winds between south-west and north-west and that most competitors preferred the smoother water available on the inshore course*

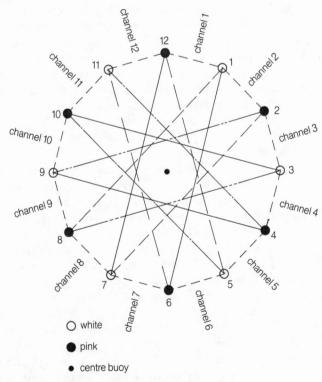

RYA 500m course in Portland Harbour

checked annually using the highly accurate Tellurometer system already described.

Boats wishing to make a run over the Portland course first decide which lane best suits them and although in the early years there was some disagreement about this, most helmsmen are prepared to settle for the same lane as one can fine tune the angle of heading by sailing through a lane diagonally without adding much to the distance sailed. In a moderate wind, the nearest lane to a square reach is normally favoured but in heavy conditions it is usually possible to go for a broader reach. As the run only has to be one way there is no need to keep changing the lane in order to offer return runs. A number of boats, like *Crossbow*, are designed for running on one tack only but fortunately most designers have favoured the starboard tack! Really fast boats actually need to sail a curved course, pointing up as they accelerate and then steadily bearing off during the run as speed continues to increase.

In order to time boats over the course, start and finish boats were placed on either side of the circle, sighting across the adjacent pairs of buoys that form the 'gates' to the lane. They were in radio communication and pairs of stopwatches in either boat were punched as the bow of the competing boat passed through the gate. Written records were maintained on both timing boats and although this proved to be an accurate and very reliable system its great drawback was that only one competitor could be handled at a time. In the early years, 60 seconds, which corresponds to 16·2 knots, was a good time for crossing the circle and two minutes distressingly common. As a result, long queues of boats would form when the wind was good, to the frustration of all concerned.

The obvious solution was to devise a method of timing which would permit more than one boat to be on the course at any one time. Although it took several years, this is in fact quite easily achieved. It is necessary only to use watches which are synchronized and running constantly instead of starting and stopping them for each run. As each competitor passes the start gate, the watch's 'split' button is punched and the time of day written down together with the boat's name. The same thing happens at the finish gate and subsequently, time-of-day 'B' is subtracted from time-of-day 'A' to give the time taken for that particular run. Using this method it is easily possible for boats to follow each other at 10 second intervals and be timed with perfect accuracy, although it does require a great deal of concentration from the timing crews. This basic method can be made more sophisticated by using modern sports timing equipment. For instance, it is not actually necessary for the timing equipment to be near the start or finish of the course. Provided callers with radio are accurately sighting the starts and finishes, the actual timing gear can be kept warm and dry in a caravan on the shore. The Omega equipment currently used at Portland prints on paper the identity number of the competitor, the starting time and the elapsed time of the run. The only thing that can wreck the system is if boats start but don't finish or worse, finish without starting! Even this can be coped with by 'aborting' the run provided it is spotted by the observers.

The basic 'Portland' system is also used at Brest except that they have a direct telemetry link from the mark boats to a computer ashore which calculates, stores and finally prints out the results. It is also adapted without any difficulty to other types of course. A quite different timing system is used at the Pall Mall Speed Trials at Veerse Meer. Here, fixed transits are set up on the shore and TV cameras aligned to look exactly along them. A third camera is permanently looking at a super-accurate digital clock. The signals from the three cameras go to a mixer and then onto video tape. The resulting recording shows a split screen with a picture of the starting posts on the left and finishing posts on the right plus the clock face in the corner. The clever part is that is that it does not matter if the video machine runs fast or slow because the correct time is always recorded together with the picture. This method is actually more accurate than the Portland one because it cuts out operator error; people who have to shout 'now!' or push a button. Furthermore, if there is any doubt or dispute, the recording can be re-run and scrutinized as often as necessary. This very clever system was studied and designed by Wim Thijs, the engineer elder brother of Derk Thijs who set the first sailboard record at Portland. The only difficulty that has arisen with it is that because the cameras have a narrow, fixed viewing angle it can be difficult to identify something that flashed across the field of view, especially a sailboard that looks exactly the same as hundreds of other sailboards. To get over this, they had to use a voice channel on the recording tape and put a spotter with a radio on the course to describe exactly which craft was crossing the line.

The big problem at Veerse Meere is that the course is essentially a fixed one. They did have another set of transits but it took quite a time to move the cameras and get everything set up correctly again. In 1983 therefore, the Pall Mall event was moved to a new site with multiple courses but there was no wind on its inaugural week. A type of course which gets over this difficulty of fixed courses was first tried at the Schweitzer Speed trials at Maalea Bay, Maui in 1980. An accurate 500m baseline was set up and concrete markers set at either end. Using poles mounted on the concrete markers as 'backsights', 'foresight' poles could

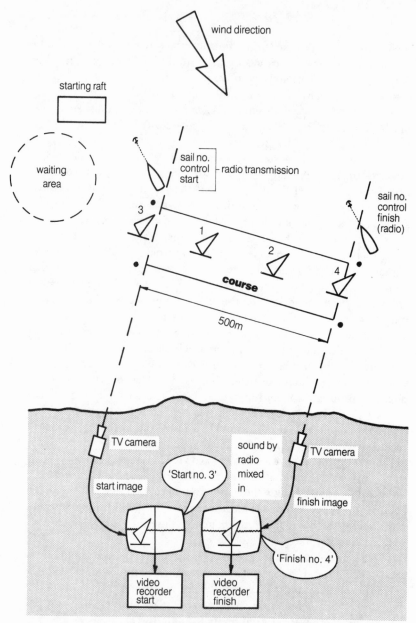

*As an improvement on purely manual timing, this ingenious set-up of TV cameras and video recorders was devised by Wim Thijs for the Pal Mall trials in Holland. Precisely aligned cameras take the place of transit posts and the system has the big advantage that everything is recorded and can be re-checked at any time*

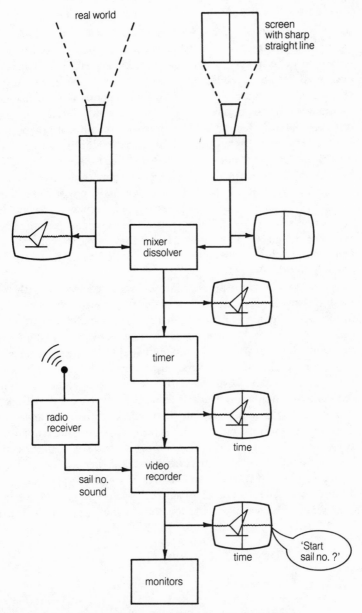

*Showing in more detail how each channel of the Dutch TV timing system works. The final TV image shows the competitor crossing an 'imaginary' line on the screen which also displays a digital timer. A voice channel carries the radio signal from the control boat which announces the identity of each starter/finisher*

be set up at any desired angle to suit the wind direction. Normal surveying instruments are used to check that the two transit lines are parallel. By this method, a fixed base-line could be used to create courses over an arc of about 30 degrees. Maalea Bay was chosen because it is a weather shore where a very strong wind pours down between two mountains onto the beach. Like all offshore winds, it tends to be gusty, but Jaap Van der Rest set a new sailboard World Record there in 1980.

In the same year, Tim Colman took the same idea further when setting up a private course at Portland. He set up three markers to form a double baseline of 1000m. As well as being 'swingable' like the Maalea Bay course, this had the value that *Crossbow* actually crossed two complete courses while sailing 1000m. As often happens, the wind may be slightly better towards the beginning or end of a run in which case the better of the two timings could be chosen. Using this course in November 1980, *Crossbow II* achieved the fabulous speed of 36 knots which remains the outright World Record today.

From 1977 onwards an alternative inshore course along the Chesil Bank had been provided as part of the RYA Speed Week, in the first instance for the benefit of the sailboards. It gradually became apparent that most of the other boats also went faster on this inshore course, especially the hydrofoils which do not like the choppy conditions which are found on the circular course in strong winds. After Tim Colman made it clear that even *Crossbow* preferred this course, the arguments for retaining the circular one were weakened. The *apparent* drawback to the inshore course is that it can only be used over a narrow range of wind directions but it turns out that this is the only really good wind direction anyway. Craft which need to sail a bit higher or lower than the course in use are forced to sail slightly further, but this is no different from the round course. A much more serious drawback, especially for the hydrofoils, is lack of depth. Boats such as *Icarus* run on the inshore course in mortal fear of hitting the bottom and ripping their expensive foils off.

# 10
# The Portland Speed Weeks

Because one team has held the World Sailing Speed Record since its inception in 1972, the 'Crossbow Story' forms a separate chapter and some of the exploits of *Icarus* and *Mayfly* are covered in the chapter on hydrofoil record-breakers. However, particularly in its early years, the Portland event was responsible for encouraging a rich variety of experimental craft. It turned out to be just the catalyst required to cause people who had some bright idea in the back of their mind to actually roll up their sleeves and build it. Most yachting events don't in fact encourage radical experiment since virtually every race or competition has some form of limiting parameters or rules. The WSSR competition, on the other hand, has the absolute minimum of rules except for sail area limits. For the first two years, the sponsor even paid 'appearance money' to help cover competitor's expenses.

There were, of course, some wildly eccentric craft and for this reason some people chose to regard the whole event as a bit of a joke. But in the words of the song 'They laughed at Orville and Wilbur . . . but who's got the last laugh now?' For those who had eyes to see, even the oddest of craft, and some were decidedly odd, contained the germ of an idea which would eventually prove useful. Speed Week soon developed a special atmosphere somewhat akin to some of the early aviation meetings. Many of the boats had a lot in common with early aircraft, being things of sticks, string and canvas. One went there with the pleasurable anticipation of being surprised by something completely unexpected and a stroll around the beach at Castle Cove could be quite a mind-bending experience. After about five years, it became clearer what type of craft was liable to be successful and therefore most of the really far-out boats faded away. Although speeds continued to be improved upon, Speed Week thereafter lost much of its appeal as an 'ugly bugs ball' to the regret of many of the original competitors. Lest we forget some of the fascinating boats and people who competed in Speed Week over the years it is therefore worth briefly reviewing it year by year.

# *1972*

In this pioneer year, no one knew what to expect but they very soon found out that Timothy Colman's Macalpine-Downie designed long, light proa was the most effective boat present by a large margin. Second fastest boat was the hydrofoil-equipped Tornado *Icarus* which just managed to stay within 5 knots of *Crossbow*'s speed of 26·3 knots, and *Icarus*'s 'baby sister' *Mayfly* was the fastest and most impressive of the smaller boats. The other boats of interest were:

*Tango Papa* (19·6 knots), a standard Tornado catamaran to which Terry Pearce and Ian Fraser had added a 15ft (4·5m) weighted spar sticking out over the weather quarter in an effort to reduce the bow-burying tendency. This made little difference but *Tango Papa*'s performance provided a very useful benchmark, proving at the same time that the Tornado is far faster than any conventional dinghy but that claims that it could sail at 25 knots were wildly optimistic.

*Trifle* (16·7 knots), Major-General Ralph Farrant's 42ft (12·8m) Kelsall-designed offshore trimaran showed that it is difficult to get an offshore boat 'wound up' in the confines of Portland Harbour. Having a much lower sail area/displacement ratio than a boat such as *Crossbow*, she would have needed a gale-force wind to achieve her maximum speed.

*Foiler III* (13·6 knots): Gerald Holtom spent a number of years developing foils as stabilizers rather than trying to make them lift the boat out of the water. The idea is that relatively small stabilizing foils make it possible to use a slim, easily-driven main hull. His boat was quite fast and easily handled but ill-health prevented him from completing the 52ft (15·8m) offshore version of which it was the prototype. It was left to Eric Tabarly to make use of the idea with his *Paul Ricard*.

*Kotaha* (13·6 knots), designed and built by the Danish naval architect Leif Wagner-Smitt, was an extremely interesting reversible hydrofoil proa with 10 sq metre rig. Beautifully constructed and finished, it showed considerable promise and it was disappointing that Wagner-Smitt never bothered to follow it up after this first year.

*Miss Strand Glass* (6·3 knots): hydrofoil pioneer Christopher Hook designed this ambitious boat which featured a fully-immersed lifting hydrofoil system with automatic incidence control plus manual over-ride. Unfortunately he could not control the weight of all the ironmongery: at 800lbs (362·9kg) all up, the boat was too heavy to lift.

*Leif Wagner-Smitt with the elegant and efficient* Kotaha *with which he competed in the first RYA Speed Week* (Yachting World)

# *1973*

*Crossbow* raised her speed a further 3 knots and was now more or less out of reach of the rest of the fleet. *Icarus* was again second but failed to improve her speed. By far the most interesting boat was:

*Clifton Flasher* (16·2 knots): a 12-man Bristol syndicate headed by TV designer Chris Robilliard and boatbuilder Nigel Irens constructed this radical 27ft (8·2m) proa with a five-element wing sail rig. The sesqui-plane layout of the rig made it possible to keep the individual wings down to a weight of 24lbs (10·7kg) each. They were built of doped fabric over polystyrene frames to a Wortmann glider section of 12 per cent thickness/chord ratio and they revolved as a set round a single pivot rather than individually. Like *Crossbow*, *Clifton Flasher* was a one-way boat and her rig folded down to enable her to be towed home after a run. On her first appearance she demonstrated great but unpredictable power.

*Digereedo* (15·3 knots): this attractive boat resulted from a collaboration between Peter Shaw who had been half of the *Thunder* 'C' Class cat project and Rodney Garrett who had built a clever little hydrofoil boat called *Mosquito*. The unique feature of *Digereedo* was that her main lift foil was made to fold flat and pass through a trunking in the hull thus making her more practical than most hydrofoils. Both the main and the steering foils could be adjusted for angle of attack while sailing, with a particularly neat linkage for the rudder foil which could be adjusted by twisting the tiller extension. There were inevitable teething problems and for unknown reasons Garrett and Shaw did not continue development of the boat after 1974.

*Miss Strand Glass II.* This was a completely new boat by the pupils of Forde Park School with an even more mind-bogglingly complicated control system. This time they managed to keep the weight down to 500lbs (223kg) but this was still far too heavy for successful foiling.

*Shooting Star* (9·1 knots) was the first of a series of boats designed by the Weymouth engineer Reg Bratt to embody his twist-free 'high-boom rig'.

*Flip-Flap* was an attempt by T. Edmunds to produce a pure 'space-frame' boat with no hull at all. Like others before and since he found that this was impractical because it was difficult to get up enough speed to make the hydrofoils work. That is why most successful

Miss Strand Glass *attempted to solve the tricky problems of automatic foil incidence control but was a victim of severe overweight* (Yachting World)

hydrofoils have been built around boats such as the Tornado which are fast and seaworthy in their own right.

# *1974*

This was a year without *Crossbow* and in her absence, the star of the show was another Macalpine-Downie design:

*British Oxygen* (24·26 knots), rather sportingly entered by Robin Knox-Johnston who realized well enough the difficulties he would face trying to wind up this 70ft (21·3m), 13 ton offshore catamaran within the confines of Portland Harbour. He had a plan to come charging in through the harbour entrance but the wind direction was wrong. This thrilling boat never had a chance to show what she could do before being wrecked by a Frenchman in the Single-handed Transatlantic Race. She was eventually replaced by *Sea Falcon*, a modification of the same design in which Knox-Johnston planned an assault on a record for the nautical mile. At the time of writing, however, this plan has yet to come to fruition.

*Clifton Flasher* (22·14 knots) put up her best performance, thanks to a general sorting out of the control system including trim tabs on the wings, which made it possible to feed in the power a bit more gradually. Her main problem seemed to be that the 27ft (8·2m) main hull was over-powered by the rig and the syndicate never had sufficient funds for a new one. They did try a new planing outrigger hull which was too heavy and therefore discarded. 'The Flasher' was one of Portland's successes: a genuinely original and worthwhile project carried out by a bunch of enthusiastic amateurs. Had the funds been available to build a double-sized version, they could well have had an outright world record boat on their hands.

*Mayfly* (19·38 knots) started the week with a new, fully-submerged foil system with automatic incidence control but the system collapsed and the old foils were re-fitted. Using them, she put up a speed way in advance of all the other small boats and faster than anything in 'C' or 'B' Class too!

*Watergate* (15·39 knots): Bristol boatbuilder Hywel Price has entered for almost every Speed Week with a series of spectacular and completely different boats. This one was a 23ft 7in (7·1m) scow with a Tornado rig. She had a horrendous amount of weather helm but was still the fastest monohull.

*Boreas* (15·04 knots): by fitting it with his semi-wing, high-boom 10 sq metre rig, Reg Bratt, or rather his jockey Mark Keddie, managed

*The ingenious and successful 'cascade' aerofoil rig of* Clifton Flasher *which was made up from five short asymmetrical, flapped wings* (Yachting World)

to push the speed of this Unicorn cat up to this creditable speed which became the record for the 10 sq metre class.

*Minoi II* (12·86 knots) was a foil conversion of a 470 dinghy by Claude Tisserand of France. Since this was not much faster than a normal 470, there did not seem to be much advantage in pursuing this particular line of development.

*Miss Strand Glass* (12·59 knots): this version was loosely based on a Tornado catamaran with foils on the lee side only. These were of super-cavitating section but the boat suffered from the old problem of excessive weight. Christopher Hook also fielded a second design: *Miss Bosham*, a lightweight trimaran built up from various kayak components. The main point of interest was a new form of self-tending rig that looked like a bi-plane banked 90 degrees. It did not work out too well but you certainly could not accuse him of running out of ideas.

The success of *Clifton Flasher* had created a lot of interest in wing masts and several more appeared this year. The most interesting was on a

The 'high boom rig' developed by Reg Bratt on his catamaran Boreas (Yachting World)

*Hydrofoil pioneer Christopher Hook watching his self-setting rig experiment* Miss Bosham (Yachting World)

little catamaran named *Tackwing* which, as its name implies, was an attempt to make a tackable solid wing. The method used was to have the solid wing attached at its mid-point to a short mast via a universal joint. In order to tack, it was inverted so that its head became its foot and *vice versa*. In addition, it was set at an angle which should have helped to reduce heeling force. The boat failed through simple structural inadequacy and very unfortunately was not developed further.

If Christopher Hook is every Englishman's idea of a dotty scientist, then Didier Costes is every Frenchman's. A quiet, charming nuclear physicist, he has spent a number of years playing around with a collection of pieces of bent aluminium which come together annually to form the extraordinary *Exoplane*. This is the kind of craft which attracts a small crowd of puzzled looking people who don't quite like to admit that they are trying to work out which direction it sails in. They will be wrong in either case because *Exoplane* is a symmetrical proa which reverses direction rather than tacking. The boat itself, with its curved, reversible, steerable hydrofoils is intriguing enough but the real interest lies in the rig, which represents an attempt to completely eliminate heeling force. The sail is something like an umbrella, set to leeward of the

*The technically attractive* Tackwing *was unfortunately not developed*
(Yachting World)

*The amazing* Exoplane *in one of its many versions* (Guy Gurney)

boat on the end of a spar at an angle of something like 45 degrees to the horizontal so that heel is exactly balanced by lift. It is a very impractical craft which spends 95 per cent of the time on the beach being repaired but just occasionally Costes gets everything right for a few minutes and goes skipping away at an impressive rate – usually in the wrong direction. Like a lot of the 'wild' Portland competitors, *Exoplane* is a failure as a boat but serves to demonstrate a very important idea: that of the no-heel rig.

# *1975*

*Crossbow* returned this year in a sorted-out form and broke the '30 knot barrier' with a best speed of 31·1 knots. It turned out that 30 knots was no particular barrier though it was beginning to look as if 40 knots might be. It was a useful speed politically because it exceeded the claimed but unratified one by Steve Dashew's *Beowulf*. Once again, a lot of the technical interest was in the smaller boats.

*Bluey*, designed and built by Cmdr. George Chapman, featured a most interesting and clever collapsible wing mast. A series of wooden frames slid up and down the mast and a sleeve sail was sewn over these frames to form the wing. In addition, there was a trailing edge flap made like a normal, fully-battened sail so that the rig could tack. This was a considerable breakthrough because it was a wing rig that could be lowered and stowed like a normal sail. The Gallant rig developed by Jack Manners-Spencer for cruising yachts embodies some of the features of the Bluey rig but without the trailing-edge flap. *Bluey* herself was also a hydrofoil boat with a layout similar to *Mayfly* but considerably heavier and hence slower.

*Streaker*, built by P. J. Bromley, was a somewhat over-optimistic effort to do away with the hull of the boat. An inclined Tornado rig was precariously supported on two small kayaks and a water-ski but it was shown once again that however clever the rig, it is wise to build on the basis of a fast and reasonably seaworthy hull.

An omen for the future was provided by the two-man sailboard entered by Mike Todd and Clive Colenso. Everyone, including the two sailors, regarded this as a bit of a laugh but they had to admit that the speed achieved, 13·5 knots, was quite impressive.

# 1976

*Crossbow II* made her debut and just managed to exceed the speed of her predecessor. It was apparent that the new boat had lots of potential but also that her steering was a problem.

Two other boats, both old friends, claimed World Records: *Icarus* with 20·7 knots in 'B' Class and *Mayfly* with 21·1 in 'A'. It was rather ignominious that the smaller boat was now faster than the larger one although in theory at least there is no virtue in length once a boat is flying on hydrofoils. The old aeronautical tenet of 'simplicate and add lightness' was also a factor in favour of *Mayfly*.

One of the more interesting things that happened this week was that two 'Sydney Harbour' 18ft (5·4m) skiffs appeared, Ray Alderman's *Sponsor Needed* and Peter Legrove's *Otis*. A group which had built these boats in England was trying to create a professional racing circuit along the Australian lines but were running into a lot of resistance from the yachting establishment. Their importance from our point of view is that they give an important cross-reference of speed. Admittedly, they were almost certainly not up to the standard of a *real* Sydney skiff and the crews not as skilled but they were at least the same kind of thing. Therefore, the best speed achieved, 14·7 knots by *Sponsor Needed*, seems quite remarkably slow. In comparison, a perfectly standard Hobie 16 cat notched up 17·6 knots the same week. There does not seem to be anything freakish about the results achieved by *Sponsor Needed*. The wind strength was adequate for other boats to break records and she made a total of 22 attempts with an average speed of 12·1 knots. The inescapable conclusion is that planing dinghies – even extreme ones like an 18ft (5·4m) skiff – are just not all that fast.

Clive Colenso rather bravely tried to sail with a specially made 10 sq metre wing-sail on a sailboard. Although a powerful and experienced board sailor, he found it too much for him to handle. One mistake seems to have been in making the sail so big, as even 6 sq metres is considered large for a normal sailboard rig. He also discovered, as others have before and since, that solid sails are more critical of angle of attack than cloth ones. One moment there is no power, and the next too much.

In the 10 sq metre Class, Reg Bratt had put his semi-wing, high-boomed rig onto a new boat named *Auster* which had little foils under the bows to stop it from diving. In spite of this she was not faster than his earlier boat. An Italian named Orlandini brought a very pretty little cat named *Artemide* which had a different variation on the high-boom rig idea. A sail cut a bit like a yankee jib was sheeted to the end of a spar sticking up from the stern and she recorded a respectable if unexciting 13·1 knots.

# 1977

This was probably the most fruitful and interesting year in the whole history of the RYA Speed Week. There were 48 entries including a number of very innovative boats, plenty of wind and new World Records in every class except 'C' where there was no entry. The inshore course along Chesil Beach was used for the first time and its smooth water helped to raise the speeds of a number of the smaller boats.

Although the event was again dominated physically by *Crossbow II* which raised her own record to a new figure of 33·8 knots, probably the most significant performance was that of Derk Thijs whose 19·1 knots on the Windglider sailboard really shattered the 10 sq metre Class. Till that moment, it looked as if the 10 sq metre Class would provide an interesting development area with a variety of hull and rig possibilities being tried out. Then, along came Thijs on his Windglider with a mere 7 sq metres of sail and completely blew their doors in. It was not only the small boats that had a shock for this speed by Thijs put him in the same range as the fast cats in 'B' Class such as Hobie and Tornado. Except for those who were able to dismiss this performance as some kind of freak, it was clear that sailboards were going to be a more and more dominant force in speed sailing.

*Icarus II* was an attempt to double up on the success of the earlier boat and hopefully to provide some competition for *Crossbow*. She was a 26ft (7·9m) catamaran with two Tornado rigs, one stepped in each hull, and a two-rung ladder hydrofoil layout. She flew on her first outing but her welded aluminium foils were not sufficiently strong and collapsed. Later in the week they were repaired but she never got going again. 'Big Icarus' was sailed for a further two years with gradually increased confidence until she foundered and broke up in 1980. She was rebuilt in 1983 but

Icarus II *on hydrofoils. This boat above all proved Murphy's square law (something twice the size will be four times the trouble) (Guy Gurney)*

again suffered serious damage. With James Grogono giving his time to the new boat, 'Little Icarus' was campaigned by his brothers Andrew and Alan. Between them they managed to raise the old war-horse's speed to 22·2 knots before breaking the mast.

*Mayfly* had been completely rebuilt by Ben Wynne including brand-new solid metal hydrofoils. He managed to get the Department of Mechanical Engineering, University of Newcastle upon Tyne to make these using sophisticated engineering methods including numerically-controlled machine-tools. This enabled Wynne to specify a NACA series 6 section rather than the simple ogive used before and to incorporate sectional twist so that as the boat went faster the angle of attack of the foils became less. The foils were tapered both in chord and thickness and had turned-down tips to improve side-force and reduce tip-loss. She also had a larger and better-cut sail and fairings on her cross-beams. The inshore course gave her the really smooth water that she needed in order to show her best, and Wynne was rewarded for his considerable efforts with a new record speed of 23·0 knots. This made her the second-fastest boat in the competition after *Crossbow II*.

Another boat whose performance cannot be ignored in 'B' Class was the standard Hobie 16 which achieved the really remarkable speed for a boat of this type of 19·8 knots. The 'secret weapon' was the former world champion of the class, Jeff Canepa, which only goes to show what can be done by putting a really good man at the helm. This was considerably faster than the apparently better-engineered NACRA 5·2 which only managed 16·7 knots. In fact there were three production cats sailing which all produced exactly the same speed, 16·7 knots: the NACRA 5·2, the Dutch *Aesticat* and a standard Shearwater MkIII named *Buzby*. This was a rather impressive performance by the Shearwater, whose basic design was 20 years old, but it was noticeable that she threw a tremendous amount of spray into the air compared to the other boats, and spray is a sign of drag.

Another illustration that conventional monohulls were barking up the wrong tree was provided by a very attractive GRP version of the Norfolk Punt named *Golden Jubilee*. According to the Portsmouth yardstick, the Punt is one of the fastest of dinghies but what this really means is that she is very fast under her own local conditions of smooth water and light winds. In the rough and tumble of Portland Harbour she managed 13 knots – exactly ten knots slower than the speed achieved by *Mayfly* with less sail area.

The Thijs family, Derk, Beb and Wim, delighted everyone with their triple sailboard but in order to be reasonably stiff this needed a rather

*Derk, Wim and Bep Thijs on the three-person sailboard* (Yachting World)

heavy hull with the result that its sail area/displacement ratio was markedly worse than a one-man board.

Another 'first' this year was provided by Keith Stewart with his little kite-propelled catamaran. It was extremely slow, but a least showed that it is possible to pull a boat along with kites. The odd thing is that Keith Stewart, who was first in the field, and has been back to Speed Week virtually every year since, has never yet achieved any worthwhile speed. Part of the reason seems to be that he is generally trying to demonstrate some practical feature of his kite designs such as stability in the air, or the ability to launch from the water, that have been inimical to high performance. Therefore, he was quickly overtaken in speed when a more efficient type of kite appeared.

Winner of the prize for interesting design was Jon Montgomery's inflatable catamaran *Sisi*. A lot of clever design had gone into this boat in order both to keep it light and to improve on the basic 'sausage' shape of a simple inflated tube. This can be achieved by fitting two inner tubes inside an oval shaped envelope and by fitting a rigid bow, while still retaining the ability to pack the whole thing up into the boot of a car. This boat eventually developed into the present *Catapult*.

# *1978*

If 1977 was a vintage year for Speed Week, 1978 was the nearest it has yet come to a complete flop. The dates of the Week are chosen so as to be as close as possible to the Autumn Equinox and neap tides but this time the most basic ingredient of sailing – wind – was almost completely absent. This was a great shame because there seemed to be the ingredients of an exciting drama.

The excitement was caused by the appearance of an apparently viable challenger for the outright record, *Slingshot* from the USA. This interesting boat was owned by a group of rich adventurers from Chicago under the leadership of Karl Thomas whose boast was that he tried to break new ground in a different field of human endeavour each year. One of his previous projects had been the attempted crossing of the Atlantic by balloon. He was forced to ditch in mid-Atlantic and then had four days in a liferaft during which he had time to think about the World Sailing Speed Record.

The boat, which was designed by Karl Thomas's brother George, was something entirely new – a giant planing dinghy something like a greatly enlarged 10 sq metre sailing canoe, 60ft (18·2m) LOA; there was a maximum hull beam of 4ft 6in (1·3m) and a maximum overall beam of 42ft 6in (12·6m). At rest, she seemed to be a trimaran with little floats on the ends of twin-pole outriggers. The clever part was that the outrigger could be winched across so that the whole length stuck out on one side. This made her like a reversible *Crossbow I* but had the drawback that the inboard float was pressed up alongside the main hull and was barely clear of the water when the boat was dead level. The long, slim U-sectioned bow gradually flattened out towards the stern and there was a surprising amount of rocker so that when at rest a considerable length of bow was waving around in the air. She had a rather, low, snug rig with a total of 700 sq ft of sail, approximately half the area set by *Crossbow II*; the main being set on a semi-wing mast, the idea being that she was designed for winds of Force 5 or more so there was no need for a lot of sail. The mast was standing on a universal joint and the shrouds were adjustable in length (as indeed they had to be because of the variable beam) so that the mast could be canted to windward.

Perhaps the nicest thing about *Slingshot* was her construction by the famous Gougeon brothers of Bay City, Michigan using their well-known WEST system of epoxy saturated cedar. Thanks to this, she had the remarkably low all-up weight of 1800lbs (803·5kg) and was beautifully

*One of the few efforts to build a really big planing boat was* Slingshot *which was prevented from showing what she could do by two unlucky accidents* (Yachting World)

smooth and fair. The worst thing about her was probably her outrigger arrangement which merely copied the worst mistakes of *Crossbow I* in her first year. Her crew of four or five tried to balance her by dashing up and down the outrigger and when she was at full stretch, they all tried to crowd onto the tiny outrigger hull which was barely big enough for the helmsman, and as a result completely blocked his view ahead. At the same time, if the boat heeled at all, the lee outrigger would dig into the water and create a tremendous flurry of spray. These faults, however, are mainly apparent with hindsight; at the time she seemed a big and exciting new boat that could genuinely give *Crossbow* some opposition. In the disappointing light airs during the week, *Slingshot* only managed a speed of 21·9 knots compared to *Crossbow II*'s 28·1, but she obviously was not a light airs boat due to her low sail area.

Karl Thomas and his friends were alleged to have spent $80,000 on *Slingshot* and obviously did not want to go home empty-handed. They therefore made an arrangement with Tim Colman that they would share the cost of keeping the course available for a further week in the hope of getting some decent breeze. They did in fact get around 25 knots but it was from the north-west which is a gusty, offshore wind at Portland. *Crossbow* managed 34·4 knots, faster than her existing record but not by the required 2 per cent. *Slingshot* fractured her mast-step and tore a sail and by the time everything was ready once more their time was up. Speed Week having been a fiasco, they decided to have the boat stored in Weymouth and return the following year.

Apart from *Slingshot*, there were two interesting hydrofoils, two kite-yachts and a mass of various sailboards. One of the hydrofoils, the intriguingly-named *Hi-Trot III*, was built and sailed by students from the Kanazawa Institute of Technology, Ishikawa, Japan. The boat, a 15ft (4·5m) catamaran, was conventional as was the foil system which was like a *Mayfly* with an incidence control system added. The students

Force 8 *showing the feeler arms which measure riding height and control the incidence of the foils* (Yachting World)

had put a lot of work into the rig: there were two masts each with a double-luffed, wrap-around sail plus complex camber and leech control. As with so many 'clever' boats however, the weight had got out of control and she would have needed a lot of puff to raise her 400lbs (178·5kg) out of the water. Sadly, neither the boat nor its sailors ever re-appeared thereafter. An attractive project which had actually been seen for the first time in 1977 was the Pattison brothers' *Force 8*, an incidence-controlled flying hydrofoil with full wing rig. One of their ideas was that a hydrofoil boat with differential incidence control should be able to achieve full roll stabilization without the need for the crew sitting out on the side. Therefore, the 'pilot' sat centrally in the main hull in a very aircraft-like cockpit while the main foils were mounted below minimal floats at the ends of a crossbeam. The incidence-control system was basically automatic with Hook-type feeler arms to control the riding height but with a manual over-ride system. The rig was quite ambitious: a solid wing mast with a large trailing-edge section made from two layers of Melinex sheet with battens. There always seemed to be a good deal of difficulty in controlling this sail, and in the first two years the boat used to porpoise on and off her foils severely, but the Pattisons were serious chaps who would keep going away, changing things and trying again.

A good deal of amusement was provided by the four-man sailboard *Gel ar Mor* sailed by 'Les Crocodiles d'Elorn' which introduced a new manoeuvre to sailing, the 'ripple tack' as each of the rigs went about in sequence. There were lots of one-man sailboards all ready and waiting to do great things as soon as the wind arrived because this section of the sport had now become frankly commercial in outlook with several board manufacturers out to capture the World Record. On a technical level, they were beginning to get round to the much smaller, specialized speed boards though this process still had some way to go.

Ian Day and Paul Jeffree from Christchurch brought a new approach to the kite-yacht idea. They were impressed by the efficiency of a new type of commercially-available steerable kite called the Flexifoil. Made of spinnaker sailcloth, these kites are wing-shaped and have a gauze opening along the leading edge into which the wind blows and inflates the wing to its proper aerofoil shape. A single glass-fibre spar along the leading edge keeps the wing extended laterally and its ends provide the mounting points for the two control lines. Most kites fly fully-stalled; just a tethered wind-break in the sky, whereas the Flexifoil which is free to rotate round its spar flies like a proper wing and is therefore much more efficient. 'Efficient' in this context means both that it exerts a lot of pull on its strings and that it flies close to the wind. If you stand still and

*Faster! Faster!*

fly a Flexifoil directly upwards, it will reach an angle of about 70 degrees from the horizontal or 100 degrees off the true wind direction. If you then translate this into a plan diagram of a boat sailing to windward it will be found that the kites are producing a thrust-line as favourable as a typical sloop rig. There are three big advantages: (1) the kites experience

Jacob's Ladder *with her stack of Flexifoil kites* (the author)

*Close-up of* Jacob's Ladder *showing control system* (the author)

a stronger, cleaner wind than at sea level and are not knocked about by the boat's motion; (2) the lines can be made to pull from the gunwale so that there is no heeling force; and (3) the kites can be steered so that they swoop around the sky and take out more kinetic energy than if they stayed in one place.

The Day/Jeffree team were only just starting to play with their Flexifoils this year and came along with a rather horrid little 12ft (3·6m) catamaran. The light winds allowed them to do little more than stooge quietly around the harbour but at least it did demonstrate that they could steer and indeed, sail to windward. Keith Stewart, in contrast, returned with a much more interesting-looking boat like an elongated kayak with a small outrigger, but his kite was a great zeppelin of a thing whose main virtue was that it floated.

# 1979

Another somewhat dismal year due to the lack of both wind and money. Players had ended their involvement with Speed Week after the 1977 event and in 1978 Smirnoff had provided both funds and liquor but, alas, for one year only. For 1978 therefore, the RYA staggered on with a budget cut to the bone including all officials paying their own hotel bills. There were no records during the week but high drama afterwards, as we shall see in a moment!

There were a couple of days of reasonable south-westerlies which served to show that a number of boats and boards were raring to go. *Slingshot* raised her speed to 22·6 knots which was not very impressive considering that little *Mayfly* went 22·0 on the same day. The *Jacob's Ladder* team was back having replaced their original mount with a Tornado catamaran. They managed to fly a stack of 14 Flexifoils and achieved the quite respectable speed of 13·1 knots thereby. The Pattisons had improved the rig controls of *Force 8* and got 16·3 knots out of her and even Didier Costes managed a run of 14·4 knots with the amazing *Exoplane*.

The real head of steam was among the sailboards. Ten Cate had entered a powerful works team headed by their No. 1 jockey Jaap Van de Rest, backed up by Jan Marc Schreur and the husband and wife team of Jaap and Erica Keller. The US parent manufacturers of the Windsurfer, Windsurfing International, had sent over Ken Winner and Matt Schweitzer with a couple of sleds of the type being developed in Hawaii for wave-riding and jumping. Faced with this kind of fire-power, most amateurs were outclassed and even the World Record holder Derk Thijs was nervous when he saw the special light-weight boards that Van der Rest and Schreur had available. Britain's only pro was Clive Colenso who had recently gone into production with his own board called Olympic Gold but this was a typical all-round regatta board and no-one gave him much chance compared to the Dutch.

This seemed a correct interpretation based on the results of Friday's sailing which produced the best wind of the week. In a breeze that barely reached 18 knots, Derk Thijs went out and did 18·6 on the Windglider and Jaap Van der Rest replied with 19·2; faster than Thijs' record but not by the required 2 per cent needed to claim a new one. Colenso, on the same day, only managed 13 knots. With excitement running high, a group of competitors which included Karl Thomas of *Slingshot*, Van der Rest, Colenso and Keith Stewart arranged to have the course kept open for a few days in the hope of getting more wind. Their prayers were answered except that the wind came from the East, the worst possible heading for Portland because the sea then comes in through the entrances and the 'inshore course' becomes a lee shore.

*Slingshot* had no luck at all: commencing her very first run one of the rollers supporting her crossbeams failed. This allowed the 'long' end of the outrigger to swing aft while the 'short' end, which was close up against the hull, swung forward and pierced the main hull. Her rigging went slack and the mast hung over at a drunken angle. She was towed inshore and moored but as a final blow, her mooring parted during the night and she drifted onto rocks and was holed. Although the damage could have been repaired fairly easily, this was the end for *Slingshot*. Karl Thomas and his team just packed up and went home to Chicago, never to return.

On the same day, Jaap Van der Rest put in a run of 22·3, an almost incredible 4·2 knots faster than Thijs' record. Colenso also sailed but could manage only 14·9 knots. The Ten Cate team were jubilant as they appeared not merely to have a World Record but one which was way out of reach of their competitors. They therefore packed up their gear and prepared to go home. There then followed the most controversial episode in the history of the World Sailing Speed Record. Michael Ellison, Secretary of the Amateur Yacht Research Society was the Official Observer who had agreed to stay on at Portland and the following is a quotation from his official report:

> On Monday morning I did not hear from *Slingshot* regarding making runs but the wind was South East Force 8, no craft could leave Weymouth and club boats were being swamped and fittings were being washed ashore. Keith Stewart and Clive Colenso confirmed that they would like to try the inside course (on a lee shore with heavy breakers) and I agreed to arrange observers and indicated that as there could not be any launch the cost would be less than £100.
>
> We opened the course with Joan M. Jenkins, S. Chapman, Dan H. Whistance and myself as timers and observers soon after 14.30. Keith Stewart indicated that he could only make one run from the Navy base at 15.30 and please would we be sure to get his time. Clive made a first run of 45·68 seconds but the radio failed. His second run was 47 seconds and again the arrangement for timing was not satisfactory. His third run averaged at 42·79 seconds but three watches averaged 42·65 and the fourth read 43·20 due to the fact that the watch was started by the observer who watched the bow cross the transit and not on the word 'now'. For the fourth run, two observers watched the transits (one on each end) and four watches were started on the word 'now' and stopped when the light was switched on at the end of the course. The time for the fourth run averaged 42·33 seconds (42·30; 42·31; 42·34; 42·37). The observers present are satisfied that the times for the fourth run have been properly measured and recorded.

The significance of these times were that they worked out to a speed of 22·95 knots, just sufficient for Clive Colenso to snatch the World Record that Van der Rest had established only 24 hours before. When they heard about this, the Ten Cate team was aghast and they immediately put up a strong barrage of complaint about the manner in which the record had been claimed, and indeed innuendo about the likelihood of it being correct. All these strong feelings came pouring out at the ratification meeting on 27 November that year.

The Ten Cate team first claimed that they had been denied the opportunity of making runs on the day in question, which Michael Ellison strongly refuted. He said that he had met Van der Rest during the morning and that he was packed up and about to leave and made no mention of wanting to sail. Of course, had he thought that Colenso had the smallest chance of sailing at 22 knots, it might have been a different story! It was repeatedly pointed out that on every other occasion during the preceding week, Colenso had been struggling to attain 14 knots. Was it really likely that he could suddenly pull an extra 9 knots out of the bag?

The WSSR Committee sensibly declined to speculate on this and rejected the Ten Cate complaints. What worried them a lot more was the manner in which the timing had been made. It had been a foul day: cold, blowing a gale and pouring with rain and as Ellison had reported, the radio link between the ends of the course had failed at the first attempt. Therefore, in what seemed a rather desperate improvisation he and his helpers had driven two cars onto the foreshore so that they could sight over the transits from inside them. All four watches (on two boards) had been in one car and in lieu of radio the observer at the other end had flashed the headlights of his car when Colenso crossed the transits. It all sounded a bit 'hairy'. Ellison was given a searching inquisition by the other members of the Committee and defended himself and his team stoutly on every point. Finally, and after a great deal of heart-searching by all concerned, Colenso's record of 22·95 knots was ratified.

Subsequent events did little to calm the doubts experienced by those who wondered if Colenso really could have sailed so fast, especially on a rather ordinary production board. He emigrated to Australia but returned to compete at Portland again in 1981 when he again failed to produce even remotely competitive results. It was possibly fortunate therefore that his record lasted for less than a year when the lead was regained by Jaap Van der Rest!

# *1980*

Speed Week was in funds again having acquired as a sponsor Ten Cate, European manufacturer of the Windsurfer. In view of the foregoing, a number of people involved with the event had a somewhat uneasy feeling but in fact their sponsorship was managed with the lightest of touch, although they withdrew after a second year of sponsorship when they began to feel that their own position as both sponsor and competitor was too tricky a role to fill successfully. During the summer, Van der Rest had been to the Schweitzer Speed Trials in Maui and come home with a brand new record of 24·6 knots. As this was actually faster than the standing records in every class except the Unlimited one, Van der Rest asked to be recognized as the record-holder in those classes too. However, the Committee observed that the sail area classes have both minimum and maximum limits and that therefore it is only possible to sail in one of them at a time.

One thing that 1980 was definitely not short of was wind: one day it blew Force 8/9 and to everyone's astonishment, some of the sailboards managed to make runs over the inshore course. Yachtsmen always exaggerate the wind force, of course, but Austin Farrar who acts as measurer to the event had a proper anemometer with him which repeatedly registered 40 knots. I would never have believed that a small sailing boat could survive in such conditions. The Chesil Bank beach of Portland Harbour was, as usual the weather shore but from about 300ft

*Gale force winds at the 1980 Portland Speed Week when only sailboards and Jacob's Ladder dared to leave the beach*

(100m) offshore the water was absolutely white. What made it possible for the intrepid board-sailors to sail was that they were launching from the weather shore in very shallow water. They found that if two helpers stood in knee-deep water holding the board, the 'jockey' could get control of the rig with one foot in the foot-strap and the other on the bottom and then, on the word 'go' be released like a bullet from a gun. Nine times out of ten, this ended in a spectacular pitch over the bow but just occasionally a run was completed. The tragedy was that the wind direction was not quite right so the boards tended to run diagonally across the course finishing well offshore in the rough water whence they had to be rescued by the RYA's stalwart racing manager John Reed in his powerboat. The best speed recorded on this day was 23·9 knots by Van der Rest; some way short of his Maui record. However in view of the fact that he had to travel extra distance by sailing diagonally over the course, he was probably hitting about 25 knots.

The only record set at Speed Week 1980 was by good old *Icarus* which managed a further small improvement of her 'B' Class record, sailed by Alan Grogono and myself.

# *1981*

Another amazingly windy week and one dominated by sailboards to an unprecedented degree. Although the sailboard interest was welcome enough, it was sad that enthusiasm in the larger classes was on the wane. One very obvious reason was that a sailboard was now the second fastest sailing boat in the world and this tended to discourage the boats. In technical terms, this was 'the year of the sinker'. The West German surf-sailing expert Jürgen Honscheid came along with a board he called *F2* which was not designed as a sailboard at all. In fact it was a stock wave surfboard designed for the small, steep waves of North Cornwall. It had not sufficient buoyancy to support even a child's weight so Honscheid had to make a water-start whenever he went out.

Conditions were nearly ideal on the inshore course on two different days and it was apparent that the standard of sailing of the boards had improved immensely. This was shown by the fact that 16 different boards managed to exceed 20 knots, which only a year or two before had been considered an impossible feat. Honscheid tended to get more runs than others as a result of his amazing skill at 'carve gybing'. It's no good trying to tack a sinker because it sinks. The only way to turn round without an enforced swim is therefore a special kind of fast gybe in which the sailor leans into the turn and swishes round like a waterskier

*The inflatable catamaran,* Catapult, *sailing on the inshore course at Portland. This shows how it is possible to sail very close to the windward shore in relatively undisturbed wind* (the author)

rounding a buoy. Honscheid was so good at this that he could go on sailing up and down the course continuously for half an hour at a time. On his best day, he bettered 23 knots on six different occasions, all within a period of an hour. His best run was 24·75 knots which bettered the record of Van der Rest but not by the 2 per cent needed to claim a new one.

Honscheid was naturally very disappointed and unfortunately a number of European surf magazines chose 'not to understand' how he could be the fastest in the World but not the World Record holder. They noted with heavy sarcasm that the 10 sq metre record was still held by the Ten Cate team who by a strange coincidence were also sponsors of the event. This was completely unfair to Ten Cate who had nothing to do with the running of the event and certainly no influence on the rules. Nevertheless, the sour nature of the publicity they received as a result of the year's activities led them to pull out.

The other eye-catching incident of 1981 was *Jacob's Ladder*'s effort to turn itself into a flying boat. For their fourth year, Ian Day and his team were determined to do something really worthwhile. They had more and bigger kites, better handling gear on the Tornado, the centre-boards had been moved to a better position and planing surfaces had been added aft to stop her squatting at speed. Apart from the rather tricky launching procedure, the outfit was also showing itself remarkably seaworthy. Even in winds strong enough to keep all the boards ashore, the *Ladder* could be launched and made to sail around the harbour under perfect control for hours on end. She put in a number of very fast runs including one of 23·75 knots – just short of the World Record for 'C' Class.

On the final day of the week it blew a gale and the *Ladder* team decided to make a 'shit or bust' effort. The process for launching the kites and boat from a weather shore is rather complicated and hard to describe but basically, the boat is moored just offshore and the kites' flying lines are led back to windward and through a firmly-anchored snatch-block. The kites are laid out in a line on the ground and launch themselves with a whoosh as soon as they are turned the correct way up. With the kites up, the snatch-block is eased away to transfer the flying lines to the boat. The launch procedure went surprisingly smoothly: they put up a total of 240 sq ft of kite which was the minimum for a 'C' Class run and it was immediately obvious that they had a horrendous amount of power. When the snatch-block was eased away and the full lift of the rig came directly onto the boat, she immediately started to lift off the water but was restrained by her painter made fast to the shore. The crew, Ian Day who flies the kites and Martin Rayment who steers the boat, were just getting ready to cast off when the bows lifted to such an angle that Rayment fell overboard. The boat then leaped clean off the water and the painter broke. For a few horrifying microseconds, Ian Day went soaring away with the boat till he relinquished his grip and fell about ten feet into the water. The boat actually reached an altitude of about 30ft (9·1m) and flew about 150ft (45·7m) downwind before crashing violently into the water.

The best thing about this incident was that no one was hurt although the boat was badly knocked about. Providentially, the whole amazing sequence was captured on video and the tape has been a firm favourite at speed meetings ever since.

Oh! and I almost forgot to add that *Icarus* raised her own record once again to 24·46 knots.

# *1982*

Speed Week followed immediately after the similar event at Brest, then in its second year. Brest had been organized on a quite different basis, being set up by a promoter with the backing of the city council, and was much more generously funded than Portland which for the second time in its history was without a sponsor at all. *La Base de Vitesse de Brest* is organized from a modern marina and all sorts of facilities were specially put in ashore, such as a large bar-restaurant containing an enormous number of TV monitors which constantly showed video recordings of the day's sailing. The sponsors included the regional newspaper *Ouest France*, and Thompson who provided the quite amazing video service. In spite of all these advantages, the actual sailing conditions in Brest harbour are less favourable than at Portland being less sheltered. This did not prevent a large number of entries being attracted by the very considerable prize fund, the top prize for the week being 50,000 francs.

Brest did at least get plenty of wind and although this did not suit the '*engins*' such as the various hydrofoil boats, it was good enough for the numerous sailboards to turn in some sparkling performances. The best was 26·53 knots by Philip Pudenz from West Germany; yet another World Record in the 10 sq metre Class and a considerable advance on Van der Rest's most recent record, 25·11 set the previous year at Veerse Meer in Holland. Another feature of Brest was that a number of the large offshore multihulls such as Marc Pajot's *Elf Aquitaine* and the enormous *William Saurin* were persuaded to enter although their speeds, in the confines of the harbour, were frankly disappointing.

After the circus-like atmosphere of Brest, Portland was a drab-seeming affair. Due to lack of funds, only the inshore course was used and the small team of organizers huddled rather miserably in workmen's shelters lent by the Council. As anticipated there was a large entry of boards and only a few boats, but a number of the sailboard 'stars' had come on from Brest. There was one really good day's sailing during which sailboards poured constantly over the inshore course in an undisciplined horde which left the organizers with a nearly impossible task of allotting the correct times to the correct boards. This was made even harder by the fact that if rigs are heeled acutely towards the observer, it is very difficult to see the sail-number. A number of fast runs were missed and hard words were spoken at the next day's briefing. Some of the 'gentlemen' amateur organizers of the RYA were shocked to find the degree of professionalism that existed among the board sailors who openly declared that their earning power would be reduced if they did not go home with good results. In spite of this there were some stunning results and the hitherto unknown French board sailor Pascal Maka shattered the record so recently set by Philip Pudenz with an amazing speed of 27·82 knots.

Although there were relatively few boats taking part there was one other World Record – by *Jacob's Ladder* which finally managed to crack 'C' Class with a speed of 25·03 knots. This was a highly popular result and there could hardly be a greater contrast between the *Jacob's Ladder* team and the boardsailing pros: on the one hand the well-paid, athletic 'jockeys' sailing boards whose main purpose in life seemed to be to publicize other kinds of products such as drink or clothing and on the other the amateur experimenters, tinkering away year after year with radical ideas of the kind that only respond to repeated trial and error.

It was somewhat ironic that by the end of 1982 when the RYA Speed Week at Portland seemed at its lowest ebb, that every one of the World Records was once again held at Portland. *Crossbow* had set her outright World record of 36 knots in a privately-organized trial in 1980 and all the other class records had been achieved during Speed Weeks.

# 1983

Excellent winds and last-minute sponsorship by Johnnie Walker meant that Speed Week was considerably more successful than expected although the organization was quite shaky, particularly in respect of the issuing of results. Sailboards again dominated although there were some other interesting boats. The big news of the week was the startling new 10sq m record by Fred Haywood who reached 30·83 knots and became the first board sailor to exceed 30 knots. He did this using a new carbon-fibre wing mast (see Ch. 8) which gave a substantially better performance than a conventional sailboard rig.

The 'A' Class record, held for so long by *Mayfly*, was finally taken by *Black and White*, a tandem, sinker sailboard bravely sailed under foul conditions by Gordon Way and Glen McKinley, with a speed of 25·39 knots. Following this performance, one wondered whether any of the records would in future be safe from the assault of sailboards. Would the 'B' and 'C' Class records eventually be claimed by three- or four-man boards?

Showing that there is still life in the old boat, *Icarus* raised her own record to the height of 26·59 knots which although pleasing is woefully short of the 10sq m record. Leif Wagner-Smitt brought his new hydrofoil *Ugly Duckling* over from Denmark but although he was convinced that he had run at 30 knots and been mis-timed, this boat had serious handling problems and ended the week badly smashed up following a capsize. The *Jacob's Ladder* team put hydrofoils on to their boat but they needed much more sorting out. The same applies to a very interesting new boat named *Gamma* that was built by some of the *Clifton Flasher* team. This embodies a very promising sloping wing mast and some impressive bursts of speed were demonstrated.

The three new records set in 1983 clearly demonstrated that Portland is still unchallenged as the best venue for speed sailing but there was considerable frustration on the part of overseas competitors that it was not more professionally organized. With the sport becoming steadily more popular, and more professional, this event is under some pressure to show that it is keeping up with the times and 1984 should see some changes for the better.

I hope that this chapter will show that the achievement of Speed Week has not only been in its consistent raising of record speeds, but in the rich variety of experimental craft which have used it as their 'test bed'. Some, like the kite yachts and hydrofoils, have come to fruition largely because of Speed Week while others such as inclined rigs and tackable wings have yet to do so. It is quite clear that without Speed Week most of them would never have been built at all.

# The perils of speed sailing!

Crossbow II *starting to go down . . .*

*. . . and* Icarus II *nearly gone!*

Jacob's Ladder *heading for the heights . . .*

*. . . and* Swiss Yachting *heading for the depths!*

# 11
# The *Crossbow* story

The story of the World Sailing Speed Record is very largely the story of one man, or rather, one team: the *Crossbow* team. Since its inception in 1972 the World Speed Record has constantly been held by one of the two boats of this name. Nor has it been a matter of going out and setting a record and then waiting for someone else to beat it. For six years the record was raised continually by the *Crossbow* team in spite of a conspicuous lack of real competition at their level.

The man behind the *Crossbows*, the owner, driving-force, helmsman and in every sense 'skipper' is Tim Colman. In the small, rather clannish world of sailing, Colman's was not a well-known name before 1972 although he had been a successful Dragon helmsman at club level, coming close to winning the Edinburgh Cup at Torbay in 1957, while his uncle, Alan Colman, owned the ketch *Wishbone* which gave its name to the boom of that type.

On the other hand, on his own 'patch' in Norfolk, Timothy Colman rates one step below royalty – quite literally since as Lord Lieutenant of the County he is the monarch's representative on formal occasions. He is involved in a host of other activities being, among other things, Pro-Chancellor of the University of East Anglia and chairman of a national charitable foundation. In business too, Colman is definitely a good name to have in Norfolk. Colman's mustard has been made there for over 200 hundred years, and since merging with Reckitts of Hull, Reckitt and Colman has grown into one of Europe's larger food to pharmaceutical companies. Tim Colman is a director of that company and also of Whitbread's (sponsors of the Round the World Race) but his main business interest is with a newspaper group which publishes morning, evening and weekly newspapers in the Eastern Countries.

Most competitors and officials concerned with the World Sailing Speed Record are completely unaware of all this except perhaps to have a vague feeling that Tim Colman has something to do with the mustard of that name. One of his most engaging qualities is that when away from Norwich he is a completely private person who not only does not seek but actively avoids personal publicity and is clearly delighted to spend a couple of weeks being a sailor among sailors.

In fact he has been a life-long yachtsman. A zest for the sea seems to have shown at an early stage for he joined the navy at the age of 13 via the Royal Naval College, Dartmouth. Not surprisingly, sailing was encouraged and while others were playing cricket he spent most summer afternoons racing Dartmouth One-design dinghies. Later, as a young officer based in Malta he acquired a vintage National 12 and sailed around the island single-handed, pulling up on beaches to sleep. A long-standing member and recently appointed Admiral of the Royal Norfolk and Suffolk Yacht Club, he campaigned an International Dragon successfully for a number of years, latterly in partnership with a cousin, Christopher Boardman, who, incidentally, won an Olympic Gold Medal in the 6-Metre *Lalage* in 1936 and crewed aboard Sopwith's *Endeavour* in the 1934 America's Cup challenge. The main reason for choosing the Dragon was that it was the most competitive boat being sailed at Lowestoft but at home Colman hoards a collection of Uffa Fox books (the proper, pre-war ones) which tell of much more exotic craft such as twin sliding seat canoes and International 14ft dinghies. In fact he mentions as a highlight of his sailing career crewing as a boy for Peter Scott amongst others during the Prince of Wales Cup Week at Lowestoft. In the era when the 14s were the aristocrats of small sailing craft, the POW was one of 'the' sailing events of the year. He had known Peter Scott since childhood and indeed accompanied him on a wildlife expedition to the Antarctic in 1968.

It was therefore Peter Scott's name that caught his attention in the pages of *Yachting World* in April 1970 when the famous ornithologist and sailor was a member of a 'Forum' discussion on 'high speed sailing'. Scott was one of the very few people who had taken part in any kind of organized speed trials prior to this date.

When *Yachting World* decided to shoot an arrow in the air in 1970, Scott was the obvious choice as a guest speaker at the Forum and later as the President of a World Sailing Speed Record steering committee.

In any case, when Colman read the article in *Yachting World*, it apparently had exactly the effect intended: it fired his imagination and set him thinking. He soon started doodling giant canoes – something like a huge version of Uffa Fox's famous *Valhalla*. He had already given up the Dragon in favour of family sailing and needed a new challenge.

Would it not be better, he thought, instead of regular weekend racing, to concentrate on one big effort of, say, two weeks per year? And would not the World Sailing Speed Record idea that *Yachting World* was talking about be just the right kind of project?

Two minds seemed better than one, so he first talked his ideas over with an old friend and fellow-sailor, Tom Hall, who was enthusiastic and welcomed the idea of joining in the venture. Colman and Hall did a lot of talking, drew some more doodles and agreed on a delightfully simple strategic plan. The requirements for their boat were: 1. It should win! 2. It must be fun at every stage – otherwise they would rather quit.

From this point Colman seems to have been more or less committed to building a boat. He originally envisaged it as a two year project, win or lose. He agreed with Hall that neither of them were either qualified or had sufficient time to design the boat themselves and so they called in an East Anglian yacht designer and asked him to come up with a proposal.

The sketch that this man produced fuelled their enthusiasm but was frankly disappointing and showed one thing very clearly – that to design a record breaker, mere professional competence was not enough. What was needed was an original thinker; someone who could take an absolutely detached view of the whole field of small-boat design and had the qualities of boldness and imagination required to come up with something really new. The man whom Colman first consulted was honest enough to know that he fell short by this reckoning and generous enough to suggest another name: that of Roderick Macalpine-Downie.

The son of a Scottish land-owner and military engineer, Roderick Macalpine-Downie stands out from the generality of yacht designers like a Stradivarius among penny whistles. His character is a mixture of razor-sharp intelligence mixed with natural Scots iconoclasm. His breadth of knowledge and interest is so wide and his conversation so penetrating that people often wonder how this man came to be a mere 'boat designer' (his own phrase) rather than some kind of highly placed academic. The answer is that he does what pleases him rather than what he 'ought' to do. He drifted into yacht design after his father had died in a sailing accident and left the family saddled with a huge bill for death duties necessitating the sale of their Scottish estate.

Thus cut free from his background, Macalpine-Downie established himself at Brightlingsea in Essex where he designed a series of high-performance catamarans beginning with the Thai series. He then became, through John Fisk, involved with the International Catamaran Challenge Trophy, the so-called 'Little America's Cup'. He designed and built the first of the Hellcat series of the 'C' Class catamarans and with Fisk took *Hellcat II* to the USA and handily beat the defending *Wildcat*. After this there was a series of defences of the Cup in England. All but one of the defending craft were designed by Macalpine-Downie during the time the trophy was in England, giving him a relationship to this particular cup a bit like R. G. Mitchell's to the Schneider Trophy.

'Thai' was built by a young Brightlingsea boat-builder, Reg White, who subsequently proved to be one of the World's outstanding helmsman of high-performance catamarans. The firm became Sail Craft, builders of a range of cruising and racing multihulls, most to Macalpine-Downie design, and Reg went on to win a Gold Medal at the 1976 Olympics.

Colman wrote to both Macalpine-Downie and White in the middle of winter 1970 and arranged a meeting shortly afterwards. He expected that Macalpine-Downie would be full of ideas and was not disappointed. He too had spotted the Forum report in *Yachting World* and had felt similarly attracted to the challenge of a competition based on absolute speed. He generously volunteered his help in designing a challenger for the trophy and thus was established a partnership which has lasted to this day.

At their first meeting it was agreed to build for the first Speed Week, organized by the Royal Yachting Association and sponsored by John Player, scheduled for October 1972 and that the boat should be launched, if possible in the early part of 1972 so that it would be possible to carry out development trials on the East Coast prior to moving to Portland Harbour. Sail Craft would built the boat and their associated company Sail Spar would rig her, while Gowens were to make the sails.

Colman had always had in mind some kind of long, slim giant canoe and he was pleased to find Macalpine-Downie had no hesitation in specifying a boat of this general type. What took his breath away was the sheer audacity of Macalpine-Downie's thinking. His initial sketches showed a boat 60ft (18·2m) long with a maximum hull beam of 1ft 10in (560mm) and an overall beam of 27ft (8·2m). This was to be driven by a sloop rig of 885 sq ft and to have an all-up weight of 1,500lbs (680kg). Righting moment was to be provided by the weight of four crew sitting at the end of a 25ft (7·6m) long outrigger. Clearly he was not one of those people who thought the World Speed Record could be captured by a Flying Dutchman with an extra-large spinnaker. Unlike some designers who can be paralysed by the sight of a blank sheet of paper, he was positively exhilarated by the prospect of designing something really *outré*, that would be completely unfettered by any kinds of rules or limits or indeed by previous experience.

In conversation with Colman, Macalpine-Downie talked about a boat intended to be 'cost-effective rather than cost-efficient' and while writing about *Crossbow* in *Yachting World* he described her as 'The Most Extreme Conventional Boat Ever Built'.

Conventional? Good grief! How could he describe this over-powered knitting-needle as conventional? What he meant was that *Crossbow* was not intended to embody any new principles but only to push existing ones to their limits. She was not designed to plane, nor to rise out of the water on hydrofoils. She was to be driven by conventional cloth sails on a conventional aluminium mast. She was not to be built from carbon fibre or anything else more exotic than wood. *Crossbow*'s speed was to be derived from her very high ratios of length to beam, sail to weight and righting moment to all-up weight.

Where Macalpine-Downie was perhaps telling a bit of a fib was in describing her layout as 'conventional'. In fact I know of no previous sailing boat which was designed to be capable of sailing on only one tack. The feature arose from the rules of the World Sailing Speed Record which only required a boat to make one run over a minimum distance of 500m. Therefore, since there would obviously be a weight penalty in equipping the boat with 25ft (7·6m) outriggers on *both* sides, it was agreed to accept the limitation of being able to sail in only one direction. Starboard tack was chosen, not in the hope of obtaining right of way over others but because in the Northern Hemisphere, stronger gusts of wind *veer* rather than *back* and so free rather than head a boat sailing on starboard tack.

Work went ahead at Sail Craft, using the well known 'cold-moulding' technique of stapling thin layers of wood onto a former. In this case the hull was built up from three layers of (3mm) Gaboon, laid up at 45 degrees, giving a total thickness of (9mm) before fairing.

At first sight the idea of stepping a 55ft (16·7m) mast on such an obviously frail craft seemed to be asking for trouble but in fact the very large *overall* beam meant that the shrouds made a far greater angle to the mast than in any normal boat and hence the strain on them and therefore the compression on the mast was not at all excessive. There was an extra, short beam extending about 3ft (914mm) to port to stop the mast from falling over to windward. Clearly it would be in great danger if the sails ever filled from the port side.

The mast itself was stepped on the weather topside. Had it been stepped in the centre of the hull, the already tiny 'slot' between main and jib would have been closed up to almost nothing. On the other hand, to step it some distance out along the crossbeams would have required a lot of stiffening and hence extra weight. The mast itself was a stock cruiser section which was stepped with a permanent 60 degrees rotation to windward which was intended to give a smooth entry to the leeward side of the sail.

Twenty-seven feet (8·2m) outboard on the end of two aluminium crossbeams was mounted a tiny outrigger hull that looked like a piece of the bow of the main hull. There was just room in the stern of this little boat for the helmsman to sit down inside a hole in the deck, looking very like a canoeist. The idea was that Colman would steer with his feet but this is one area where the designer seemed to run out of ideas and when the time came for the first trials, Colman brought a pair of his childrens' pony irons down with him from Bixley and solemnly connected them up to the steering wires. These ran back to the main hull inside one of the cross-beams and thence to the top of the tiny rudder which was mounted on a stout skeg about ten feet (3m) forward from the transom. The whole assembly was made up as a box which could be withdrawn from the hull, as could the equally small dagger-board.

In designing the dagger-board and rudder, Macalpine-Downie was very conscious of the horrific amount of side-force that nearly 1000 sq ft of sail was going to develop and thus strength was the first consideration rather than hydrodynamic efficiency. Short, stubby appendages of almost square plan-shape were therefore specified.

No doubt the hardest part of the design was visualizing a suitable technique for sailing it. The basis of the whole design was that the outrigger hull should skim along just clear of the water, kept there by skilful application of sheet and helm. If this seems an impossibly ambitious idea then it did not to Macalpine-Downie whose long experience with 'C' Class cats told him that a skilled helmsman could 'fly a hull' for just as long as he wished in a suitable wind, and he did not see why the same thing should not apply in the case of *Crossbow*. The sails were to be trimmed by a multi-part purchase with three ends giving respectively 3:1, 8:1 and 16:1 advantage. The crew would haul in the slack of the sails with the 3:1 purchase, then harden them down with the 8:1 and finally the 16:1 while the helmsman had the bitter end to hand so that he could release it in emergency. As well as trimming the sheets the crew were supposed to provide live ballast by moving their weight up and down the outrigger as necessary.

By May the various parts were ready and *Crossbow* was assembled for the first time on Brightlingsea hard. The completed boat was then rolled down to the water on air rollers with help from a crowd of interested spectators and towed carefully out to a mooring. Perhaps fortunately the wind was light on this first day of trials. A motor-boat towed *Crossbow* out of the narrow confines of the river into the broad acres of the Blackwater Estuary where the main was hoisted and the jib unrolled for the first time. As the crew sheeted in, Colman felt that the boat was hardly moving – certainly there was no impression of speed. Then he glanced down at the speedometer and was astonished to see it reading 12 knots! Already she was sailing faster than most keelboats ever manage without seeming to move at all! The next thing that happened was that the slight noise of contact with water was lost and Colman realized that he was airborne. Assailed by a moment of sudden panic, he let go of the mainsheet which brought the 'pod' back down onto the water with an undignified smack. 'Why did you do that?' Roderick reproved him. 'It's supposed to run clear of the water, you know.'

This remark nearly led to disaster because it made Colman feel that he should be braver in handling the sheets in future. The following weekend therefore, when *Crossbow* was roaring up the river with a fresh breeze, he felt positively reluctant to let go of the sheet even when the outrigger was flying through the air at some 20 knots. When he eventually did let go it was almost too late: higher and higher he soared as if trapped in some piece of berserk fairground machinery. The crew either slithered down the trampoline to the main hull or clung to the webbing like human flies. Eventually the boat came to a standstill with the rig more or less flat on the water and the helmsman feeling both vulnerable and foolish, hanging on precariously, 27ft (8·2m) up in the air. Fortunately for all, having served up a sharp reminder that she was not to be trifled with, *Crossbow* relented and after a few teetering seconds, fell back right side up. On a subsequent trial she almost went over the other way; the outrigger filled and sank taking the skipper with it, so that only his hat remained in view. Far from leaping to the rescue, Roderick and Reg were rendered helpless with laughter at this Keaton-like performance.

Colman always says that one of the most remarkable things about this boat was how much of it was right first time, a major tribute to its designer. He obviously expected that there would be 'teething troubles'. After a few trial sails it became obvious that there was one serious fault – the 'pod'. Interestingly enough, it proved *Crossbow*'s most enduring problem; every year that she sailed there was some kind of change made either to the windward hull itself or its 'under-carriage'.

First it was too small. The multipart mainsheet proved completely impractical: even with the 16:1 purchase they could not budge it an inch when *Crossbow* was sailing hard and friction from numerous blocks made it impossible to let out any quantity in a hurry. A winch was obviously needed and a powerful one at that. With the sheets being controlled by winches, the crew would also be needed to sit or kneel on the windward hull and it was clearly too small to accommodate them. From his steering position in the stern, Colman could not see if people sat in front of him and when the hull 'splashed down' the after part was drenched with spray. Perhaps most important, when the little hull touched the water it immediately created a large amount of drag, being so short and chubby compared to the main hull. The idea of dragging something like a slimmed down eight-foot rowing dinghy through the water at 25 knots with four people sitting in it was clearly ludicrous. Elegant though it was, 'the pod' simply had to go.

Macalpine-Downie could quite easily draw a new and improved pod but with the date of the Speed Trials now growing alarmingly close, there was no time to build a new one. It was therefore agreed to use the hull of a Shark catamaran which Sail Craft could supply 'off the shelf'. Although this tended to spoil the appearance of *Crossbow*, because it had quite a different profile, at least it ran through the water a lot easier. The main shrouds came down to bridles which were set up so that the windward hull would always run with somewhat bow-up trim and it is safe to say that this was the fastest 18ft (5·4m) sailing boat of all time.

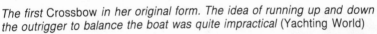

*The first* Crossbow *in her original form. The idea of running up and down the outrigger to balance the boat was quite impractical* (Yachting World)

The problem of visibility remained because there was still sufficient room for the helmsman only at the extreme stern of the hull.

If Timothy Colman thought that he was going to have two weeks of jolly sailing at Weymouth without too much to worry about before or afterwards then he was much mistaken. As the date for the trials drew nearer, the logistical problems of campaigning *Crossbow* began to loom larger and larger, until they seemed to assume the proportions of a full-scale military operation. Actually, Colman was in his element here whether arranging transportation of a 60ft (18·2m) load or charming the local boating fraternity to help with its reassembly on the sea-front at Weymouth. Eventually it seemed as if the whole of East Anglia was buzzing with *Crossbow*, *Crossbow*, *Crossbow* by the time October arrived.

It was on her first appearance at Portland that *Crossbow* and her team made their greatest effect. It is worth remembering that at the time of the first Speed Week there were still plenty of people around who thought that a Flying Dutchman would win, or alternatively that a standard Tornado cat would win because they had been timed (it was said) at 25 knots, or that the hydrofoil boats would easily beat any kind of conventional boat.

When competitors, officials and the Press actually arrived at Portland they were fairly amazed to see this very large and very strange-looking boat, beautifully painted in royal blue with the name perfectly lettered on each quarter and with the initials of two Royal yacht clubs (RNSYC, RNSA) on the transom. Her people were fairly impressive too. Apart from the actual crew with their royal blue Guernseys embroidered in red with the name *Crossbow* there was a long standing friend of Tim Colman's family, Percy Spurgeon, originally a paid hand in his uncle's yacht *Wishbone* in the thirties, and friends and helpers aboard the fishing boat *Amigo* chartered with memorable owner Ron Hill. Not least impressive was 'the skipper' himself striding around the diminutive Castle Cove Sailing Club in yachting cap and yellow sailing boats, or rushing from Weymouth to Portland in a large BMW in search of some vital spare part. It was certainly enough to give other competitors something of an inferiority complex as they assembled more modest craft on the tiny and inconvenient sandy beach in front of the club. In one way or another, it was immediately clear that *Crossbow* was in a class of her own.

In the trials at Brightlingsea, the crew had worked out a routine for sailing *Crossbow*. In such a boat one cannot simply push off from the beach and go sailing. Prior to making a run, *Crossbow* would be moored

*The first 'sidecar' was too small. This picture shows the second one with Tim Colman steering with difficulty from the stern with his view completely blocked by Roderick Macalpine-Downie* (Yachting World)

to the stern of *Amigo* which in turn would anchor in a suitable spot from which to release. The mainsail would then be hoisted and sheets freed well off. Colman used the dory to keep in touch with the Committee boat, and after requesting a run would wait until the course was clear and the timing boats in position on appropriate channels. In later years a walkie-talkie radio made life easier. The boat would then be allowed to hang back from *Amigo* on a long tow line that ended in a bridle arrangement whose purpose was to make the boat lie about 45 degrees off the wind. When everything was ready, the jib was unrolled and as soon as it began to fill, Colman gave the order to slip the mooring line.

As the boat bore off and gathered way, the crew would be winding furiously on the two Lewmar winches to bring in the main and jib sheets, the aim being to accelerate smoothly until the sails were fully sheeted and the weather hull skimming the waves. Colman would encourage his crew by giving a running commentary so that they would know without looking round when they entered the course and how fast they were going. As soon as they had passed the second timing gate, sheets were eased, the jib rolled up and main dropped. After that it was simply a question of waiting for the *Amigo* to come chugging round the course at a stately 7 knots and take them in tow again. At a speed of around 25 knots, which was typical for the first year, *Crossbow* took only 40 seconds to cross the course and her whole run from slipping the mooring to easing the sheets was little more than a minute. Yet from finishing one run to being ready to start another took at least one hour! This meant she could only make a maximum of six runs a day and, as a week's sailing normally only gave two or three days of good wind, one can see that her chances of finding perfect conditions were severely limited.

They also found that the little 'Shark' hull was far from satisfactory as a weather hull. Because the weight of four men would practically sink it, it was still necessary for the crew to keep off while the boat was gathering way and they then had to clamber up the trampoline to their winching positions as she started to lift. Colman still had a very poor view and still got immersed with spray when the hull was touching the water. If the weather hull touched down heavily during a run, the drag was so horrible that it immediately removed any chance of it being a good run. For the time being, however, they were stuck with it.

For the first three days of the week, winds were around ten knots only and from the east, the worst direction for Portland Harbour. *Crossbow* made run after run at speeds around 18 knots mainly to allow the crew to get the feel of the boat. Then, on the fourth day the wind blew over 20 knots and the mast fell down. Not a single wire or fitting broke, the spar itself simply folded up. Because of the very good angle of the shrouds, it had not been thought necessary to fit any struts or spreaders to the mast. However, as the top panel of the mast was unstayed the spar showed the tendency, well known to all dinghy sailors, for the top-mast to bend away to leeward and the lower part to bend correspondingly to windward. Because of the rotated section, the inner forestay was also supposed to act as a lee shroud; but not well enough as it turned out. The failure resulted mainly from the tricky geometry rather than an over-light section, but having now seen this fold up like a child's drinking straw, it was thought prudent to go for a heavier one. As soon as he could get ashore, Macalpine-Downie went straight to the nearest telephone and called Doug Beach at Sail Spar with a request to send down a new mast of heavier section. This possibility had been foreseen and suitable lengths of aluminium alloy section were being kept on one side at Sail Spar. However, they were completely 'bare' pieces of tube not in any way made up into a mast and not even joined together into a single length.

The Sail Spar people loaded up a van with the pieces of section plus a big pile of tools and fittings and set off for Weymouth 200 miles away. Meanwhile, *Crossbow* had been hauled out onto Weymouth beach and her crew were hard at work on the promenade stripping the fittings off the broken spar. Luckily the mast was pretty simple and the job of building up a new one not all that complex. After working through the night it was finished the following day and the boat was re-launched and ready by the evening.

Ironically, the day that *Crossbow* spent ashore produced the strongest wind of the week. While she was confined to the beach, her competitors did their utmost to take advantage of the chance to grab her position as fastest boat so far. However, the hydrofoil-equipped Tornado *Icarus*, which was the only boat with any chance of threatening her, tried a little too hard and ripped off one of her transoms putting her back on the beach as well.

The following day, *Crossbow* was back in contention. There was still wind, around 20 knots, though not as much as on the day she missed. The new mast looked good and the crew felt more confident in their handling of the boat. They were soon rewarded by a run of 24·4 knots and then another of 26·3. That was the end of the wind and of the first year's sailing. In some ways it had been a disappointment: they had not achieved the hoped-for 30 knots and they had discovered that *Crossbow* had severe limitations in the number of runs she could make in a given period of time. On the other hand they had recorded a speed of 26·3 knots which won them the John Player Trophy and prize by a substantial margin and established an irrefutable World Record.

The winter of 1972 gave the opportunity for some rethinking. The most important thing to be changed was the windward hull and Macalpine-Downie designed one to be built by Norfolk Broads boatbuilders, Eastwood Whelpton Ltd. Tim Whelpton was another Dragon sailor, a long standing friend of Colman's, and keenly interested in the *Crossbow* project. For 1973 he not only built an immaculate new hull but also joined the crew, replacing Tom Hall who pulled out because of pressure of work. Whelpton was welcome as a crew member not only for his expertise as a sailor and boatbuilder, but also because of his very considerable physical strength – he was alleged to be one of the strongest men in Norfolk and a great asset as a winch-winder. There was another change when Nigel Agar, a Norfolk farmer, replaced Reg White who was so busy with his own sailing programme that he hardly had time to devote to *Crossbow*.

The new windward hull was 24ft (7·3m) long and, much to Macalpine-Downie's satisfaction, matched the main hull in appearance. The 'skipper' now got a forward cockpit and a steering wheel instead of pedals. There were also three 'fox-holes' aft wherein the three winch men and the tailer could stand. This was not only more comfortable but reduced their air-drag. The system now was that the man furthest aft

*The larger sidecar allowed Colman to sit forward with the winch-winders standing behind him in 'fox-holes'* (Yachting World)

handled the jib-sheet on his own while the much more powerful main employed both a winder and a tailer.

There were also new sails, by Austin 'Clarence' Farrar, the man who had made the famous wing mast for Macalpine-Downie's 'C' Class catamaran *Lady Helmsman*, and was regarded as the leading expert in sails for large multihulls. It was decided to move the whole rig aft one foot and at the same time take some sail area off the jib and put it into the new mainsail. The boom was shortened and the mast height raised by five feet from 55 to 60ft (16·7–18·2m) giving a worthwhile improvement in aspect ratio.

Although the considerably longer outrigger hull was expected to be a big improvement in terms of reduced running resistance at high speeds, Macalpine-Downie also considered ways to keep it out of the water entirely. He had seen the way that hydrofoils had been effectively used by other boats the previous year and therefore decided to use one as an 'anti-splash-down' feature. A diamond shaped foil was made up and fitted to the underside of the small hull. The idea was that as soon as *Crossbow* was running at a respectable speed the foil would provide lift and go on doing so until it came entirely clear of the water.

In practice, this was only partly successful. The foil did provide lift while the boat was accelerating and would help to keep the windward hull just clear of the water but if it flew high and then dropped suddenly, the foil lacked the power to prevent a 'splash-down' and also threw a lot of spray in its original version.

The last but not least of the changes was the cutting of five feet of length off the stern of the main hull. Macalpine-Downie considered that the boat was not reaching anything like her maximum hull speed and that she was carrying unnecessary weight and skin friction drag penalties, so a saw was taken to the stern. The amputated piece now has an honoured position in the bar of the Royal Norfolk and Suffolk Yacht Club.

# 1973 Speed Week

There were only two days of good wind in 1973 Speed Week and on the second of these in a breeze which only just reached 20 knots, *Crossbow* achieved a speed of 29·3 knots, the best speed achieved by anyone that year and a new World Record. The boat was clearly much improved and the main feeling at the end of the week was one of frustration at not being able to see what she could really achieve.

All of the *Crossbow* team felt that the 1973 campaign had been a bit of a let down. They still held the World Record to be sure, but the elusive 30 knots still seemed to be some way off. More sailing in stronger winds was what *Crossbow* needed and so it was decided, instead of laying her up, to position her at Grafham Water, near Huntingdon, one of the largest reservoirs in England. Unlike Weymouth, it was within reasonably easy reach of both Norwich and London and as there was a sailing club there were facilities such as launching ramps and changing rooms.

The plan was to position *Crossbow* at Grafham and leave her ready rigged and as nearly as possible in a 'go' condition. Then, when really strong winds were forecast, the crew could be contacted by telephone and rush off to Grafham at a moment's notice. Of course, it was not only the crew who had to rush to Grafham, but also a locally recruited team of timers. A surveyor had been called in to set up two alternative 500m courses 20 degrees apart on an approximate south-east–north-west line so that the boat would be able to sail at right angles to the hoped-for south-westerly gale. The distance was marked by transit posts stuck in the ground. *Crossbow* was taken straight to Grafham from Weymouth with the intention of leaving her there until Christmas.

In the event, despite magnificent help from an enthusiastic team of helpers at Grafham, the plan was as great a disappointment as the rest of 1973. 'Operation Grafham' went into action only three times; the last occasion being in a full gale in December. During this last exercise, they had some spectacular bursts of speed during which *Crossbow* probably sailed as fast as she has ever done but it proved impossible to get a good, steady run over the course. Although Grafham is pretty open and

*Crossbow*'s rig is pretty high, they soon discovered that wind coming over the land is never anything like as steady as a sea wind. The gale came rolling and tumbling across the countryside and *Crossbow* alternately leaped and plunged as the gusts hit her. Furthermore, the wind direction was never quite right for the fixed transits so that either the boat had to take a less than ideal angle or sail further than 500m. Lastly, the crew, who had all dropped their work and driven like demons to Grafham, were never really in the right frame of mind to get the best out of the boat, and they were not able to work together properly as a team on these hastily arranged occasions. Also, of course, it was damned cold! After the third try when the speeds had not exceeded her Weymouth best, Colman decided, without opposition, to pack the boat up for the year.

# *1974 season*

*Crossbow* did not come out in 1974 as Colman felt the team had devoted enough time to the project for the time being and a mere repeat of earlier years ran the risk of failing to meet the second objective, 'it had to be fun'. In her absence, the best performance at Speed Week was that of another Macalpine-Downie design, the 70ft (21·3m) catamaran *British Oxygen*. *BO*, however, was designed as an offshore racer, not a record breaker, and her speed of 24·26 knots fell some way short of the record.

# *1975 season*

1975 was *Crossbow*'s final fling. Indeed she only really owed her continued existence to the fact that everyone concerned felt that she must be given a fair chance to pass the magic figure of 30 knots. The conditions under which she was likely to be able to do this were in fact incredibly narrow. To raise her previous best speed she would need at least 25 knots of wind, yet it was generally felt that it would be impractical to handle the boat in much over 30 knots due principally to the buffeting the rig received while being towed back between runs. So here they were with a boat so specialized that it could only sail on one tack, in smooth water, and only wanted to sail in a wind between 25 and 30 knots! The remarkable fact is that these conditions did in fact materialize!

The only significant technical change to the boat had been the replacement of the hydrofoil (which had been knocked off in a 'splash-down' and now resides at the bottom of Grafham Water) by a metal plate which the designer described as the 'planing shoe'. With the benefit of hindsight, it might have been more sensible to have designed the outrigger hull as a planing boat in the first place, although this could have led to problems at low speed; but since it had not been, efforts were concentrated on making its repeated high-speed take-offs and touchdowns as trouble-free as possible. With the new 'shoe' in place the outrigger would tear sheets of spray from the surface but it did at least stay up high and bounce from wave to wave instead of ploughing in.

Tuesday, 30th September was *Crossbow*'s great day. In a breeze of approximately 25 knots she recorded a run of 31·09 knots. The 'barrier' was broken and *Crossbow*'s was a happy team.

There followed what turned out, with hindsight, to have been an error. The Committee, perhaps encouraged by the sponsors who were keen for some good publicity, decided to ratify the new World Record immediately. In the meantime Colman had to leave Weymouth to attend to some urgent business after agreeing that Macalpine-Downie would sail the boat in the unlikely event of stronger wind.

As it turned out, Thursday, 2nd October did produce more wind so Macalpine-Downie immediately arranged to sail. In a breeze somewhere between 25 and 30 knots he recorded a speed of 31·24 knots – *Crossbow*'s best ever – but this did not exceed the record set two days previously by the required 2 per cent and thus could not be claimed as a further record. If only the Committee had not been in such a hurry to ratify the first record, then the higher speed could have been registered.

This last occasion was one that I remember well because it was the only time I ever saw *Crossbow* looking pressed. Over the years one had grown used to seeing this large boat cruising gracefully across Portland

Crossbow I *at high speed* (Yachting World)

Harbour at what always appeared to be a rather gentle pace. Because of her great length she gave very little impression of speed. This time, however, she was really working. Her lean, knife-like bow bore down on the water and threw the chop of Portland Harbour angrily away. From her transom a white, 'U' shaped groove ran straight back for about 200ft (60·9m) while the little outrigger bounced crazily from wave-top to wave-top leaving a big white splash to mark every impact. This was *Crossbow*'s last run – she had shot her bolt and was thereafter consigned to an honourable retirement in a shed at Whelpton's Boatyard in Norfolk. Although it had proved much harder than expected, she had fulfilled her design objective: that of sailing at 30 knots. The extraordinary thing is that her entire sailing career consisted of no more than two hours of actual sailing time.

# *Crossbow II*

Timothy Colman describes the decision to build again as 'inevitable'. As we have seen, campaigning *Crossbow I* consisted of a very small amount of sailing and a very great deal of sitting and waiting. These long pauses gave ample opportunity to think of all the possible improvements that could be made. After three years of this, Macalpine-Downie's notebook was not so much bulging as exploding with ideas waiting for a chance to be tried.

The first decision to be taken was absolutely crucial: whether to go for another 'one-way' boat or not. Everyone agreed that in theory a one-way only boat should be faster but their experience had been that practice and evaluation – all the things that come under the heading of tuning – was vital and that the extreme difficulty of building up sailing time with *Crossbow I* had been crippling. It was therefore decided from the outset that the new boat must be capable of sailing on either tack.

Colman decided the requirement for the new boat very simply: it should be capable of raising the World Record to 40 knots. It was agreed that in general terms the improvements would come from:

1. better power/weight ratio;
2. greater righting moment;
3. more efficient rig and better sails;
4. better sheeting/winching/sail-handling arrangements; and
5. less critical transverse stability.

After agreeing these headings it was up to Macalpine-Downie to come up with a practical design that embodied them. He was still very troubled by the symmetric/asymmetric question. Clearly, one could expect to go faster in a boat in which the main weights were disposed on one side and in which the rig was designed for one particular wind direction. In a boat designed to sail *equally well* on either tack it is necessary to have everything disposed symmetrically or else have some kind of variable geometry arrangement. If on the other hand you decide that you only want to sail *well* on one tack and that it is sufficient to be able to sail *slowly* on the other tack, then things become a little easier.

From this beginning, and with typical originality, Macalpine-Downie started to design a boat that would be partly symmetrical and partly not; able to sail on both tacks but only designed to sail fast on one.

An early decision was to go for another 'displacement' boat. Although he was quite tempted to plunge into the new area of hydrofoils he observed from the 'state of the art' shown by other Speed Week competitors that there were still many unknowns in this field and that it would be very difficult to come up with something with a good chance of success without a lengthy period of development, which is why they had rejected the idea of foils originally for *Crossbow I*. Long, thin hulls still seemed to offer the best chance for the time being. This narrowed the choice to a catamaran or trimaran and in the context of high-speed sailing the latter seems to be merely a proa with a superfluous extra hull, like *Slingshot*. However, with a catamaran the rig presents big difficulties. If, as in *British Oxygen*, one elects to have a single tall mast in the middle of the boat, there are terrific engineering problems, with attendant weight and cost, involved in making the cross-beam structure strong enough to have the mast stepped on it.

How about having two masts, one in each hull? This is an attractive solution which has been tried a number of times but there is a fatal flaw. When sailing to windward (which high speed boats in effect always do) one rig interferes with the airflow to the other. This was an effect well known in aircraft circles in the days of bi-planes and known as 'inter-plane interference'. But they found a way round it, didn't they? High performance biplanes nearly always had 'staggered' wings, that is to say one ahead of the other. Now, if one had staggered masts in a normal catamaran, one would be rather far forward in its hull and the other rather far aft which would lead to an odd weight distribution and other difficulties. But how about having the masts in the normal position and staggered hulls? This solution, which as far as I know is unique, is the one adopted for *Crossbow II*. The two hulls and rigs are similar but the lee hull runs 13ft (3·9m) ahead of the windward one and both sails receive 'clean air'.

Once the rig has been split into two it becomes possible to achieve an increase in sail area while at the same time reducing the height of the masts, lowering the centre of effort and increasing the aspect ratio. For the new design Macalpine-Downie specified a sail area of 1,300 sq ft which could be achieved with two masts of 56ft (17m), a substantial increase of area compared to *Crossbow I*. In rigging the two masts, he followed the well known bi-plane system of cross-struts and diagonal wire braces by which it is possible to achieve a remarkably rigid, box-like structure. A great advantage is that it is not necessary to have any rigging on the windward side of the windward mast or the lee side of the leeward mast because all forces are resolved in the gap between the two masts. Thus it was possible to use the full width of the boat by having the masts stepped at the point of maximum beam. It was decided to dispense with foresails which it was felt added more complexity than speed.

A problem inherent in any large Bermudian sail is the high forces required at the clew in order to hold the sail in the correct shape for windward sailing in high apparent wind-speeds. With *Crossbow I*, in spite of her multi-part mainsheet and Lewmar winches, they were never able to get the sails sheeted in as hard as they should have been and they never achieved the desirable situation of being able to recover the sheet quickly after being compelled to ease it out to avoid a capsize. This led Macalpine-Downie to consider something like a wishbone rig in which the clew is extended all the time and the sheet serves to turn the whole sail like opening or closing a door. Wishbones, as the name implies, are curved so as to accommodate the curvature of the sail, but a wishbone strong enough to contain the clew forces on *Crossbow II* (estimated at 2 tons) would be horribly heavy. However, accepting, for the second time, that the boat needed to sail only slowly on port tack, he devised what he called 'wish-booms' which were straight spars on the windward side of the sail only. These were so angled that there is more tension on the leech than foot and there were topping-lifts to limit this. Powerful tackles on the ends of these wish-booms were used to heave the sails out to the required position before starting to sheet in. Of course the wish-booms produced a heavy thrust on the masts which had to be contained by another pair of struts and wires. In fact the rig was beginning to look a bit like Clacton pier although Macalpine-Downie states that there is less wire per square foot of sail area than on *Crossbow I* and furthermore that a lot of the strutting is in the plane of the apparent wind and so adds little significant drag.

Having thus produced a rig in which the sails needed only to be swung towards the centre-line in order to sheet them, the next object was to make it do this as quickly as possible. The first step was to link the two rigs together so that they were finally all controlled by one line and then to connect this one line to a very powerful winching system. For this, Lewmar were called in because of their great experience of linked winch systems for offshore racing yachts. They came up with a system in which three handles turned one drum. Macalpine-Downie would have preferred a pedalled system but this would have involved a major development programme in itself. The winching system was built into the boat in such a way that three people could stand well-braced in individual fox-holes each winding furiously on their individual handle. A fourth man 'tails' the winch from the aft end of the windward hull and effectively controls the amount of power being taken from the rig. He is in voice-pipe communication with the helmsman who occupies the foremost fox-hole some 25ft (7·6m) away.

The hulls were again to be 60ft (18·2m) long and basically semi-circular in under-water section. They have rather more bow overhang than *Crossbow I* and are a bit fuller aft. In order to raise the cross-beams, and crew, a respectable height above the water, there is a kind of raised superstructure above the sheer-line. Although the two hulls are similar, only the starboard one is fitted with cockpits, sail-handling and steering gear, and hence is considerably heavier than the port one. The helmsman sits well forward steering with twin, underdeck tillers.

A surprising conclusion about *Crossbow I* was that she was 'too strong and too heavy'. With the new boat, this was to be remedied by reducing the skin thickness to an alarming-sounding 6mm before fairing – and without timbers of any sort. Taken as a whole, the design was a typically bold and imaginative piece of work by Macalpine-Downie. She was still conventional in that she was to be a displacement boat driven by cloth sails, but at the same time bristling with new ideas and new solutions to old problems.

A somewhat different team undertook the building. The hulls were entrusted to Randall Leavitt, a solitary wood-working genius who operates, in the traditional English manner, from a ramshackle wooden shed behind his home in Tollesbury, Essex. Leavitt had built several immaculate prototypes for Macalpine-Downie but *Crossbow II* was by far the biggest job he had ever tackled. It also so happened that 1976 was the hottest summer in British history, so poor Leavitt found himself working through sweltering days followed by hardly-less sweltering nights in order to complete the two hulls in time for the 1976 Speed Week. In spite of these difficulties, the final result was an absolute miracle of light-weight wood construction: so thin yet so fair and smooth. As soon as the hulls could be prised out of Leavitt's shed, the *Crossbow* team were waiting with a trailer which had been specially constructed to transport the whole of *Crossbow II* behind a Range Rover. The hulls were rushed to Norfolk where Tim Whelpton was waiting to complete and fit out the whole boat. Meanwhile, International Yacht Equipment of Southend were at work on the spars and equipment while 'Clarence' Farrar was labouring over a hot sewing-machine at Martlesham.

Because of the high cost of these very big sails, it was agreed that Farrar would initially make up just one and then wait until it could be hoisted on the boat and checked before proceeding with the second sail. This turned out to have been a sound decision because when the first sail was hoisted it was found that the 'droopy' foot pulled upwards and produced an excessive fullness in the lower part of the sail. This fault was then designed out of the second sail and the first one was re-cut to match it.

The trouble was, *Crossbow II* was getting seriously late. It was not until 17th September that she was assembled for the first time at Upton and 'Clarence' got his chance to hoist the first sail the following day. It had been hoped to have sea-trials at Lowestoft in early September but now it was simply a question of whether or not the boat would get to Portland in time for Speed Week beginning on the 25th. Farrar and his men worked shifts to complete the second sail. When a dinghy sail can be made in a day, a week sounds a reasonable time but it has to be borne in mind that these sails were made from a special $11\frac{3}{4}$ ounce narrow-woven Terylene that took some handling at the best of times. Each sail had 130m of seaming, each seam being triple-sewn.

At the same time as Farrar was tatting away like the Tailor of Gloucester's mice, Tim Whelpton and his men were working like demons to complete the fitting out and rigging. To a well-organized man like Tim Colman, it was all rather frustrating.

When Whelpton and Agar finally arrived at Portland after twelve hours of driving at a steady 30 mph (the trailer begins to snake at 31 mph) they were greeted by strong winds and bucketing rain – hardly the best conditions for setting up a new boat. The strongest wind of the week blew on the first day, Saturday 25th, but they simply were not ready to sail. On Sunday *Crossbow II* was under way for the first time and a number of problems became apparent. There were various quite minor problems with the rig which could be either overcome or tolerated but the serious difficulty was lack of steering at speed.

*Crossbow II* was built with conventional skeg rudders aft in each hull. When the weather hull lifted, its rudder, which was only intended for low speed, was naturally waving around uselessly in the air and the lee rudder apparently lacked the power to give the helmsman control. For this reason her runs were a bit of a gamble and on several occasions were 'aborted' when the boat failed to exit through the correct gate. Colman was not too happy with this as he had visions of losing control and colliding at high speed with a timing or spectator boat. Apparently there was a problem in setting the two rigs to drive equally – even with improved sails a two inch adjustment of tack tension alters helm balance by the maximum amount that can be controlled.

Another worrying and rather unexpected problem was that the weather hull seemed to leap up and down a lot. This had always been a *Crossbow I* problem but it had been hoped that *Crossbow II*'s much bigger and heavier windward hull would be steadier and that it would prove possible to hold it in the ideal position just skimming the waves, instead of which she was leaping and plunging just like the old boat.

In spite of all these difficulties, there was plenty of speed potential. Everyone felt that she would easily better the old boat's best performance and she confirmed this on the Wednesday when, in a wind that was barely touching 20 knots, she was timed at 31·8 knots, a new World Record.

By *Crossbow* standards, 1976 had been a bit of a shambles with a completely untested boat thrown together at the last moment. However, Colman had announced that he hoped to reach the boat's potential in a two year campaign and so was prepared to make a maximum effort for the second year. As Colman seemed to be perfectly serious about giving up after 1977, Macalpine-Downie went home with plenty of food for thought.

To solve the steering problem he proposed to fit a bow rudder in the lee hull. It seemed as if the aft rudder was running in disturbed water and that there was insufficient separation between it and the dagger-board, so it made no sense to increase it in size and in any case there could be strength problems. As an interesting sideline, it is worth noting that the original drawings of *Crossbow II* showed air rudders mounted forward of the masts. These were abandoned as being risky in the short time available but it would have been interesting to see if they worked.

When 1977 Speed Week arrived, it was a very different *Crossbow II* that was launched at HMS *Osprey*. Well organized and fully ready in every respect, she looked hungry for speed. Preliminary runs were promising to say the least. On 2nd October, in only 10 knots of wind, she reached 23·7 knots – more than twice the wind speed. Steering was no longer a problem and a new planing shoe seemed to be doing useful work. The following day there was a modest increase of wind: *Crossbow* ran three times and recorded a best speed of 29·4 knots. The crew were getting the rig nicely sorted out and the boat was obviously nowhere near her potential.

The 4th of October was her day of triumph and disaster: a typical warm-sector day with a grey sky and a solid 20 knots of breeze pouring steadily over the Chesil bank onto Portland Harbour. Reluctant to be

*Crossbow II at speed. Although an apparently complex boat she set more sail lower down than her predecessor and was much easier to handle* (Yachting World)

drawn on any forecast of speed, Colman had nevertheless announced that he hoped to reach 35 knots – would this be the day? The first two runs were exactly the same: 31·3 knots. During the third run there was a lull and she only managed 29·4. For the fourth run of the day, the wind had risen to 24 knots and she flashed across the course at 33·8 knots looking perfectly under control and with plenty in hand. As she eased sheets and luffed up to stop it was apparent that something was wrong: her port hull was settling in the water. She was immediately taken in tow by her regular nanny-boat, ably handled by Arthur Meech, and towed slowly towards the beach in a sinking condition.

When she was hauled out of the water it was found that she had an eight inch hole on the starboard side of the port hull; whether from hitting a piece of flotsam or simply from excessive water pressure was not known. It was not at all difficult to repair but it turned out to be irrelevant because the wind was finished for the week.

*Crossbow II* had made only ten runs in her 1977 form and set a new World Record on her tenth. Colman had said that he wanted to give the new boat two years and now he was once again under pressure from the team to change his mind and give the boat another chance. It was obvious she had more to come and Macalpine-Downie was still dissatisfied with the amount of up-and-down movement by the windward hull. In her first year she had leapt and plunged just like the first boat. The fitting of a planing surface under the windward hull had converted the plunging into smacking, but what he could not understand was why the windward hull could not be held at a steady height in the way that he had done years before in the 'C' Class cats. Even the most hopeless of Hobiecat helmsmen can master this trick, so why couldn't they manage it in the much bigger boat which ought, one would think, to be steadier rather than livelier?

In an effort to solve this problem, Macalpine-Downie made a detailed examination of films and photographs of *Crossbow* sailing, in an effort to see what was going on. Eventually he came to the conclusion that the sails were at fault. When they were fully sheeted and the boat accelerated, they would begin to stretch into a fuller shape. More fullness meant more drag and heeling force so up would go the windward hull. When the hull leaped up, the crew would be forced to ease sheets and as soon as they did this the sails sprang back into their original flatter curve, the abrupt drop in drag consequently dumping the hull heavily back into the water. In other words there was an unstable relationship between wind strength and heeling force. Of course, this is hardly a new problem: the whole thrust of what sailmakers and sparmakers have tried to achieve during the last twenty years is a rig combination that automatically flattens off in gusts and returns to a full shape in lulls. The sad fact was that *Crossbow II*'s rig seemed to be achieving the exact opposite.

Unfortunately the reasons seemed to be very closely tied up with Austin Farrar's philosophy of sailmaking. He had always maintained that for sails subjected to such enormous stress as *Crossbow*'s, it would be impossible to rely on a 'stiff' cloth and sails which had the shape permanently built in. In an article for *Yachting World* published in June, 1977 he put this quite clearly:

> However with sails as large as *Crossbow*'s – her two identical mainsails are each 650 square feet – the wind force is so great that nothing short of plywood would hold a shape on its own and we have to rely on stretching the material to pull the shape into the sails where it is required.

The trouble with this method was that it necessarily implied using a fairly elastic cloth. In the same article, Farrar pointed out that a hard-finish cloth in the same weight would be practically like metal and impossible to handle either in the loft or on the boat. So *Crossbow II* had soft cloth sails that stretched in high winds and caused the instability problem. However, this business of producing stable sails for big boats was not confined to Austin Farrar and *Crossbow*. On the other side of the Atlantic, the leading cloth-makers and sailmakers were pouring numerous thousands of dollars into research in the battle for the America's Cup. Furthermore the 12-metre is one of the few boats whose experience could be of much value to *Crossbow*. Both Hood and North had been working on entirely new constructions of sailcloth for the 1977 defence of the America's Cup. One of these was an amazingly ingenious cloth which, in addition to the normal warp and weft threads lying at right-angles to each other had a third direction of threads at 45 degrees. More practical, however, was the new breed of 'two-ply' cloths: basically two layers of cloth on top of each other with or without interweaving or inter-sewing between them. This was before the second step was made to cloths laminated from one layer of cloth and one of non-woven plastics sheet such as Mylar.

After learning about this, Macalpine-Downie proposed that new sails be ordered from the English loft of North. This was not an easy decision to make: as well as being very expensive, the choice of North implied a lack of confidence in Farrar with whom he had worked for a number of years.

Speed Week 1978 was a flop: the wind never rose above 15 knots. This was doubly disappointing because the new sails seemed to be a real improvement and it seemed likely that the old 'leaping and plunging' problem had been licked at last. The boat was not only fast but stable and could be held with the weather hull running at a much more even height. She demonstrated her remarkable efficiency by running at a speed of 27·7 knots in a breeze of only 12 knots!

One of the reasons that Colman had agreed to bring the boat out for a third time was that at last there was a supposedly serious challenger in the form of *Slingshot* from the United States. However, in the winds available that year, this intriguing boat did not seem to be too sharp a threat as her best speed during the week was 21·16 knots. On the other hand, an American challenge to a British held World Speed Record was something that the national press could get their teeth into. The extrovert Carl Thomas, owner of *Slingshot*, seemed to quite enjoy this kind of thing but Colman found personal publicity distasteful in spite of being in the publishing business himself. Perhaps he felt that sailing was an area in which he could get away from publicity rather than create it. In any case, this seemed to be another reason to stick to his decision to make 1978 the final year.

This was not quite the end of the 1978 story however, for both Colman and Carl Thomas agreed to share the cost of keeping the course open for another few days in the hope of finding wind. After waiting for three more days they were rewarded with a wind strength of just over 20 knots. Crossbow made a run of 34·4 knots – her best to date but not a new record because it did not exceed the previous one by the required 2 per cent. *Slingshot* damaged her mast-step and never made a decent run. Carl Thomas left the boat at a local boat-yard and returned to America disappointed.

Although *Crossbow II* was clearly a better and faster boat in 1978 and only needed the right conditions to raise her own record substantially, this time Colman was adamant that he was not going to campaign her again for the time being. For one thing he had just been appointed Lord Lieutenant of Norfolk, which would place a further large demand on his time and for another his son had reached the age of wanting to be taken sailing – in a Mirror Dinghy, not *Crossbow*! He also felt that the whole team was in some danger of losing their enthusiasm for the competition and he for one had no intention of continuing just for the sake of it.

After returning from Portland, therefore, *Crossbow* was carefully washed down and put away in a barn, deep in the Norfolk countryside. However it seems as if the urge to have 'just one more go' is nearly

*This close-up of* Crossbow II *shows how three linked winch-handles drive one drum which controlled the entire rig via a single sheet. Note the planing 'shoe' under her windward hull* (Yachting World)

irresistible so it was no tremendous surprise that after missing out a year, it was announced that *Crossbow II* would be returning to Portland Harbour at the end of 1980.

Very little was done to the boat but Colman decided that it ought to be possible to improve her chances by changing the circumstances under which she sailed. He felt that the format of the 'Speed Week' was too restrictive because although the organizers would always give *Crossbow* priority, there was inevitably some delay as a result of sharing the harbour with a lot of other boats – some of which had their own legitimate claims on class records. He therefore proposed to wait till after Speed Week 1980 was over when he could have the Harbour to himself. He also decided to abandon using the circular 'offshore' course and concentrate on the inshore one along the Chesil Beach causeway. It was discovered that this course could be made considerably more flexible by setting up a series of transits at different angles so that the run did not have to be made parallel to the beach. Furthermore, it was found that one set of timers could view and time more than one transit at a time; thus times could be recorded for passages across both 'AA' and 'BB' transits on only one run.

The organizers of the Week were a bit miffed to find that Colman was apparently boycotting their event especially as a new timing system had virtually eliminated the queuing that had been so tiresome in earlier years. The weather gods seemed to take the same view because Speed Week 1980 enjoyed every possible strength and direction of wind after which the weather became sullenly quiet and cold. Nevertheless *Crossbow* was positioned at Portland Harbour, timing and observation teams arranged and then the whole team went on stand-by to await suitable weather.

They finally got strong winds in mid-November and on the 17th *Crossbow* made a series of runs in winds ranging from 25 to 30 knots. Her best recorded run was 36·0 knots which was subsequently ratified as a new World Record and has remained the undisputed Outright World Sailing Speed Record since.

It is obvious that the whole *Crossbow* team would dearly like to be the ones to finally crack the 40 knot barrier. Although 30 knots proved to be no real barrier, it does seem as if 40 knots will be a very hard nut to crack. For instance it is difficult to imagine progress beyond this speed with cloth sails and there may also be quite difficult problems with rudders and centre-boards. One's feeling is that the *Crossbow* team will want to go on trying to achieve the magic figure of 40 knots and then sit back in the knowledge that this would be a very hard record to break.

# 12
# What makes
# sailing boats fast?

If you want to learn *in detail* about the numerous factors that affect the
speed of yachts and the methods used to measure them, then it would be
wise to direct your attention to one of the excellent existing works on the
subject, such as those by Marchaj or Kay. Nothing I write can possibly
replace the work of real scientists who have studied the subject for years.
When reading such books it is, however, all too easy to get bogged down
in detail and lose sight of the main thrust of the arguments. What I
attempt to do here is describe *in the broadest possible terms* what makes a
sailing craft fast.

We can begin with a basic statement:

High power/weight ratio and low resistance = Speed
*Factors affecting power/weight ratio*
– weight
– sail area
– efficiency of sail plan
*Factors affecting resistance*
– weight
– smoothness
– form

## Examination of the factors: *resistance*

**Weight**  In any vessel that floats, the total weight of the vessel is exactly
equal to the weight of water that it displaces and so the all-up weight of a
ship is always referred to as *displacement*. In planing or hydrofoil craft,
some or all of the weight is supported by dynamic lift and therefore the
word *displacement* is no longer appropriate.

The nature of the vessel and the use to which it is to be put have a
critical effect on weight. A cargo vessel is only useful in terms of the

amount of cargo it can carry and is inherently incapable of being light. When considering the performance of merchant ships, we start by assuming that we are talking about carrying a lot of weight as efficiently as possible. The same applies to any vessel designed to carry some kind of payload: in the case of a warship, weapons, armour and stores; and in the case of a cruising yacht, living accommodation, stores and people. To achieve very light weight we therefore need a specialized vessel which is not required to carry anything other than her crew – minimum of one person for World Sailing Speed Record.

The vessel itself must be as light as possible and this can be achieved by good structural design and by using strong, lightweight materials. Because it calls for special materials, light construction is always expensive construction and this makes it attractive to keep the size of the vessel down. The ultimate in this direction would seem to be a very small sailboard, hardly more than a water-ski, made from a minimal amount of very strong materials. Another reason for keeping the structural weight of the vessel down is that the crew then forms a high proportion of all-up weight and is available as moveable ballast. Again the small sailboard in which the crew is at least ten times heavier than the craft would seem to be the ultimate.

Ballast (other than moveable ballast such as the crew) should be eliminated if possible because it only adds to the all-up weight. Fixed ballast is a poor way of achieving stability because it has no useful effect at all until the boat is heeled. This has been realized by the designers of small offshore racing boats who nowadays minimize ballast to that which is required to achieve self-righting. In a small boat such as a racing dinghy, the crew form a high proportion of the all-up weight and can add very usefully to stability by moving their weight to windward; but in a larger vessel, crew weight becomes less significant so other ways of stabilizing her have to be found (see Power).

**Smoothness** Only the bow of a boat and the leading edge of its keel and rudder really feel moving water against them. After a short distance, the water flow is slowed by friction with the hull and eventually a thin layer becomes attached to the hull and moves along with it. This is undesirable in itself because it adds to the displacement of the vessel but further down-stream the situation becomes worse because the attached layer of water gradually gets thicker and finally breaks down into turbulence. The turbulence uses up energy and is experienced as drag. It is obviously important to delay the onset of turbulence as long as possible and this is achieved by good hull shape and by hull surface smoothness. Marchaj

223

says that every imperfection of surface of more than 2 microns in height is significant and should be eliminated if possible in order to maintain laminar flow (smooth flow without turbulence between the hull and the moving water). Very conveniently, 2 microns is about the smallest imperfection that can be felt with the finger-tips.

**Form** For a displacement craft, the ideal section is a cylinder because a circle has the least wetted surface for a given volume. Waterline length is the most important dimension of a displacement hull because speed is limited to approximately the speed of movement of a wave of the same length as the waterline (Vmax = approx. $1 \cdot 5 \times 2\sqrt{WL}$). Fineness ratio is also very important because finer hulls make less pronounced waves. For a given displacement, the longer and slimmer the cylinder, the lower will be the resistance. In practical terms, a shape something like a rowing eight approaches the ideal, having a semi-circular underwater section, very gently tapered ends and a fineness ratio of around 1:25. However this shape has no stability and therefore cannot carry any sail.

Keelboats of all types are a compromise between low resistance and low ballast weight. You can have narrow beam and a lot of ballast or less ballast and more beam. Rating rules tend to obscure the clarity of this situation but it can always be boiled down to this basic compromise between ballast stability and form stability.

The cylinder hull-form can be given stability in other ways than by adding a ballast keel to it:

− Two (or more) hulls joined together by beams form a multihull whose stability is derived from the big separation between centre of buoyancy and centre of gravity when it heels.

− A long spar extended to windward and having at its end a weight (such as the crew) forms a flying proa. *Crossbow I* used this layout.

− Hydrofoils on the ends of spars can be used to provide stability.

**Form of non-displacement craft.** Planing demands a suitable hull shape which will always have more wetted surface than the ideal cylinder. Typically, it demands broad, flattened after sections and straight aft buttock lines, an angle of attack between the water-flow and the fore-body and a reasonable aspect ratio. Very long, slim hulls do not plane well because of their poor aspect ratio.

Hydrofoils which lift the boat out of the water can eliminate hull drag entirely but they have their own drag which depends on their efficiency and the amount of weight they are having to carry.

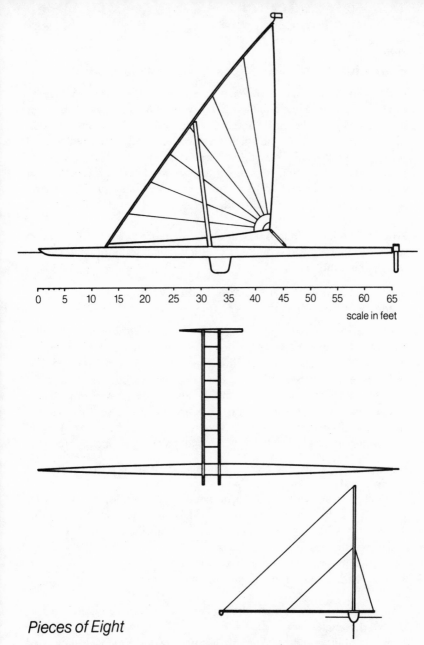

0    5    10    15    20    25    30    35    40    45    50    55    60    65

scale in feet

## Pieces of Eight

*The author published this sketch of a possible record-breaker when the World Sailing Speed Record was announced in* Yachting World. Pieces of Eight *was to have been based on a rowing-eight hull with an aluminium ladder as a cross-beam. The sail would have been a second-hand genoa set as a lateen rig.* Crossbow *was a better idea!*

225

# Examination of the factors: *power/weight ratio*

**Weight** When the size of a given boat is increased, sail area is increased by the square of linear dimensions but weight increases as the cube of them. Thus it is inherently more difficult to achieve high power/weight ratio in larger craft. In a displacement craft, length is needed both to achieve fine hulls and for seaworthiness and this inevitably brings weight with it. To escape from this situation, we would need a type of boat which does not depend on its length for speed. This could be either a planing craft or a flying hydrofoil.

**Power** The most obvious way of obtaining more power is to add more sail but usable sail area is limited by the amount of stability available. To increase stability:

– add ballast. But this also increases all-up weight.
– add beam. But this increases wetted surface.

Of the two, beam tends to be a more effective way of increasing stability. If not restricted by rules, the beam of boats tends to go on increasing until a scow form results. The scow can be fast but only if it is sailed heeled, otherwise there is too much wetted surface. It is more sensible to split the boat in the middle and create a catamaran.

Ballast is much more useful if it is movable and the best thing to use as movable ballast is the crew who have to be on board anyway. We can follow the course of a kind of 'arms race' of ballast movement as follows:

– work-boats with shingle or sand-bags which can be shifted to windward;
– small boats in which crew sit on windward gunwale;
– racing dinghy with crew sitting out vigorously beyond the gunwale;
– racing dinghy with crew on trapeze or sliding seat;
– catamaran;
– catamaran with crew on trapeze; and
– proa with crew on the end of long outrigger.

**Sail power** is only useful if the rig has a favourable aerodynamic drag angle (the angle between the lift developed by the sail plan and the resultant of lift and drag. The smaller this angle, the more close-winded the rig). Why? Imagine a vessel sailing directly down-wind in a wind force of 10 knots. After it has attained a speed of 5 knots, it will experience an apparent wind of only 5 knots. If boat speed rises to 6 knots, apparent wind falls to 4 knots and so on until there is insufficient power to push the boat along any faster. In a powerboat heading dead into wind, the opposite is true: boat speed is added to wind speed to find apparent wind, the wind that the boat actually feels. Now imagine a boat sailing on a square reach: as soon as it starts to move, its own forward speed modifies the wind speed and direction and a vector diagram shows that *the faster the boat sails, the more the apparent wind increases and comes ahead.* Eventually, the boat cannot sail any faster because the apparent wind is too far ahead. Therefore, only a close-winded boat can be a fast one.

**Sail efficiency** results from the following:

– shape as close as possible to the appropriate airfoil. A fully-battened sail set on a streamlined, rotating mast is good but an asymmetrical solid wing mast whose camber and twist can be controlled to suit different wind strengths would be considerably better;

– high aspect ratio. Efficiency of an airfoil is in direct proportion to its

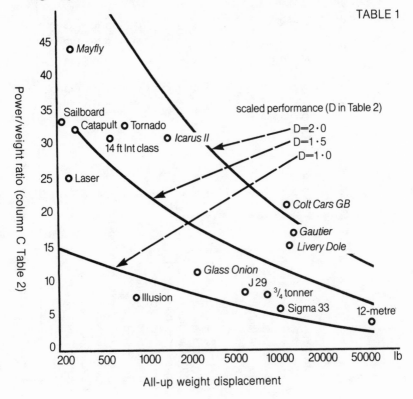

TABLE 1

TABLE 2

## Displacement and sail area ratios of various sailing craft

| Yacht (type) | No. of crew | Displ. (lb) (kg × 2·2) | $^3\sqrt{}$Displ. =(A) | Sail (sq ft) (sq m × 10·8) | $^2\sqrt{}$Sail =(B) | Sq ft/lb × 100 = (C) | B/A = (D) |
|---|---|---|---|---|---|---|---|
| 12-Metre (heavy keelboat) | 10 | 60,000 | 39·1 | 2,160 | 46·5 | 3·6 | 1·19 |
| Gautier III (light tri) | 4 | 13,250 | 23·7 | 2,228 | 47·2 | 16·6 | 1·99 |
| Livery Dole (light tri) | 3 | 12,300 | 23·1 | 1,765 | 42·0 | 14·9 | 1·82 |
| Colt Cars GB (v.light tri) | 3 | 12,050 | 22·9 | 2,500 | 50·0 | 20·8 | 2·18 |
| Sigma 33 (cruiser/racer) | 4 | 10,101 | 21·6 | 523 | 22·9 | 5·2 | 1·06 |
| $\frac{3}{4}$-Tonner (keel racer) | 4 | 8,600 | 20·5 | 680 | 26·1 | 7·9 | 1·27 |
| J 29 (keel racer) | 4 | 6,840 | 19·0 | 559 | 23·6 | 8·1 | 1·24 |
| Glass Onion (keel racer) | 4 | 2,720 | 14·0 | 288 | 17·0 | 11·2 | 1·21 |
| Icarus II (hydrofoil) | 3 | 1,500 | 11·5 | 470 | 21·7 | 31·3 | 1·89 |
| Illusion (model 12-metre) | 1 | 854 | 9·50 | 64 | 8·0 | 7·5 | 0·84 |
| Icarus I (hydrofoil) | 2 | 722 | 8·97 | 235 | 15·3 | 32·5 | 1·70 |
| International 14 (planing dinghy) | 2 | 610 | 8·50 | 190 | 13·5 | 31·2 | 1·62 |
| Mayfly (hydrofoil) | 1 | 340 | 6·98 | 150 | 12·2 | 44·1 | 1·75 |
| Catapult (inflatable cat) | 1 | 320 | 6·84 | 107 | 10·3 | 32·0 | 1·51 |
| Laser (planing dinghy) | 1 | 300 | 6·70 | 75 | 8·7 | 25·0 | 1·30 |
| Sailboard | 1 | 200 | 5·85 | 67 | 8·2 | 33·5 | 1·40 |

(*Large Sailing Hydrofoils* by J. L. Grogono. © 1983)

span to chord ratio. Practical considerations prevent boats from having really high aspect ratios like a sailplane's wing; and

– low drag. As well as shape, drag will come from rigging, fittings and the smoothness of the sail surface. Smoothness is especially important near the leading edge so a solid wing mast with a perfect surface will be a big advantage. Film-laminated sailcloth is a lot smoother than a normal woven cloth but a perfectly smooth solid surface is better.

**Other rig improvements** The following are worth considering:

– sloping rig to reduce heeling force and produce useful lift; and
– rig consisting of a number of elements which have high aspect ratio individually but are not as tall as a single-element sail (Planesail, Clifton Flasher).
– Elevated (kite) rig which experiences stronger, steadier wind.

# Conclusions

This very simplified picture of the factors affecting speed leads us to the following conclusions:

1. The speed of single-hulled ballasted yachts is in proportion to the square root of their waterline length. Except in special cases such as surfing down waves, they cannot break away from this speed limit because they are trapped in a vicious circle of displacement, wetted surface and stability.
2. Planing craft can break away from the waterline length limitation. The most efficient planing craft are the smallest ones because they have the highest power/weight ratio and the highest ratio of crew weight to all-up weight. This is borne out by the very high speeds attained by sailboards and the relatively poor ones attained by large planing dinghies.
3. Long, slim, lightweight hulls have a high speed potential which is limited by the amount of stability that can be built in and what is practical or seaworthy.
4. Hydrofoils offer a very high speed potential which is not linked to the size of the craft.
5. Brute force is no substitute for efficiency – either of hulls or sails. High lift to drag ratio of the total hull and rig system is essential.

# Predictions

The speed of sailboards has risen so dramatically that it surely cannot have reached its ultimate. Thirty knots has been attained and 35 would seem to be within reach of present technology. Beyond this, the inefficiency of soft sails will begin to be felt. Water-skiers have been towed at over 50 knots which shows that there is nothing inherently impossible in standing on a tiny planing surface at very high speeds. With sailboard sail-plans of substantially better lift/drag ratio there seems little to prevent speeds from continuing to rise.

Hydrofoils have shown great promise in recent years and are limited mainly by the lack of funds needed for their expensive engineering. This could change if there were a real cash incentive in winning the World Sailing Speed Record. Meanwhile, the leadership in hydrofoil development is likely to pass to those interested in ocean racing where there is more money available through sponsorship. Very good engineering will be needed to produce a reliable offshore flying hydrofoil but when this becomes available it will result in a substantial improvement of offshore speeds.

The current World Sailing Speed Record holder *Crossbow II* inherits the title given to her predecessor of 'most extreme conventional boat ever built'. She was designed to achieve 40 knots and has actually reached 36. With detailed improvements and in ideal conditions she probably could attain 40 knots but very little more because of her soft sails. A further scaling up of this concept would be very expensive and would bring only small gains because of the difficulty of maintaining the same power/weight ratio at a larger scale. Therefore it is unlikely that a *Crossbow*-type boat will ever exceed 40 knots by much.

The success of *Jacob's Ladder* shows the great potential of the 'elevated rig' concept. The efficiency of the soft-cloth kites can obviously be improved and the boat used up till 1982 was not very suitable. Therefore, if the flying element were replaced by something like a high-performance sailplane, radio controlled perhaps, and the water element was replaced by a suitably designed hydrofoil boat, then a very efficient combination could result. Potential top speed? At least 50 knots!

# World Sailing Speed Record: record rules

### (Copyright: Royal Yachting Association)

## 1. General

The purpose of these rules is to enable attempts to be made on the World Sailing Speed Records in any part of the World under comparable conditions. They do not form the conditions of any prize or trophy, nor are they sailing instructions.

The establishment of the World Sailing Speed Records is subject to the following rules and may only be established under the jurisdiction, and with the approval, of a National Authority affiliated to the International Yacht Racing Union. The National Authority shall appoint an independent official to observe the attempts.

The record shall be held by the helmsman and shall be recorded in his name and nationality together with the name of the designer, builder, owner and the name of the yacht.

The record in each class shall stand until it has been exceeded by at least two per cent of the previously existing record. Every request to ratify a record will be considered in time and date order. The time used for this purpose will be the local, civil clock time at the place the record attempt is made and the moment the competing craft enters the course will be considered to be the time of the run.

It should be noted that if the National Authority of a prospective contestant is unable to administer these Record Rules then it is permissable to apply direct to the Royal Yachting Association for guidance and assistance.

## 2. World records

The World Sailing Speed Record will be held by the helmsman anywhere in the World who establishes the fastest speed, which is ratified in accordance with these Rules.

In addition, records can be established in the following IYRU sail area divisions:

| | |
|---|---|
| 10 Square Metre Class | (up to and including 10 sq.m.) |
| 'A' Class | (from 10 sq.m. up to and including 13·94 sq.m.) |
| 'B' Class | (from 13·94 sq.m. up to and including 21·84 sq.m.) |
| 'C' Class | (from 21·84 sq.m. up to and including 27·88 sq.m.) |
| Unlimited Class | (over 27·88 sq.m.) |

A boat may nominate only one class before each attempt on the record. If it is desired to attempt more than one class, a separate run must be made for each class attempt with the appropriate sail area.

A fee of £25 will be charged by the RYA for the ratification of all World Records.

## 3. The course

The record shall be established over a minimum of half a kilometre on water (not ice), which shall be measured to an accuracy of one per cent.

The course may be defined by posts and transits ashore or by buoys afloat.

## 4. Watches and timekeepers

The timekeeping shall be carried out by officials who have been approved by the National Authority.

The time taken for the yacht to complete the course shall be measured by timepieces whose accuracy shall be confirmed. If separate timing stations operate at each end of the course each shall make use of at least three timepieces. If one timing station shall be used, whether ashore or afloat, it shall operate at least three timepieces simultaneously unless one electronic timing device of proved accuracy is being employed. If both start and finish lines are being monitored on videotape, one such device shall suffice.

Signals for actuating the timepieces may be visual, auditory, mechanical or electrical, but in all cases the same system shall be used at either end of the course, and shall be considered acceptable by the official observer appointed by the National Authority or by the Royal Yachting Association.

# 5. Calculation of speed

Time shall be recorded to the nearest one tenth of a second and in calculating the speed the arithmetic mean of the time shown on the watches used shall be taken.

The speed shall be calculated to the nearest tenth of a knot with allowance made for the resolved component of any tidal stream and/or current on the course. A course where the tidal stream and/or current is liable to be in excess of two knots is not considered suitable for a sailing speed record attempt.

# 6. Manual power

A yacht shall use human power only other than battery power for instrumentation. There is no objection to various methods of power transmission, such as hydraulic, provided there is no element of power storage beyond that associated with materials in their conventional sailing application.

# 7. Measurement

In the sail area divisions, all record claims must have their sail(s) measured immediately following the record attempt, by a qualified measurer. The observer should, following a record run, ensure that no means of power or stored energy has been used, by checking the hull.

# 8. Means of propulsion

Prior to and during the attempt, the yacht shall accelerate from rest, and shall be propelled only by the natural action of the wind on the sails, spars and hull, and water (not ice) on the hull.

# 9. Crew

At least one person shall be on board from the moment the yacht accelerates from rest until she has finished her attempt.

# 10. Notice of intention to make record attempt

One month's notice of an attempt on any record must be given to the Royal Yachting Association.

# 11. Ratification of records

Pending the official ratification of a record by the Royal Yachting Association, the helmsman, builder, designer or any other interested parties shall not cause a record to be published or circulated without the words 'subject to official ratification by the Royal Yachting Association'.

A request for ratification must reach the Royal Yachting Association within 30 days of the run being made. No record will be considered for ratification until 30 days have elapsed from the time of the run.

The following documents are to be submitted to the Royal Yachting Association:

(a) A plan showing the course, together with a report from the official surveyor, covering measurement of the course and tidal stream/and or currents.

(b) Timekeepers' report and calculations.

(c) Typewritten list of the names of the timekeepers and course surveyors.

(d) Report of the official observer which shall verify the accuracy of all measuring equipment.

## 12. Interpretation

In the case of dispute over any of these rules, the decision of the Royal Yachting Association shall be final.

**NOTE:** In November 1983 the International Yacht Racing Union gave its official recognition to the World Sailing Speed Record Committee as the world authority in respect of the rules for speed records under sail and as the official ratifying body for such record claims.

# Results of RYA Speed Weeks, Portland Harbour

## 1972

(In 1972 and 1973, there were no sail area classes but the results are given here as if there had been. It is not clear if the 1974 speeds were formally ratified.) Speeds in knots. * indicates a record speed but it is not clear if the 1974 speeds were formally ratified.

| Class | Boat | Description | Owner/helmsman | Speed |
|---|---|---|---|---|
| Unlimited | *Crossbow* | 60ft (18·2m) proa with 1,000 sq ft sloop rig | Timothy Colman | 26.3* |
| 'C' | — | | | |
| 'B' | *Icarus* | Tornado catamaran with hydrofoils | *Icarus* Syndicate | 21·6 |
| 'A' | *Mayfly* | 15ft (4·5m) cat with hydrofoils | Philip Hansford | 16·4 |
| 10 sq m | *Kotaha* | Hydrofoil outrigger | Leif Wagner–Smitt | 13·6 |

## 1973

| Class | Boat | Description | Owner/helmsman | Speed |
|---|---|---|---|---|
| Unlimited | *Crossbow* | Shortened 5ft (1·5m), new sidecar with hydrofoil | Timothy Colman | 29·3* |
| 'C' | *Lady 'B'* | Hellcat III S | Keith Sanger | 17·7 |
| 'B' | *Icarus* | New single rear steering foil & wider beam | *Icarus* Syndicate | 20·0 |
| 'A' | *Hobie 14* | Standard Hobie cat | Hank Pauloo | 14·5 |
| 10 sq m | — | | | |

## 1974

| Class | Boat | Description | Owner/helmsman | Speed |
|---|---|---|---|---|
| Unlimited | *British Oxygen* | 70ft (21·3m) offshore catamaran | Robin Knox-Johnston | 24·26 |
| 'C' | *Clifton Flasher* | 25ft (7·6m) proa with 5-element wing rig | Flasher Synd./Nigel Irens | 22·14* |
| 'B' | *Orlando* | Standard Manta cat | G. E. Ward | 16·31* |
| 'A' | *Mayfly* | Now with metal foils | Philip Hansford | 19·38* |
| 10 sq m | *Boreas* | Unicorn cat with foils & semi-wing rig | Reg Bratt | 15·04* |

| Year / Class | Boat | Notes | Crew | Speed (knots) |
|---|---|---|---|---|
| **1975** | | | | |
| Unlimited | *Crossbow* | Sidecar now has planing skid underneath | Timothy Colman | 31·1* |
| 'C' | *Stampede* | 25ft (7·6m) Cruising cat | Rory Carter | 16·4* |
| 'B' | *Hobie 16* | Standard Hobie cat | Hank Pauloo | 16·9 |
| 'A' | *Mayfly* | As before | Hansford/Grogono | 19·4 |
| 10 sq m | *Boreas* | As before | Reg Bratt | 14.1 |
| **1976** | | | | |
| Unlimited | *Crossbow II* | 60ft (18·2m) slewed bi-plane catamaran | Timothy Colman | 31·8* |
| 'C' | *Clifton Flasher* | As before | Flasher Synd./Nigel Irens | 20·4 |
| 'B' | *Icarus* | As before | *Icarus* Syndicate | 20·7* |
| 'A' | *Mayfly* | As before | Ben Wynne | 21·1* |
| 10 sq m | *Auster* | New 18ft (5·4m) cat under old 'high-boom' rig | Reg Bratt | 14·6 |
| **1977** | | | | |
| Unlimited | *Crossbow II* | Better steering and planing shoe added | Timothy Colman | 33·8* |
| 'C' | — | | | |
| 'B' | *Icarus* | As before | *Icarus* Synd./Andrew Grogono | 22·2* |
| 'A' | *Mayfly* | New foils and sail | Ben Wynne | 23·0* |
| 10 sq m | *Windglider* | Standard sailboard with special sail | Derk Thijs | 19·1* |
| **1978** | | | | |
| Unlimited | *Crossbow II* | New sails | Timothy Colman | 27.7 |
| 'C' | *Gel ar Mor* | Four-man sailboard | 'Les Crocodiles d'Elorn' | 10·5 |
| 'B' | *Icarus* | As before | *Icarus* Synd./James Grogono | 19·5 |
| 'A' | *Mayfly* | Added sitting-out wings and fairings | Ben Wynne | 18·7 |
| 10 sq m | *Windglider Ranger* | Lighter than normal board | Derk Thijs | 15·3 |
| **1979** | | | | |
| Unlimited | *Slingshot* | 60ft (18·2m) proa | Slingshot Synd./Karl Thomas | 22·6 |
| 'C' | *Smoothy* | 'C' class cat with C/F hulls | John Vigurs | 14·2 |
| 'B' | *Icarus* | As before | *Icarus* Syndicate | 18·9 |

| Class | Craft | Description | Holder | Speed |
|---|---|---|---|---|
| 'A' | *Mayfly* | As before | Ben Wynne | 22·3 |
| 10 sq m | Ten Cate Special | Lightweight speedboard | Jaap Van der Rest | 19·2 |
| **1980** | | | | |
| Unlimited | *Icarus II* | 26 ft (7·9m) cat with 2 Tornado rigs | *Icarus II* Syndicate | 9·8 |
| 'C' | *Jacob's Ladder* | Tornado cat with 'Flexifoil' kite rig | Day/Jeffree | 18·6 |
| 'B' | *Icarus* | As before | *Icarus* Syndicate | 23·8* |
| 'A' | *Nothing's Happening* | Production version of *Mayfly* | Terry Crumpton | 17·5 |
| 10 sq m | Ten Cate HP | Special sailboard | Jaap Van der Rest | 23·9 |
| **1981** | | | | |
| Unlimited | — | | | |
| 'C' | *Jacob's Ladder* | As before | Day/Jeffree/Rayment | 23·75 |
| 'B' | *Icarus* | As before | *Icarus* Synd./Andrew Grogono | 24·47* |
| 'A' | *Seafly 14* | Production version of *Mayfly* | B. de V. Brest/T. Crumpton | 16·45 |
| 10 sq m | F2 | Sinker board | Jurgen Honscheid | 24·75 |
| **1982** | | | | |
| Unlimited | — | Boards moved and planing surface aft | | |
| 'C' | *Jacob's Ladder* | As before | J. L. Syndicate | 25·03* |
| 'B' | *Icarus* | Hydrofoil trimaran | *Icarus* Syndicate | 18·01 |
| 'A' | *Loisir 3000* | | Gahagnon/Cunin | 16·83 |
| 10 sq m | *Ellesse* | Sinker board | Pascal Maka | 27·82* |
| **1983** | | | | |
| Unlimited | *Icarus II* | Total rebuild (but sank again) | R. Downhill | 21·41 |
| 'C' | *Jacob's Ladder* | Hydrofoils added | Day/Rayment | 24·48 |
| 'B' | *Icarus I* | Longer rear foil (better steering) | A. Grogono/J. Fowler | 26·59* |
| 'A' | *Black & White II* | Sinker tandem sailboard (the first?) | G. Way/G. McKinley | 25·39* |
| 10 sq m | *Maui/Pryde* | Sinker sailboard + partial wing rig | Fred Haywood | 30·83* |

# History of the World Sailing Speed Records

(In 1974, which was the first year of 'class' records, the best speeds achieved at Portland do not appear to have been formally ratified as records, but they are included here nevertheless)

| Boat | Owner/helmsman | Country | Place | Date | Speed |
|---|---|---|---|---|---|
| **Unlimited Class (Outright World Sailing Speed Record)** | | | | | |
| Crossbow | Timothy Colman | GB | Portland | October 1972 | 26·3 |
| Crossbow | " | " | " | October 1973 | 29.3 |
| Crossbow | " | " | " | October 1975 | 31·1 |
| Crossbow II | " | " | " | October 1976 | 31·8 |
| Crossbow II | " | " | " | October 1977 | 33·8 |
| Crossbow II | " | " | " | 17 November 1980 | 36·0 |
| **'C' Class (from 21·84 up to 27·88 sq m sail area)** | | | | | |
| Clifton Flasher | Flasher Synd./Nigel Irens | GB | Portland | October 1974 | 22·1 |
| (NF)[2] | W.S. Bradfield/Don White | USA | Port Jefferson, NY | 18 November 1978 | 24·4 |
| Jacob's Ladder | Ian Day/Martin Rayment | GB | Portland | 13 Oct 1982 | 25·03 |

## 'B' Class (from 13·94 up to 21·84 sq m sail area)

| | | | | | |
|---|---|---|---|---|---|
| Orlando | G. E. Ward | GB | Portland | October 1974 | 16·31 |
| Hobie 16 | Hank Pauloo | USA | Portland | October 1975 | 19·9 |
| Icarus | Icarus Syndicate | GB | Portland | October 1976 | 20·7 |
| Icarus | " " | " | Portland | October 1977 | 22·2 |
| (NF)² | W.S. Bradfield/Don White | USA | Port Jefferson, NY | 17 October 1978 | 23·0 |
| Icarus | Icarus Syndicate | GB | Portland | 8 October 1980 | 23·8 |
| Icarus | " " " | GB | Portland | 1 October 1981 | 24·47 |
| Icarus | " " " | GB | Portland | 14 October 1983 | 26·59 |

## 'A' Class (from 10 up to 13·94 sq m sail area)

| | | | | | |
|---|---|---|---|---|---|
| Mayfly | Philip Hansford | GB | Portland | October 1974 | 19·38 |
| Mayfly | Ben Wynne | " | Portland | October 1976 | 21·1 |
| Mayfly | " " | " | Portland | 3 October 1977 | 23·0 |
| Black and White | G. Way/G. McKinley | " | Portland | 15 October 1983 | 25·39 |

## 10 sq m Class

| | | | | | |
|---|---|---|---|---|---|
| Boreas | Reg Bratt | GB | Portland | October 1974 | 15·04 |
| Windglider | Derk Thijs | Holland | Portland | October 1977 | 19·1 |
| Ten Cate Special | Jaap Van der Rest | " | Portland | 21 October 1979 | 22·3 |
| Olympic Gold | Clive Colenso | GB | Portland | 22 October 1979 | 22·95 |
| Ten Cate Special | Jaap Van der Rest | Holland | Maalea Bay, Maui | 18 July 1980 | 24·63 |
| Ten Cate Special | " " " | " | Veerse Meer, Holland | 13 November 1981 | 25·11 |
| Mistral Special | Philip Pudenz | W. Germany | Brest, France | 28 Sept. 1982 | 26·53 |
| Ellesse Special | Pascal Maka | France | Portland | 13 October 1982 | 27·82 |
| Maui Special | Fred Haywood | USA | Portland | 16 October 1983 | 30·83 |

## Standing records for various ocean races and passages

| Race or route | Distance (nautical miles) | Elapsed time | Date | Yacht/Ship | Length overall ft (m) | Skipper | Speed (knots av) |
|---|---|---|---|---|---|---|---|
| Whitbread Round the World Race (3 stops) | 27,430 | 120d 6h 34m 14s | 1981/2 | Flyer | 76ft (23·1m) | Cornelis van Rietschoten (Holland) | 9·5 |
| Round the World Race (1 stop) | 27,120 | 134d 6h | 1975/6 | Great Britain II | 77ft 2in (23·5m) | Rob James (GB) | 8·4 |
| Single-handed round the World (1 stop, not racing) | 27,120 | 167d | 1973/4 | Manureva ex Pen Duick IV | 67ft (20·4m) | Alain Colas (France) | 7·3 |
| Transpacific Race Los Angeles – Honolulu | 2,225 | 8d 11h 1m 45s | 1977 | Merlin | 67ft (20·4m) | Bill Lee (USA) | 11·0 |
| Round Britain (and Ireland) Race | 1,950 | 8d 15h 3m 10s | 1982 | Colt Cars GB | 60ft (18·2m) | Rob James (GB) | 9·4 |
| Newport–Bermuda Race | 635 | 2d 14h 29m | 1982 | Nirvana | 80ft (24·3m) | Marvin Green (USA) | 10·16 |
| Sydney–Hobart Race | 630 | 2d 14h 36m 56s | 1975 | Kialoa | 79ft (24m) | John B. Kilroy (USA) | 10·1 |
| Fastnet Race | 605 | 2d 23h 2m 10s | 1983 | Condor II | 80ft (24·4m) | Bob Bell (GB) | 8·4 |

**Transatlantic**

| | Distance (nm) | Time | Year | Yacht | Length | Skipper | Knots |
|---|---|---|---|---|---|---|---|
| Fastest, Sandy Hook–Lizard | 2,925 | 8d 16h 33m 17s | 1984 | *Jet Services* | 60ft (18m) | Patrick Morvan | 14·03 |
| Fastest monohull yacht Sandy Hook–Lizard | 2,925 | 12d 4h 1m | 1905 | *Atlantic* | 185ft (56·3m) | Charlie Barr (USA) | 10·3 |
| Fastest E–W (Plymouth–Newport) | 3,000 | 14d 13h 54m | 1981 | *Brittany Ferries GB* | 65ft (19·8m) | Chay Blyth (GB) | 8·57 |
| Fastest single-handed E–W (Plymouth–Newport) | 3,000 | 17d 23h 12m | 1980 | *Moxie* | 50ft 1in (15·6m) | Phil Weld (USA) | 6·96 |
| Fastest E–W (Teneriffe–Martinique) | 2,640 | 10d 12h | 1968 | *Pen Duick IV* | 67ft (20·4m) | Eric Tabarly | 10·47 |

**Day's Runs**

| | Distance (nm) | Time | Year | Yacht | Length | Skipper | Knots |
|---|---|---|---|---|---|---|---|
| Greatest claimed by clipper (but impossible to prove) | 465 | 24h | 1854 | *Champion of the Seas* | 266ft (81m) | Alex Newlands (GB) | 19·37 |
| Greatest generally accepted clipper | 369 | 24h | 1855 | *Flying Cloud* | 225ft (68·5m) | Capt. Cressy (USA) | 15·37 |
| Greatest by yacht(s) | 380 | 24h | 1970 | *Sea Bird* | 61ft (18·5m) | Marc Pajot (France) | 15·83 |
| | 380 | 24h | 1981 | *Sea Falcon* | 70ft (21·3m) | Robin Knox-Johnson | 15·83 |
| Greatest by monohull yacht (claimed) | 341 | 24h | 1905 | *Atlantic* | 185ft (56·3m) | Charlie Barr | 14·2 |

## Time and speed for a 500 metre distance

| Time in seconds | Speed in knots | Time in seconds | Speed in knots |
| --- | --- | --- | --- |
| 24 | 40.9 | 61 | 16.1 |
| 25 | 39.3 | 62 | 15.8 |
| 26 | 37.8 | 63 | 15.6 |
| 27 | 36.5 | 64 | 15.4 |
| 28 | 35.1 | 65 | 15.1 |
| 29 | 33.8 | 66 | 14.9 |
| 30 | 32.7 | 67 | 14.9 |
| 31 | 31.7 | 68 | 14.5 |
| 32 | 30.7 | 69 | 14.3 |
| 33 | 30.3 | 70 | 14.1 |
| 34 | 28.9 | 71 | 13.9 |
| 35 | 28.1 | 72 | 13.7 |
| 36 | 27.3 | 73 | 13.5 |
| 37 | 26.5 | 74 | 13.3 |
| 38 | 25.8 | 75 | 13.2 |
| 39 | 25.2 | 76 | 13.0 |
| 40 | 24.5 | 77 | 12.8 |
| 41 | 24.0 | 78 | 12.6 |
| 42 | 23.4 | 79 | 12.5 |
| 43 | 22.9 | 80 | 12.3 |
| 44 | 22.3 | 81 | 12.2 |
| 45 | 21.9 | 82 | 12.0 |
| 46 | 21.4 | 83 | 11.9 |
| 47 | 20.9 | 84 | 11.7 |
| 48 | 20.5 | 85 | 11.5 |
| 49 | 20.1 | 86 | 11.4 |
| 50 | 19.7 | 87 | 11.2 |
| 51 | 19.3 | 88 | 11.1 |
| 52 | 18.9 | 89 | 11.0 |
| 53 | 18.5 | 90 | 10.9 |
| 54 | 18.2 | 91 | 10.8 |
| 55 | 17.8 | 92 | 10.7 |
| 56 | 17.5 | 93 | 10.5 |
| 57 | 17.2 | 94 | 10.4 |
| 58 | 16.9 | 95 | 10.3 |
| 59 | 16.6 | 96 | 10.2 |
| 60 | 16.4 | 97 | 10.1 |

# Index

Ada 25
Aero Research Ltd. 50
Aesticat 174
Agar, Nigel 205, 214
Aikane 87
Airborne lifeboat 49
Aitken, Sir Max 77
Albacore 49
Aldeburgh 125
Alderman, Ray 171
Allday Aluminium 126
Allegre 98
Alter, Hobie 52
Amateur Yacht Research
  Society (AYRS) 92, 123,
  147, 149, 183
America 17, 19, 20
America's Cup, The 17, 68,
  71–3, 218
American vessels 12–17
American War of
  Independence 15
Amiens, Peace of 18
Amigo 202, 203
Appollonio, Howard 118,
  126
Arab sailing vessels 4
Architectura Navalis
  Mercatoria 11
Ariel 25, 30 (illus.), 30, 34
Artemis 172
Astro-navigation 36
Atlantic (schooner) 67–8,
  67 (ph.)
Auster 172
Auzepy-Brenneur,
  Charles 82
Avenger 42, 43 (ph.), 44,
  49

Baines, James 27–8
Baker, J. G. 112–14
Baltimore clippers 14–15,
  20, 22, 24–5, 28–9
Barbary pirates 6–7
Barlovento 87
Barr, Charlie 67–8
Beach, Doug 204
Beach yawls 19–20
Bell, Alan 121
Bellerophon 8
Beowulf V 151–2, 170
Bermuda 'fitted
  dinghies' 40–1
Bermuda Race, The 64
Bermudian rig 41
Bestevaer 82
Birch, Mike 100

Bisschop, Eric de 86
Black and White
  (sailboard) 131, 190
Black Ball Line 27, 37
Black Prince 25
Black Soo 77, 78 (ph.)
Blackwall frigates 20
Blue Charm 77
Bluey 170–1
Blyth, Chay 68, 97
Boardman, Christopher 195
Boeing Jetfoil 109, 116
Bond, Bob 147
Boreas 165, 167 (ph.)
Boston Whaler, The 105
Bourne End Week 46
Boxall, Jerry 99
Brabazon, Lord 56
Bradfield, Prof. W. F.
  131–3
Bratt, Reg 164–5, 172
British Oxygen 98–9, 165,
  208, 211
Britannia 20, 69–70, 69
  (ph.)
Brittany Ferries GB 68, 98
Bromley, P. J. 171
Brown, Woody 86
Bruynzeel, Cornelis De 79
Brynhild 48–9, 48 (ph.)
Burgess, Starling 72
Buzby 174

California Gold Rush 21–2
Cambria 66
Canepa, Jeff 174
Canoe Club, The 46
Caribbean, The 13
Castle Cove Sailing
  Club 153, 161
Cape Horn 21–2, 37
Catamarans 83–102, 85
  (des. by Herreshoff illus.)
Catamaran Yacht Club 59
Catapult 175, 187 (ph.)
'C' Class catamarans 53–63
Centre-plates 40, 44
Ceramco 82
Champion of the Seas 28,
  37
Chapelle, Howard I. 12,
  14, 16
Chapman, Frederick Hendrik
  af 11, 12
Chapman, Cmdr
  George 170
Chapman, S. 183
Chapman Sands Sailing
  Club 53, 55
Charles, Daniel 97

Chaworth-Musters,
  Robin 94
Chebec or Xebec 6–7,7
  (illus.), 13, 29
Cheers 95
Chichester, Sir Francis 95
Chilvers, Peter 134
Chinaman 25
Choy, Rudy 86
Chrysolite 31
Clifton Flasher 100, 163,
  165, 166 (ph.), 190
Club Med 82, 95–6
'Cod's head and mackerel
  tail' 12
Colas, Alain 82, 94–5
Colbert, Jean-Baptiste 7
Colenso, Clive 137, 142,
  171–2, 182–4
Colman, Alan 194
Colman, Timothy vi, vii,
  viii, 49, 151, 152, 160,
  162, 177, 194–221
Colt Cars GB 96 & (ph.)
Contender (dinghy) 47
Cook, Capt. James 52, 84
Cooke, Brian 94
Coronet (dinghy) 50
Costes, Didier 168
Coulnakyle 25
Cressy, Capt. (& Mrs) 37
Crocco (& Ricaldone) 111
Crossbow 49, 104, 110, 128,
  137, 152, 156, 161, 162,
  163, 170, 176–7, 194–210,
  (phs.) 201 & 203 & 206 &
  209
Crossbow II 134, 137, 160,
  171, 172, 176, 177, 190,
  192 (ph.), 210–221, (phs.)
  216 & 220, 230
Cruising Association,
  The ix
Cruising Club of America
  (CCA) 65
Crystal Trophy 93
C/S/K (Choy, Seaman,
  Kumalae) 86–88
Cunningham, Lindsay 52
Currey, Charles 46
Cutty Sark 24–5, 28–9,
  31–2, 35–6, 38, 51

Dashew, Steve 148, 151–2,
  170
Darby, Newman 134
Daring 42, 46–7
Dartmouth, RN
  College 195
Dauntless 66
Day, Ian 179, 187–8

# Index

Deane, Anthony 7
De Havilland (Flamingo & Mosquito) 50
Dell Quay Dory 105
De Quincey, Roger 46
Design 222–230
*Dhows* 4
*Digereedo* 163–4
*Diligente* 16, 16 (illus.), 17, 20
Di Mauro, Tony 61
Displacement 222–230
Displacement & Sail Area Ratios of Various Craft 228 (table)
*Disque d'Or* 82
*Doctrine of Naval Architecture, The* 7
*Dolphin* 88
*Dominion* (catamaran) 86
*Donald Mackay* 28
*Dorade* 64
Drag 103–106, 222–30
Drake, Jim 134
Drakkar (type of Viking ship) 8–10
Duggan, G. Herrick 86
*Duke of York* 18

*East Anglian* 46
Eastern Multihull Association 52
East India Company, The 24
Eastwood Whelpton Ltd. 205
*Eb and Flo* 88
Edinburgh Cup 194
Edmunds, T. 164
*Elf Aquitaine (I)* 68, 99, 100, 102, 189
Ellison, Bessie 46
Ellison, Michael 183
*Elorn, Les Crocodile de* 179
*Emma Hamilton* 55
Emus, Alan 47
*Endeavour* (catamaran) 51, 147
*Endeavour II* 73
*Endeavour III* 195
Epoxy-Kevlar and Epoxy-CF laminates 142
*Excalibur* 79
*Exoplane* 168–170, 170 (ph.), 182

Fairey Fox 49
Fairey Marine 50
*Falcon* 23, 23 (illus.), 25
Falconer (*Marine Dictionary*) 6

Farmoor Reservoir 153
Farrant, Maj. Gen. Ralph 93, 162
Farrar, Austin viii, 55, 56, 60, 61, 143, 185, 206, 214, 218
Fastnet Race 64, 74
Feluccas 4
Fireball 105
*Fiery Cross* 25
Firefly 49
Fisk, John 53, 54, 55, 88, 147, 148, 196
5–O–5 dinghy 50
'Flexifoil' kites 179–81, 180 & 181 (phs.), 182
*Flip-Flap* 164
*Flyer* (hydrofoil) 109
*Flyer* (Round the World Race) 82
*Flying Cloud* 26, 37
Flying Dutchman 50
*Flying Feline* (hydrofoil) 118, 119 (ph.)
Flying Fifteen 46
*Flying Fish* (hydrofoil) 117, 118 (ph.)
*Flying Spur* 25, 38
*Foiler III* 162
Follett, Tom 95–6
*Force 8* 178 (ph.), 179, 182
Forlanini 111
Forde Park School 164
Fowler, John 122
Fox, Uffa 40, 42, 46. 47, 48, 49, 50, 64, 70, 77, 146, 195
Fraser, Ian 162
French Revolution, The 15
Frers, German 82
Frigates 11
Froude, William 103
F2 (Fun and Function) 186

*Gallant* 47
'Gallant' rig 171
Galleys, Graeco-roman 2, 6 (French), 29
*Gamma* 190
Gardner, William 67
Garrett, Rodney 164
*Gel ar Mor* 179
*Georgiana* 20
Gick, Phil 46
Giles, J. Laurent 74, 79–81
Giles, Morgan 42
Gilruth, Robert R. 112
Glass fibre (GRP) 79
Gliksman, Alain 98
Glue 50

Gokstad ship 8, 9 (ph.)
*Golden Cockerel* 88
*Golden Jubilee* 174
*Goodwill* 87
Göttingen wing section 57
Gougeon Bros 176
Gowens (sailmakers) 197
Gower, Capt. 17, 19
Grafham Water 207–8
*Great Britain III* 97
*Great Republic* 27
Griffiths, John 25
Grogono, Alan 128, 174, 186
Grogono, Andrew 130, 174
Grogono, Bernard 120
Grogono, James viii, 120–30, 147, 174
*Guinness Book of Records* 58, 147
*Gulfstreamer* 98
Guns (influence on design) 10
Gurney, Alan 81

Hall, Tom 196, 205
Hansford, Philip 110, 124–30
*Happy New Year* 20
Harris, Bob 52
Hasler, Col. 'Blondie' 73, 96
Haylock, Teddy 49
Hayman, Alan 154
Hayman, Bernard 147, 149, 150 (ph.), 154
Haywood, Fred 134, 143, 143, 190
Heckstall-Smith, B. 70
*Hellcat* 53, 54 (ph.), 196
*Hellcat II* 54, 197
Hemmings, Jack ix
Henderson, Michael 93
Herreshoff, Nathanael 71, 77, 85
Heyerdahl, Thor 83
Hickman sea-sled 105
Hill, Ron 202
*Hi-Trot III* 178
Hobiecat 52, 171, 172, 174
Holt, Jack 49, 50
Holtom, Gerald 162
Honolulu (beach catamarans at) 86
Honscheid, Jürgen 137, 140, 142, 186
Hood (sailmakers) 218
Hook, Christopher 112–114, 132, 162, 167, 168 (ph.)
Hope, Linton 77

Hornet (dinghy)   49, 50,
   146
Howarth, David   4
Howell, Bill   88
Howland & Aspinall   25
Hubbard, Dave   61
Hunloke, Maj. Philip   70
Hunting Surveys   148
*Hustler*   126
Huxley, Aldous   vi
Hydrofoils   100–102,
   103–19, 120–33, 206

*Icarus*   107, 109, 120–3, 123
   & 129 (phs.), 149, 160–3,
   171, 186, 188, 190, 205
*Icarus II*   173–4, 173 & 192
   (phs.)
Illingworth, Capt.
   John   73–7, 79
Illingworth & Primrose
   (designers)   76
*Infidel*   81
International Canoe
   Trophy   46–7
International Catamaran
   Challenge Trophy   52, 55,
   58–9, 196
International 14ft
   dinghy   41, 46, 50
International Offshore
   Multihull Rating
   (IOMR)   93
International Offshore Rule
   (IOR)   65
International 10 sq m
   canoe   47
International Yacht Racing
   Union (IYRU)   47, 147,
   150, 151
Irens, Nigel   100, 163
Iroquois catamaran   88–90,
   90 (ph.)

*Jacob's Ladder*   180–1, 180
   & 181 & 193 (phs.), 182,
   187–8, 189, 190, 230
*James Baines*   28, 37
James, John   121
Jardine, Matheson   24
'J' Class   68, 71–3
Jeffree, Paul   179
Jenkins, Joan   183
*Jessie* (illus.)   85
*Jet Services*   99, 102
Johnnie Walker   144, 152,
   190
John Player (inc. Trophy)
   127, 149, 152, 197, 205
Jollyboat (dinghy)   49, 50,
   146

Joubert (designer)   98
Jumpahead (catamaran)   52

*Kamiloa*   86
Kanazawa Institute of
   Technology   178
Kay, J.   222
Keay, Capt.   30
Keddie, Mark   165
Keiper, Dave   101
**Keller, Jaap and Erica**   182
Kelsall, Derek   92–3, 97,
   162
Kevlar   138
*Kialoa*   81
King, Bill   81
Kites & kite-yachts   175,
   179–81, 187–8
Knox-Johnston, Robin   99,
   165
*Kon-Tiki*   83
*Kotaha*   162, 163 (ph.)
Kumalae, Alfred   86

*Lady Helmsman*   56, 58–9,
   59 (ph.), 60, 143, 147, 206
*Lalage*   195
Lambert, Comte de   111
Landstrom, Bjorn   8
Lang, Oliver   28
Laser (dinghy)   105
Lateen rig   4, 5 (ph.)
Learmont, Capt. James   37
Leavitt, Randall   213–14
Legrove, Peter   171
Lewis, Dr David   90
Lewmar (winches)   203,
   212–13
*Lightning*   28, 28 (illus.)
Linton, Hercules   29
Little America's Cup,
   The   53, 58–9, 196
*Livery Dole*   97
Lloyds (scantling rules)   71
Logs (chip or patent)   35
Long, Huey   68
Lubbock, Basil   29

Macalpine-Downie,
   Roderick   viii, 52–5, 88,
   91, 98, 162, 165, 196–200,
   205–6, 208–21
Mackay, Donald   26–7, 37
Mackinnon, 'Bee'   52
Maka, Pascal   142, 189
Manners-Spencer, Jack   171
'Manu Kai' (series of
   catamarans)   86
*Manureva*   95
Marchaj, C. A.   222
March, Rodney   61

'Mariners' Mirror', The   37
Marshall, Wilson   67
Mason, Andy   140
'Maxi' yachts   65
*Mayfly*   107, 110, 112–20,
   124–30, 125 & 131 (phs.),
   149, 161–2, 165, 171, 174,
   182, 190
McKinley, Glen   190, 196,
   197
McMullen, Mike   94, 99
Measured miles   146
Medina, River (Measured ½
   mile)   47
Meech, Arthur   217
*Merlin* (dinghy)   49, 50
*Merlin* (ULDB)   81
*Midnight*   77
Milestone, Bill   44, 45
   (ph.), 46
Milovitch, Dimitri   143
*Minitaree*   99
*Minoi II*   166
*Mirrorcat*   91–2, 91 (ph.),
   94, 98
*Miss Bosham*   167, 168 (ph.)
*Miss Nylex*   60
*Miss Strand Glass*
   (hydrofoil)   132, 162
*Miss Strand Glass II*   164,
   164 (ph.)
*Miss Strand Glass III*   166
Mitchell, R. G.   197
Mitchell, 'Tiny'   146
*Monitor*   110, 112–14, 114
   (ph.), 132
Montagu Whalers   40
Montgomery, John   175
Moore, Beecher   viii, 44, 49,
   53, 146, 147
Moorson's Registered
   Tonnage   31
Morris, Stewart   41
Morvan, Patrick   99
*Moses H. Grinell*   17
Mosquito (hydrofoil)   164
*Moxie*   98
Moy, Thomas   110
Mudie, Colin   74, 90
*Multihull International*
   (magazine)   ix
Multihull Offshore Cruising
   and Racing Association
   (MOCRA)   93–4
Murphy, Ken   86
Mylar (sail material)   143, 218
*Myth of Malham*   74–6, 75
   (ph.), 81

NACRA 5.2
   (catamaran)   174

## Index

National Maritime
    Museum   58
*Navahoe*   69
Navigation Act, 1849   24
Newick, Dick   95, 98–9
*(NF)²*   120, 131–3
Nicholson, Charles E.   71
Nigg, Don   116–18, 132
*Nonsuch*   33 (ph.)
Norfolk dinghy   41
Norfolk punt   174
North (sailmaker)   218

O'Brien, Bill   52
*Observer* Singlehanded
    Transatlantic Race
    (OSTAR)   82, 91, 94–6,
    98
*Ocelot*   60
*Ondine*   68
Opium trade   22, 24
*Ormen Lange*   8
Oseberg Ship, The   8
*Osprey*, H.M.S.   18
*Outlaw*   77
Outrigger canoes   83–4

Pacific Multihull
    Association   151
Pajot, Marc   68, 99, 189
Palmblad, Eric   111
Panama Canal, The   21
Pangallo, Biagio   7, 8
Parducci, Alan   134
Parham, Maj-Gen.   55, 57,
    60
*Patient Lady (I–IV)*   61, 62
    (illus.)
Pattison brothers   179, 182
*Paul Ricard*   68, 101, 111,
    162
Pearce, Ken,   51–2, 147
Pearce, Terry   162
*Pearl*, H.M.S.   16
*Pelican*   18
Pelly, Philippa   ix
*Pen Duick IV*   87, 94–5
Petty, Sir William   17, 84–5
Philips, Horatio   111
*Pieces of Eight*   225
*Pintail*   42, 43 (ph.)
*Pionier*   79
Piver, Arthur   87
Planing   104–6
Planing dinghies   42–3, 105
*Polynesian Concept*   88
Portland Harbour (see also
    'Speed Trials')   153–5,
    185
Portsmouth Yardstick   94
Power/weight ratio   222–230

Price, Hywel   165
Primrose, Angus   76
Prince of Wales Cup   42,
    46, 195
Prout Bros   52, 88
Pudenz, Philip   189
*Punjaub*   28

*Queen*   18
*Quest II*   56, 59 (ph.)
*Quest III*   60

*Rainbow*   25–6
Rake (of masts)   12, 15
Rand Corporation, The   134
*Ranger*   72–3, 72 (ph.)
Rating (rules &
    formulae)   44, 64–6, 74,
    85, 93
Rayment, Martin   188
*Reales* (French oared
    warships)   6
Reed, John   186
*Rehu Moana*   90
*Reindeer*   19–20
*Reliance*   71–3
Ricaldone (Crocco &)   111
Roach, River   148
Robertson, Don   52, 88
Robilliard, Chris   163
Round Britain Race   88, 91,
    98–9
Route du Rhum   100
Royal Corinthian Yacht
    Club   124
Royal Norfolk and Suffolk
    Yacht Club   195, 207
Royal Ocean Racing
    Club   64
Royal Western Yacht Club
    (of England)   82
Royal Yachting
    Association   50, 127, 149,
    153, 189, 197, 231–3
Royal Yacht Squadron   23,
    69, 93
Rutan, Bert   111
*RTL Timex* (ex *Three Legs of
    Man III)*   98

Sailboards   134–44, 175
    (3-person, ph.); 179
    (4-person); 186 (sinker)
Sail Craft   57, 89, 197, 199,
    201
Sailing canoes   46–7
Sail Spar   197, 204
*Satanita*   69, 70
Saunders, S. E.   42
Schreur, Jan-Marc   182
Schweitzer, Hoyle   134

Schweitzer, Matt   182
Scott, Peter   41, 44, 46, 49,
    146–7, 149, 195
*Sea Falcon*   99, 100 (ph.),
    165
*Sealion*   56
Seaman, Gary   137, 138–9
Seawanhaka Cup   86
*Sea Witch*   26
*Serica*   25
Severin, Tim   4
*Shamrock III*   71
Shaw, Peter   61, 163
Shearwater (catamaran)   52,
    174
*Shooting Star*   164
Shuttleworth, John   98
Sibbick (designer)   77
Simpson-Wild (designer)   94
Singlehanded Transatlantic
    Race – see *Observer*
    Singlehanded Transatlantic
    Race
'Sinker' sailboards   140–1
*Sir Thomas Lipton*   95
*Sisi*   175
Skegs   141
Slave trade, The   15–16
Sliding seats   45, 50
*Slingshot*   105, 176–8, 177
    (ph.), 182, 183, 211, 219
Small Boat Association,
    The   46
Small Boat Racing
    Association, The   41
Smirnoff   152
Smith and Dimon   25–6
*Snark*   42
*Snowgoose*   88, 89 (ph.), 92
Somerville, Hugh   vi
Southampton University   56
*Sovereign of the Seas*   28
Spanier, Barry   143
Sparkman and Stephens
    (designers)   64, 81
Speed Trials: Brest   153,
    157, 188–9;
    Burnham-on-
    Crouch   123–4, 147–9;
    Karlskrona   153;
    Kiel   135; Maalea Bay
    (Maui)   157, 160, 185;
    New Zealand   153; Port
    Jefferson (USA)   132,
    152; Portland
    (Weymouth)   58, 99, 123,
    127, 135, 136, 143–4,
    153–5, 160–91, results
    of   235–7; San
    Diego   152; Solent   59,
    88, 146–7; Veerse Meer

(Pall Mall) 153, 157, 158–9 (illus.) 189
Spencer, John 8
*Staghound* 21, 26, 27 (illus.)
*St Ann* 11–13, 12 (illus.)
Statens Sjohistorisk Museum 12
Steers, George 17
'Stepped' hydroplanes 106
Stern, Dr Vic 93
Stevens, Commodore 17
Stewart, Keith 175, 181–3
Storm Trysail Club 65
*Stormvogel* 79–81, 80 (ph.)
*Streaker* 171
*Strongbow* 82
Suez Canal 24
*Sunny South* 17
Sutton Hoo ship 8
*Swift* 13–15, 14 (illus.)
*Swiss Yachting* 193 (ph.)
Sydney Harbour 18ft dinghies 41, 51, 171–2
Symonds, Sir William 20

Tabarly, Eric 68, 87, 94, 111, 162
*Taeping* 25
*Taitsing* 25
*Tango Papa* 162
Tatiboet, Joseph 86–7, 88
Tea trade, The 24–5
Techetchet, Victor 84
Tellurometer 148, 148 (ph.), 156
*Temeraire* 7
Ten Cate 137, 152, 182, 187
Terlain, Jean-Yves, 99
Thai Mk IV (catamaran) 52, 196
Thames 'Raters' 44–6
Thames Sailing Club 44
*Thermopylae* 25, 37, 38
Thijs, Bep 174–5
Thijs, Derk 136, 157, 172, 174–5, 182
Thijs, Wim 157, 174–5
Thornycroft, Tom viii, 42
*Three Cheers* 99
*Thunder and Lightning* 46
*Thunder* (catamaran) 61, 163
*Thunder* (international 14) 44
*Tigercat* 52

*Tonnant* 8
*Toria* 91–3, 94
Tornado catamaran 51, 56, 61, 63, 63 (ph.), 121, 136, 148, 162, 165, 172
*Transat en Double* (race) 102
Transatlantic Race 64, 66–8 (1905 Emperor's Cup)
*Transit* 17–18
TransPac (trans Pacific Races) 81, 86, 88, 95
*Trapeze* 44–46
Treatise on Shipbuilding (Chapman) 11
*Tre-Sang* 73
*Trifle* 93, 162
Trimarans 84, 95–9
Tryggvason, Olav 8
*Tsulamaran* 88
*Tweed* 28
12-Metre Class 73
Twist (of sails) 55, 60

*Ugly Duckling* 190
'Ultra-Light Displacement Boats' (ULDB) 81
University of Newcastle upon Tyne 130, 174
University of New York (State) 131
US Navy (interest in hydrofoils) 112–13
Utne, Finn 56

*Vagabond* 44, 45 (ph.)
*Valhalla* 195
*Valiant* 46
*Valkyrie* 85 (illus.)
Val trimaran 98
Van der Rest, Jaap 131, 137–9, 138–9 (phs.), 140, 182–4, 185, 187, 189
Van de Stadt, E. G. 77–80
*Vendredi Treize* 82, 96
*Victory*, H.M.S. 32
Viking ships 8–10
Vilamoura Race 99
Villiers, Alan 36
*Vital* 100
*VSD* 102

Wagner-Smitt, Lief 162, 163 (ph.), 190
Waight, Bill 48
*Waikiki Surf* 86
Walker, Brian 49

Walker, John 109
*Wardance* 88
*Watergate* 165
'Water start' (on sailboard) 140–1
Watson, G. L. 20, 69
Wave-making resistance 103–5
Way, Gordon 190
*Weathercock* 60
Webb, William 26
Weld, Phil 98
WEST construction system 176
West of England Dinghy 41
Whelpton, Tim 205, 214
Whistance, Dan H. 183
Whitbread round the World Race 65, 82
White, Reg 55–6, 58, 61, 89, 197, 200, 205
*Wildcat* 55, 197
*Wildwind* 148, 152
*William Saurin* 97, 189
Williams, Geoffrey 95
Willis, John 28
*Williwaw* 101, 101 (ph.)
Windglider 135–7, 172, 182
Windsurfer, The 134–5, 137, 184
*Windward Passage* 81
Wing masts 56, 58, 60–2, 142–3, 170, 172
Winner, Ken 182
*Wishbone* 194, 202
Wishbone boom or wishboom 56
Winter, John 41, 46
Woolstenholme, Andrew ix
World Sailing Speed Record, The 110, 133, 145–60, 221; (Committee) 150, 184, 195; (courses) 151; (measurement) 149, 151, 153–60; (results) 239–41; (rules) 231–3
Wynne, Ben 130, 174

*Yachting* 52
*Yachting World* 49, 122–3, 147, 195, 197, 218
Yacht Racing Association, The 41, 46
Yarborough, Earl of 23
*Young America* 52

*Zeevalk* 77